SECRET
SERVICE
MARKETING

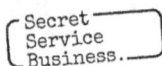

Secret Service Business.

https://secretservice.biz
Secret Service Business Pty Ltd (publisher)
de Lacy, Laura (author)
Secret Service Business Series, Book One
Secret Service Marketing: The Underground Guide to Modern Marketing for Small Skill-or-Service Businesses
ISBN Paperback: 978-0-6450683-0-6
ISBN eBook: 978-0-6450683-1-3
BUSINESS

(✱) green hill

https://greenhillpublishing.com.au/

Typeset Calluna 10/16
Cover Image by Adobe Stock
Editing by Isabelle Russell, New Zealand
Interior illustrations by
Tatsiana Teush, Poland
Cover and book design by
Green Hill Publishing

A catalogue record for this book is available from the National Library of Australia

SECRET SERVICE MARKETING

The Underground Guide to Modern Marketing for Small Skill-or-Service Businesses

LAURA DE LACY

For the owners of small skill-or-service businesses – bruised and battered by the pandemic, natural (or not so natural) disasters, or just the day-to-day slog of building a business.

CONTENTS

PART ONE

MISSION CRITICAL

In the world of small business, marketing gets a pretty bad rap... and rightly so.

Most business owners have a horror story or two to tell. There are those of us who've spent thousands of dollars on a fancy new website but had no new customers to show for it. There are those who have been lured into airtight advertising contracts by grand claims and false promises, with no recourse when leads fail to flow in. Then there are the tales of SEO woe (the result of pushy phone salespeople promising to get websites ranking first in a Google search) and money wasted on crash courses claiming to contain the latest social media wonder-strategy for generating leads or likes.

It's little wonder that, when it comes to modern marketing, we're dazed, defensive and completely confused.

But there's a good reason modern marketing feels like mission impossible – the function of marketing has changed beyond recognition. Where once an ad in the Yellow Pages directory or local paper could drive a steady flow of leads to our phone or premises, it's no longer that straightforward (or so it seems). We're bombarded with so many marketing options from advertising sales reps, web designers, online gurus, business coaches and the like that it's difficult to determine who or what to trust.

Out of sheer confusion, many of us end up taking an expensive scattergun approach to marketing our business. In trying to find a winning combination of marketing activities, materials, systems and strategies that generate a return on investment, we can find ourselves more frustrated and overwhelmed than ever, not to mention racked with guilt because we're not blogging or Insta-posting like the experts say we should be – as if we're failing our businesses by not employing every marketing strategy known to mankind.

But what if there was an easier way?

The good news? There is.

Secret Service Marketing is a real-world, no-nonsense approach to marketing for small business owners who sell skill- or service-based outcomes, designed to get big results on a small budget. It's about making the most of who we are and what we've got and making smart marketing decisions – free of guilt and frustration.

While marketing should be a little challenging, it shouldn't feel overwhelming, forced or fake. If it does, it's because we're trying to fit a square peg in a round hole by taking a mainstream marketing approach – an approach developed around the needs and budgets of big, goods-based corporations, not small skill-or-service providers; an approach that's so wrong for us in size and shape that it's barely an approach at all. And yet we've persisted with it, having no other alternative... until now.

Armed with the *Secret Service Business Series*, there's finally a clear alternative – an underground approach that flies in the face of mainstream marketing principles. Your mission – if you choose to accept it – is to cast off the shackles of mainstream marketing... and go underground.

CHAPTER 1.

THE MODERN MARKETING MINEFIELD

We've all heard the reports; small business praised as the backbone of the economy and the lifeblood of our communities. And rightly so. Of the 2.4 million businesses in my home country of Australia alone, 97.5% fall under the banner of small business[1] with similar percentages elsewhere. Given our reliance on small business goods and services – not only to fulfil our day-to-day needs but to fund our livelihoods through employment – there's no doubt that without its small business backbone, the global economy would be brought to its knees.

What's overlooked by small business spectators, however, is an important insight. Of all businesses, around 78% fall into one collective category;[2] a category that, despite the immense number of businesses it contains, flies largely under the radar, rarely receiving any focused attention, assistance or accolades.

SSBs: Sustaining Lives & Lifestyles

From sherpas in Nepal to stockbrokers in New York City, *small skill-or-service businesses* (shortened from here to *SSBs*) are essential to every community and economy in the world. The sector might be *small* by name but it's certainly not small in cumulative size, contribution or importance. In Australia, one in 10 adults operate an SSB.[3] In emerging economies it's even more. We are the self-employed builders and bookkeepers, health professionals and hairdressers, makers and bakers, landscapers, lawyers and locksmiths. We provide expertise to help people maintain, organise, enjoy and improve their lives. Most of our businesses are not particularly fast-growing, nor do they dwell at the cutting edge of innovation. Yet, we are imperative to our economy and crucial to our communities, sustaining lives and lifestyles through mastery of our respective fields.

Despite our overwhelming contribution to society, resources and initiatives designed to foster the growth of SSBs are few and far between, as outlined in a rare service-focused parliamentary report:

> 'Services receive a proportionally smaller share of government assistance than other sectors. [...] At around 30 per cent, the share of government assistance going to the services sector is much smaller than its share of output or employment of around 75-85 per cent.'[4]

This imbalance stems not from government complacency but rather, a lack of clarity about how to support the growth of businesses that provide a largely intangible product. Supporting the growth of *goods-based* businesses is quite straightforward for policy-makers – simply invest in initiatives to drive innovation and exportation. Supporting the growth of *service-based* businesses is less clear-cut.

The Neglected Needs of SSBs

The main growth opportunity for SSBs lies in marketing – specifically in winning leads, customers and projects away from larger businesses. The trouble is that modern marketing for SSBs requires a different approach to the one we're commonly taught or exposed to. Although well-intentioned, publicly-funded marketing training programs tend to target small businesses as a whole. They focus on strategies such as ecommerce and social media, which aren't necessarily in alignment with the needs and time constraints of SSBs. As a result, SSB owners often come away from these sessions feeling burdened by their newfound knowledge. Instead of feeling empowered, we feel inadequate, as if by not implementing every digital marketing strategy, we are failing our businesses and ourselves.

Not only is governmental marketing assistance out of sync with the real-world needs of SSBs, so too is the help provided by training institutions and private enterprises (such as business consultants, marketers and web designers). The information and services they deliver are often – inadvertently – more complicated, expensive and less effective than they would be if developed around SSB-specific insights.

This leaves SSB owners wrestling with a proverbial catch-22: needing practical marketing tools and training to increase sales but needing sales to fund an investment in those same marketing tools. The problem is compounded due to uncertainty about what marketing tools and training to invest in, leading to a costly and unreliable 'throw it at the wall and see if it sticks' approach – wasting time and money over and over again. This 'non-strategy' leads to the dangerous trap of competing on price alone, particularly when feeling the pinch in tough times. Sadly, many SSB owners assume lowering the price of their products or services is the only way to stand out in a sea of similar providers or larger players. Others are so desperate to fit in with the 'big boys' that they sacrifice their authenticity, presenting their business as much bigger or more capable than it actually is, blurring the line between reality and possibility and making life as an SSB owner harder than it needs to be.

And those are just a couple of the landmines hidden in the field of modern marketing. But before we dig any deeper...

What is a Small Skill-or-Service Business?

The answer depends on who you ask.

Government bodies usually define the service business sector by what it is *not*. For example, 'those parts of the economy that are not agriculture, forestry and fishing, mining or manufacturing'. While this makes sense, it means that the goods-based categories of 'retail trade' and 'wholesale trade' get lumped under 'services', flying in the face of basic economics, which classifies 'goods' and 'services' as two very distinct business offerings.

While the concept of 'goods' as separate from 'services' is good in theory, the reality is not so black and white. More often than not, businesses don't fit neatly into one box or another – to the extent that many of us are unclear as to which one we belong. Take a landscape gardener whose core business is the sale and installation of irrigation systems, or a wedding dress designer whose revenue comes from the sale of dresses s/he tailors. Customers of these businesses would see themselves as buying and deriving value from a physical product (an irrigation system or a wedding dress), so they must be goods-based businesses... or are they?

For the purposes of marketing and understanding where each of us fits in the big world of small business, here is a more useful definition.

A small skill-or-service business:

- Has 0 to 19 employees;
- Draws on a body of skills, knowledge and/or resources in a particular area of expertise to satisfy customer needs or expectations;
- Primarily sells information, advice or assistance, manual labour, the use or benefit of physical resources, an experience, or a unique, handmade or customised end product to customers in its local area.

Note: A *customised end product* is a product tailored to suit the specific needs of a customer. In other words, it is made to order, not made to stock. That means the product would not appear, exist or function in its finished form without drawing on human know-how – usually through a process of consultation, assessment, design, development, installation and/or calibration. A building renovation, an irrigation system or air conditioner installation, the tailoring of a suit, creation of a floral bouquet or design and manufacture of a sail for a yacht, for example, are all reliant on human know-how and skill to determine, process and satisfy individual customer requirements. That's why, for the purposes of marketing, a business that sells a customised end product falls squarely under the SSB banner.

WHAT ABOUT RETAIL?

Retail trade is often lumped under the banner of 'services' by government and media commentators. Although it's counterintuitive, this does make sense; after all, customer service underpins retail. No matter how good their products, small retailers struggle without providing great service - now more than ever.

That's why, although retail is not its main focus, Secret Service Marketing is an equally important resource for small retailers. It is particularly relevant to those who design goods themselves, or rely on their expertise or gut instinct to source or select a boutique range of products, from one day or season to the next, whether it's fresh produce, flowers, homewares, gifts, clothing, accessories or even used cars.

However, in not wanting to be all things to all people, this book does not explore retail-specific marketing strategies such as online shopping (ecommerce) and visual merchandising. This is not to say that these areas aren't worthy of attention. Quite the opposite

> – they are crucially important and, if relevant, should be explored and implemented in conjunction with the **Secret Service Business Series** to amplify a retailer's results.

People Power

Given this definition of small skill-or-service business, it becomes easier to see why the SSB sector not only makes our economy tick but underpins modern life as we know it. It embraces:

- Business-to-consumer (B2C) services
- Business-to-business (B2B) services
- Trade services (building/construction, plumbing, electrical, mechanical, landscaping, repairs and maintenance, cleaning)
- Hospitality (restaurants, cafés, hotels, accommodation)
- Professional services (engineering, medicine, law, accounting, architecture)
- Health and fitness (physical and mental health practitioners, independent specialists, nutritionists, alternative therapists, fitness centres, personal trainers, coaches)
- Individual and group care (child care, aged care, disability care)
- Financial services (financial planning, insurance brokerage)
- Real estate and property management
- Creative services (graphic design, signwriting, custom design and production including tailoring, cake-making, floristry, etc)

- Web design, programming and information technology (IT)
- Beauty services
- Event management
- Tourism and leisure services
- Education and training
- Printing and publishing
- Consultants and agents
- Boutique food producers and winemakers
- Artists and artisans
- And more.

Despite their many obvious differences, the common thread tying these businesses together is the human insight and expertise at their core. It makes them extremely difficult (if not impossible) to automate. Human mastery fuels SSBs and always will.

The SSB Marketing Mystery

A reliance on people power is not the only thing SSBs have in common. Another is a state of confusion about how to embrace modern marketing without: 1) being ripped off, 2) breaking the bank, or 3) having no time to focus on anything other than blog posts or social media.

Marketing has changed dramatically over the last 20 years. Gone are the days of set-and-forget ads in local directories that generate all the sales leads an SSB could need. Customers are more informed, empowered and educated than ever before. When a need arises, be it for a product or service, we all know what they do next... they Google it.

Even word of mouth marketing has changed. It's no longer a small circle of family, friends and acquaintances whose opinions and experiences have the ability to sway our buying behaviour or choice of service provider. Now, we take the word of complete strangers, via online reviews and comments, as gospel.

The internet has changed the game of business in all manner of ways. We've needed to embrace internet marketing quickly to ensure we are 'fishing where the fish are.' But how? What marketing strategies work and what are a waste of time and money?

Finding the answers to these questions is complicated by the fact that internet marketing is not only relatively new to us as business owners, but to the marketing, web and design professionals we are relying on to help us figure it all out. Through no fault of their own, few professionals are equipped to provide objective marketing advice to SSBs specifically. This means SSB owners often get sold on a single, disconnected marketing activity that is highly unlikely to produce sustainable business growth.

Knowledge is Power

SSBs are built on a simple concept – the exchange of human expertise for money. This practice dates back to ancient civilisations when artisans, architects, astronomers, scribes and other specialists would trade their expert knowledge, time and skills for things of relative value. To this day, specialist knowledge has great power and value but, in this age of socialisation and globalisation, it's only as powerful and valuable as our ability to communicate what we do... or, in other words, to market ourselves.

While specialist technical knowledge gives us the power to operate as an SSB owner, specialist marketing knowledge gives us the power to survive as one. This book provides the latter. As such, it's a survival guide, designed to empower SSB owners to make smart marketing and design decisions – avoiding the common, costly dangers of traversing the modern marketing minefield alone.

What if marketing wasn't a gamble? What if it wasn't stressful? Dare I say it... what if it was possible for the marketing function to be virtually set-and-forget – much like it was back in the days of the physical Yellow Pages? With *Secret Service Marketing* and its companion guides, *The Secret Service Website Formula* and *The Modern Marketing Arsenal*, it's not only possible but probable. On the pages of these three books, you have all the knowledge you need to capitalise on your business' small size, cut through competition (without cutting prices) and create raving fans.

Marketing doesn't need to be scary. It doesn't need to be expensive. And it doesn't need to be complicated.

It just needs to be smart.

Here's how...

CHAPTER 2.

THE BIG 4 & THE BUSY/SLOW CYCLE

They say being a parent is the hardest job in the world. If that's the case, *they* must have never owned a struggling small business.

Thinking back to the early stages of parenthood and the many years I was stuck on SSB struggle street; for me, business was harder. At least when parenting a baby, I could cling to the knowledge that he wouldn't be so dependent forever. He was guaranteed to grow, gaining more and more independence while being the source of much pride and joy.

Business had no such certainty. It was not guaranteed to grow. It was not guaranteed to become independent. And it was rarely a source of pride and joy. There seemed to be no light at the end of the tunnel.

Whether we're parenting a young child or running a floundering business, we have an entity depending on us for survival. The physical, mental and emotional demands of this responsibility can be all-consuming and incredibly exhausting. Even the calmest of souls can be driven to a state of temporary insanity by a fussy baby or flailing business keeping them awake at all hours of the night.

The job of keeping a baby or business alive is as frustrating as trying to crack the code to a digital safe when the code keeps changing. Just when we think we've figured out the combination (be it to a good night's sleep, a full tummy, a successful tender or the selection of great staff), the code suddenly changes and we have to start again. The saving grace in business, however, is that there are a limited number of causes of frustration. Unlike children, SSBs are rational and more predictable. Press the right buttons in the right sequence and the safe door will creak open.

The Big 4 Frustrations

The most frustrating aspects of running an SSB fall into four categories: *cash flow* and *human resources* frustrations – which tend to affect us in short, temporary bursts – and *scaling* and *marketing* frustrations – which cause long-term, relentless stress and strain.

Cash Flow Chaos

Managing the flow of money in and out of a business can be incredibly frustrating. When times are tough, it can feel as though we're taking one step forward and two steps back – barely receiving payment from a client before the money is chewed up by an unavoidable operating expense or loan repayment. Generating enough cash flow to survive day to day – let alone to invest in marketing, technology or other proactive measures to grow the business – is the bane of existence for millions of SSB owners, even those who run seemingly profitable ventures.

Human Resources (HR) Hassles

The management of staff and subcontractors presents ongoing challenges for any SSB owner seeking to reap the rewards of expanding beyond sole trader status. Determining if the business can justify and sustain the financial commitment associated with employing staff, recruiting the right people, training them, ensuring service standards are upheld, balancing quality and profitability, keeping employees satisfied to minimise staff turnover and staying up to speed with legislation changes are just some of the HR headaches we face from week to week.

Scaling Struggles

Scalability is the capacity for a business to grow in size; keeping demand and supply in relative balance while gradually scaling up. Some SSB owners grow their business quite naturally over time. Others of us get stuck – wanting to take it to the next level but not knowing how.

Scaling struggles typically occur in two phases. The first phase is the period of time before we find the sweet spot of scalability where demand and supply meet – or, in other words, before our business finds its feet. During this frustrating time, there can be little sense of rhythm or routine from one job or project to the next. Every one comes with unique requests or challenges, requiring the development of technical abilities to undertake and complete it. Having to acquire new skills and knowledge for each job inhibits the flow of work required to scale up. In some businesses, this phase lasts for months or years, depending on the owner's level of experience and adaptability. Until we take proactive steps to help our business find its feet, it will remain highly dependent on our knowledge and intuition, and can suck us dry of motivation and entrepreneurial spirit.

If an SSB survives long enough to find its scalability sweet spot, it can suddenly gain traction and start taking on a life of its own. The challenge then shifts from finding our business' feet, to not letting it get swept off its feet. Like running on a treadmill set on too high a speed, fast growth can cause physical and mental exhaustion for SSB owners. We can feel stuck between a rock and a hard place, not knowing where to focus our time and energy. Should we focus on servicing existing clients – letting leads lapse, disappointing prospective clients and missing out on sales? Or should we focus on sales – taking the risk of over-committing ourselves, under-delivering and disappointing existing clients? Scaling a business' operations without tipping the scales is no mean feat.

Marketing Madness

Most SSB owners have experienced the repetitive cycle of marketing madness. We scrape funds together to invest in a marketing activity – often at short notice, watch and wait for leads to roll in, then face the disappointing reality that it's been a waste of money. Fast forward a few months and we repeat the same cycle. At times, we don't know where the next dollar is coming from or how we'll make ends meet. This can lead to us neglecting our physical, mental and social health and forcing ourselves to function despite constant frustration, overwhelm or full-blown anxiety.

Symptoms of poor marketing can include:

- Low or fluctuating sales
- Low or inconsistent profit margins
- High marketing expenses with a low return on investment (ROI)
- An inconsistent flow of leads
- Missed sales opportunities in busy periods
- Cash flow chaos
- HR hassles and, you guessed it...
- Scaling struggles

Marketing: The Root of Most Frustration

Poor marketing is often the undiagnosed root cause of the other frustrations. When a business' marketing is in mayhem, cash flow chaos, HR hassles and scaling struggles are inevitable. Why? Because marketing is the *only* function in a business that brings money in.

With no marketing, there's no money, and with no money, there's no business – only a hobby or imminent failure.

It's not easy to diagnose poor marketing as the cause of our frustrations, because we can be blinded by the financial stresses and strains of its symptoms. Many of us distract ourselves by looking outside the business for someone or something to blame – be it the economy, our industry, or the actions of competitors or customers. It can be confronting to admit that we are responsible for our business' financial situation and that only we have the power to change it.

Most SSB owners have an innate awareness of the importance of marketing. It's this awareness that makes us vulnerable to telephone marketers who catch us at a weak moment, signing us up for too-good-to-be-true search engine marketing campaigns or full-page ads in directories we've never heard of, let alone used. It's when we know we *should* be marketing but don't know *how*, that we start making silly, split-second marketing decisions instead of smart, strategic ones. Split-second marketing doesn't work because it's reactive. It's marketing for the sake of marketing. Strategic marketing, on the other hand, is carefully calculated and deeply purposeful. It's proactive – seeking out appropriate marketing opportunities, rather than falling for those that land in our lap.

When we're fed up with the ***Big 4 Frustrations***, taking control of our marketing can be the key to turning things around. This doesn't mean spending thousands on a new logo, nor embarking on an SEO campaign with the next telemarketer who guarantees us a top spot in Google. Quite the opposite actually. The key to taking control of our marketing is to fight the urge to take split-second, reactive steps and instead, take a calm, calculated ***step back***. This shift of direction is critical. Without it, the Big 4 Frustrations blind us from seeing the big picture (the reality that our business exists in). They cause us to make decisions based on emotion, not logic. Taking a step back forces us to detach from the frustration. Only then can we start moving forward with purpose, clarity and insight; making fully informed, rational marketing decisions.

A Simple 'Step Back' Analysis

Stepping back is just trend-spotting. It's a basic analysis of two of the most important marketing-related figures in our business – *sales* and *gross profit margin*.

Sales is the total operational revenue generated by a business in a given period of time. *Gross profit margin* (or GP%) reveals the proportion of money left over from those sales, after factoring in directly attributable costs such as materials and direct labour – known as *cost of sales*, *cost of goods sold* or *COGS*. Gross profit margin is a less familiar concept than sales but an extremely powerful one. It's not only an indicator of a business' marketing decisions (specifically, pricing and promotions) but of its overall financial health, which is why it's so important to us as business owners.

If you're feeling frustrated, take the time to do this easy exercise – not only now, but regularly. It's a simple but effective way to give context to a business' financial figures, for the purpose of marketing decision-making. That said, if your business is in utter chaos and you've reached the point where something's got to give, simply resonating with the words on the coming pages is enough. It's okay to trust your gut.

Plot It to Spot It

The best way to spot our business' big picture trends is to plot its financial data on line graphs. This allows us to see and interpret trends visually, giving the numbers more meaning. For an easy way to do this, follow the steps below:

1. Download and open the free *Plot It to Spot It* spreadsheet file (complete with auto-populating graphs) from *www. secretservice.biz/downloads.* Look up your *weekly* and *monthly* sales and COGS figures for as far back as practical (ideally two years) and enter them where indicated on the spreadsheet. The data you enter is used to calculate and present weekly, fortnightly, monthly and quarterly sales and gross profit margins in graphical format. Each set of figures (weekly, fortnightly, etc) will give you a slightly different perspective on your business. An important trend could appear in one, that is not revealed in the others, which is why all four reporting periods are necessary.

    NOTE: Ensure your sales and COGS figures are obtained using a consistent approach. That's easy for *point of sale* (POS) businesses in hospitality, health or beauty services for example, who receive payment on the same day the service is delivered. For those in *invoicing* industries, it can be more confusing. A sale or COGS purchase will often be invoiced in parts, sometimes before, or long after, delivery. Your accounting system may or may not take this into consideration so make sure that you do. This usually means *acknowledging a sale or COGS purchase at the point in time that the deal was done*, not necessarily when it was delivered, invoiced or paid.

2. Once the figures are entered, step back and take a look at the graphs. In healthy businesses with good marketing, the plotted lines will appear steady, with an upward trend in sales over time. Gross profit margins will show as stable, with temporary, subtle dips during any price promotions.

Figure 1: A healthy sales curve (total sales over time)

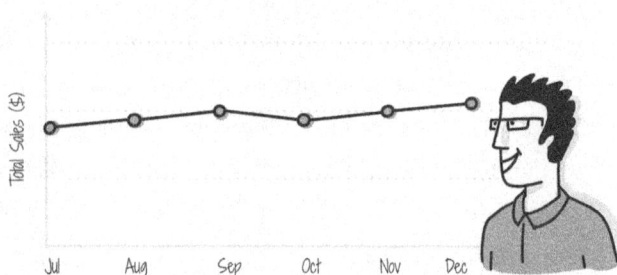

Figure 2: A healthy GP% curve (gross profit margin over time)

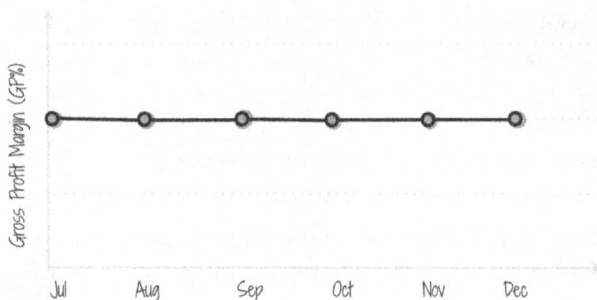

In SSBs with poor marketing, results like these are rare. Far more likely is a phenomenon I call the *Busy/Slow Cycle*, which not only affects a large proportion of SSBs, it's the bane of their existence.

The Busy/Slow Cycle

The Busy/Slow Cycle is a rhythm of business experienced by SSB owners in which sales fluctuate over time. When it rains, it pours and we're busy beyond belief, but when it's quiet, we're scratching our head, wondering where the next dollar is coming from. Somehow, we scrape through, and the cycle begins again.

Without recurring income from commission or retainer-based contracts, running an SSB can be a constant cycle of peaks and troughs – whether the extremes occur weekly, monthly, seasonally, annually or somewhere in between.

Figure 3: An unhealthy sales curve (the Busy/Slow Cycle)

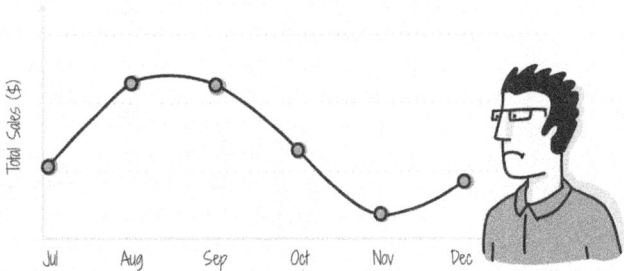

If we price jobs or projects using a quote-based system, the Busy/Slow Cycle can result in a financial double whammy. We're susceptible not only to fluctuations in sales, but to fluctuations in gross profit margins. Why? Because it's at the bottom of the Busy/Slow Cycle that we're at our most vulnerable. With unavoidable overheads to pay – rent, wages and other bills, we need to get money in quickly and can find ourselves quoting out of desperation. This means either: a) 'dropping our pants' on price, quoting lower than we usually would in an effort to increase our chances of winning the job, or b) quoting on projects that are outside our preferred field of work (either geographically or technically) to simply get work on the books. While this may generate enough cash flow to make ends meet, it can have a surprisingly big impact on our bottom line – sometimes not even generating enough from a sale to cover its costs. All that work and nothing extra in our pocket to show for it... not ideal.

Figure 4: An unhealthy GP% curve (the Busy/Slow Cycle)

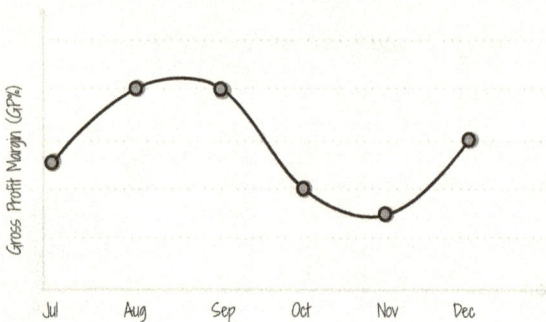

Is the Economy to Blame?

If you're thinking the curve of the Busy/Slow Cycle resembles the *economic cycle* (also called the *business cycle*), rest assured that they're completely unrelated.

Figure 5: The Economic Cycle

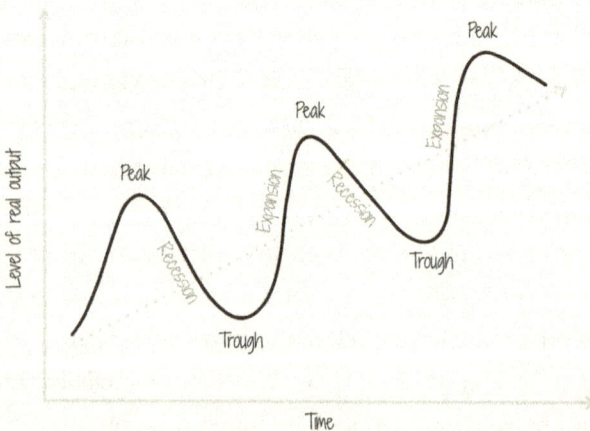

While the state of the economy does play a part in a business' performance, cyclical economic fluctuations occur over years, not weeks, months or seasons. Studies by researchers at The University of Melbourne show that the average length of a full economic cycle in Australia, trough to trough, is 45 months (3.75 years).[5] That means the economic climate has little to do with the periodic sales peaks and troughs experienced by SSBs.

In reality, if the unhealthy sales scenario above was plotted against actual economic movement, it would look something like this:

Figure 6: The Busy/Slow Cycle vs The Economic Cycle

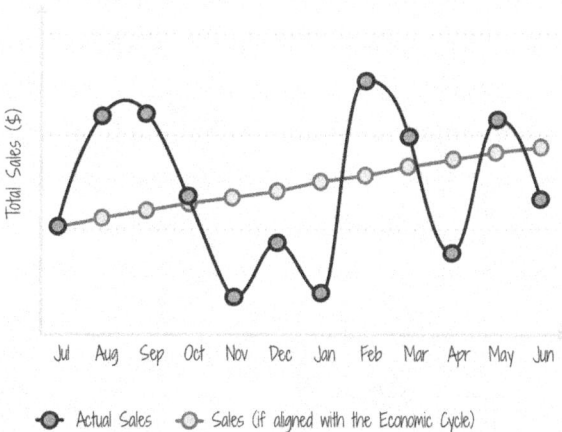

Jul Aug Sep Oct Nov Dec Jan Feb Mar Apr May Jun

Total Sales ($)

Actual Sales   Sales (if aligned with the Economic Cycle)

There is a point to all these squiggly lines...

Many of us blame the economy, the government or other external factors for our poor business performance from one year to the next but, as the last graph demonstrates, this blame is usually unjustified. All it does is solidify our position

– stuck blindly in the chaos of our Busy/Slow Cycle – and drive customers away.

Breaking the hold that debilitating beliefs such as 'it's not me, it's the economy' have over a business takes some mental gymnastics. This boils down to three steps:

1. **Acceptance** – Recognising that the Big 4 Frustrations and the Busy/Slow Cycle are within your control. While events with an unavoidable and often devastating impact such as a pandemic or natural disaster may arise from time to time, they are unusual and temporary. The vast majority of SSB frustrations and fluctuations can be relieved by moving on from past blows (including those as extreme as the pandemic) and taking strategic action. This starts with accepting that you, and you alone, have the power to change things.

2. **Accountability** – Taking full responsibility for your situation (financial and otherwise), even when caused by an outside event. This is done by dropping the use of *blame*, *excuses* and *justifications...* easier for some people than others. It's human nature to hold on to reasons why our business or bank balance doesn't look how we think it should. But the longer we cling to these reasons, the longer it takes to gain control and produce the results we want. As covered in Chapter 4, for those with the courage to end the blame game, a world of business opportunity awaits.

3. **Action** – Committing to regain control of your SSB by actioning the Secret Service Marketing methodology.

Although the Big 4 Frustrations will always exist, by practising Secret Service Marketing you'll find that their impact reduces and the peaks and troughs of the Busy/Slow Cycle begin to level out, bringing a sense of calm and order not only to your business, but your life.

CHAPTER 3.

MAKING SENSE OF MARKETING

Some business functions are more clear-cut than others. Accounting, for example, is very well defined. Although there are different methods of financial management, we're guided by fundamental rules and long-standing principles. Every business follows a semi-consistent formula for the purpose of accurate and reliable reporting.

The marketing function is more wishy-washy by nature. Although a science, it's not an exact one, which means there's a lot of confusion about what modern marketing is and how to apply it in a small business context. Many of us get caught up in the idea of marketing as 'branding' or 'advertising', simply because they are the most visual aspects and – some would say – the most fun. Common corporate definitions are no help. They usually include long-winded references to 'offerings of value' and 'exchange relationships', implying that marketing is some sort of rocket science. As you'll see shortly, it's not.

Secret Service Marketing – Methodology & Mindset

Secret Service Marketing is an approach to marketing for SSB owners, grounded in the *reality* of owning a small skill-or-service business. Most of us are time poor, on a tight budget, and in need of a marketing system that's as close to set-and-forget as possible. We're providing a *physical* service to *physical* customers so we don't want to be faffing about with blog posts or social media updates if we don't really want to. We're happy to invest money in marketing but only if we can be confident that our investment is going to provide a measurable return. For many of us, that confidence is wavering – if not completely shot.

The Secret Service approach evolved through my own humbling experiences as an SSB owner but began as a conflict of interest between my early employment and university studies. As the office/marketing manager of an SSB in the notoriously frugal hotel industry, I was taught to save money wherever possible. As a student of marketing (the traditional corporate kind), I was taught to spend it. Although I didn't recognise it then, this quandary formed the foundation of my obsession with getting big results on small budgets.

As a Secret Service Marketer, I favour simple, low- or no-cost strategies and one-time, upfront marketing investments over expensive, ongoing contracts or commitments of time and money because, at the end of the day, why spend more than you have to?

Secret Service Marketing is both a methodology and a mindset, requiring little more than a hungry mind to master. The *mindset* (a set of assumptions, attitudes and beliefs to improve business results) would be of no use without the detail of the *methodology* (a set of methods and principles to guide the marketing decisions of SSB owners) and vice versa. To reap the full benefits of both and get the most from this book, be prepared to drop any preconceived ideas or interpretations of what marketing is, as well as any emotional associations you have with it – be it confusion, frustration, guilt or distrust. Forget everything you know or feel about marketing and open your mind to a new set of knowledge and beliefs, and, I promise, marketing will finally start to make sense.

Cutting the Corporate Jargon

Making sense of marketing starts with recognising that, for SSB owners, many common business phrases have one underlying meaning. For us, the terms *business planning, business strategy, business concept, business model, strategic planning, strategic marketing, marketing strategy* and *marketing mix* are all fundamentally the same thing. They are merely variations on a theme – applicable in different ways to big businesses with multiple brands or departments – which have filtered down to us through business textbooks and our corporate cousins. For too long, this jumble of jargon has needlessly muddied the waters of SSB ownership – making us feel uneducated and inadequate and causing us to question our capabilities as business owners, when all it boils down to is a single concept: *Business Model Management*.

Business Model Management

A **business model** is the logic behind a business – the way it operates, how it creates value for its stakeholders and why it's a viable concept.[6] Business Model Management is the design, review and modification of that business model over time.

Just as a building is not stable if its footings are weak, an SSB is not scalable if its business model is unclear or outdated. A weak business model prevents a business from finding its scalability sweet spot, inhibiting it from striking the all-important balance between demand and supply. A strong business model not only makes a business stable and scalable, it simplifies decision-making, drives productivity and boosts profit potential, all while injecting a sense of direction, purpose and satisfaction into the rollercoaster ride of SSB ownership.

Business Model Management is the behind-the-scenes, planning side of running a small business. It requires business-level logic, open-mindedness, a touch of creative vision, patience and persistence. Most importantly though, it requires an understanding of what strategic options are available. Only when we know what's possible can we design a business model that makes the most of our expertise, time and resources. Without knowing our options, we're at great risk of limiting our business' market reach, earning potential and ability to serve others in a meaningful way.

A shameless business guru once told me there were only nine business models available to entrepreneurs but, the truth is, there are as many business models as there are businesses. A business model is as unique as the journey of its creator. It is born out of life experience and business acumen and should continue to evolve over time, as we do.

Perception Management

While Business Model Management is the planning side of SSB marketing, *Perception Management* is the implementation side. It's where the action happens.

Perception is our interpretation of the data that reaches us via our five senses – sight, hearing (sound), touch, taste and smell – the faculties that help us derive meaning from our world. No two people perceive the world in the same way because we interpret sensory data differently, with a unique blend of emotion, reasoning and judgement.

Figure 7: The five human senses

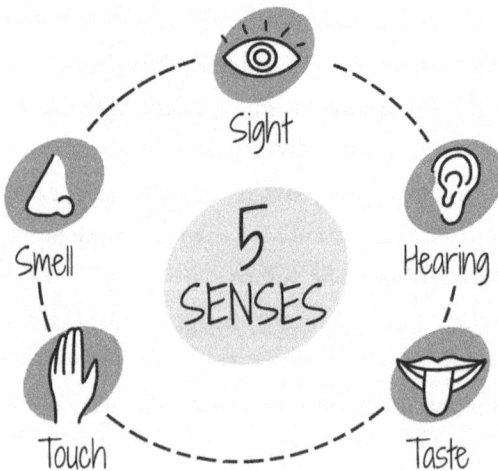

Perception Management is the understanding and improvement of the sensory experience of current and potential customers. Every little thing a customer sees, hears or experiences in or about our business before, during and after they transact with us, contributes to an overall perception or feeling about it – good, bad or indifferent. This feeling, en masse, determines our business' fate. Although we can never have full control of our customers' feelings, Perception Management is a means to steer them in the right direction.

There are two categories of Perception Management: *market* and *customer*. The aim of **Market Perception Management** is to spark and maintain the awareness and interest of potential customers in our target market and encourage them to take action – resulting in more leads and first-time customers. As a concept, Market Perception Management is most similar to the traditional, commonly-held interpretation of what marketing is: the branding, advertising and promotion used to appeal to and drive *new* customers.

The often ignored flip side is **Customer Perception Management**. Customer perception is concerned with the experience and resultant feelings of *current* and *recent* customers. It determines whether a customer's initial purchase is their only purchase or the first of many. The aim of managing customer perception is to retain customers as clients and advocates of the business, multiplying the revenue generated from a single customer over a long period of time by making their experience so positive that it inspires repeat patronage and word of mouth.

Like any other field of management, Perception Management is a deliberate and continual process. It starts by examining every customer touchpoint (point of interaction between a service seeker or customer and a business), looking at it through their eyes to determine what sensory influencers could be sabotaging their perception of the business, then taking proactive steps to fix or improve each one. Examples of sensory influencers are listed in the table below, broken down into market and customer perception.

Figure 8: An SSB's possible sensory influencers

Sense	Market Perception
Sight	• Search engine listings (ranking, body of words displayed) • Listings on online directory and comparator sites • Online reviews and testimonials • Website • Advertisements • Brochures • Business cards • Signage • Speed of communication (including time lapses or delays) • Sales paraphernalia – presentation folder and other visual resources/cues • Price and how it is communicated (quotation document, menu, etc) • Email/mail communications • Brand (including consistent application of brand elements) • Street appeal and signage (applicable to businesses that welcome walk-in enquiries) • Reception area or front counter appearance/ambience (for walk-in enquiries) • Other visual communications (clarity, composition, design, etc)

Customer Perception

- Signage
- Location
- Parking facilities
- Accessibility
- Design/presentation of premises/worksite
- Decor/lighting
- Speed of communication (including time lapses or delays)
- Presence of the business owner
- Owner/staff presentation (grooming, uniform)
- Owner/staff attitude (smile, body language)
- Owner/staff actions (what they do and how they do it, speed, etc)
- Product delivery and presentation
- Cleanliness
- Design/layout/branding of client documentation
- Customer service
- Consistency of product/service
- Customer experience
- Vehicle (model, signage, cleanliness)
- Other visual communications such as menus and posters (clarity, composition, design, etc)

Sense	Market Perception	
Hearing (Sound)	• Verbally expressed word of mouth • Telephone 'on hold' music/messaging, answering machine messages, etc • Staff phone manner (what they say, tone of voice, how long callers are left on hold) • Online videos – message, music, voiceovers, audio effects • Podcasts • Radio ads • Jingles or aural logos	
Touch	• Texture of marketing/promotional materials • Tactile components of sales presentations • Physical comfort/practicality of building entrance and reception area for walk-in enquiries	
Taste	• Promotional food samples and taste-testers • Foods/drinks provided in waiting areas or during sales meetings	
Smell	• Smell of baked goods at open inspections or sales meetings • Scratch 'n' sniff advertising	

Customer Perception
• Phone communications • Staff attitude (what they say, tone of voice) • Background music • Ambient noise • On-premise TV/videos – intrusiveness of sound
• Temperature control – effectiveness and adequacy • Physical comfort/practicality (chairs, tables, flooring, cutlery, etc) • Texture of fixtures, finishes and furniture • Door handles, toilets, taps (cleanliness, ease of use, etc) • Parking facilities – ability to manoeuvre in/out of the carpark • Physical contact during service delivery (in health and beauty services, for example) – gentleness, respect for personal space, explaining/seeking approval before commencing, etc
• Quality of any food/drinks served • Complimentary offerings for waiting customers (cup of tea or coffee and snack, bread served with olive oil and balsamic on arrival at a restaurant) • Gifts given on special occasions (Christmas, settlement of a deal, etc)
• Aromatic associations – positive (food, flowers, essential oils, perfume or aftershave) or negative (the smell of damp or mould, smells from the toilets, body odour, etc)

Although some of the sensory influencers in this list may seem trivial, the devil of SSB failure lurks in the detail. Thanks to the internet and other technological advancements, humans are processing more sensory data than ever, which means our customers are more sensitive and discerning than ever. Little errors or oversights that may have once slipped by without consequence no longer do – they all get processed and contribute to a customers' overall perception of our business. One seemingly small cringe-point can cost hundreds of thousands of dollars in initial or ongoing sales. Knowing that, we must step up our game – raising the standard at every customer touchpoint to meet or exceed customer expectations.

Breaking down the *action* side of marketing into tens or hundreds of sensory influencers puts the depth and breadth of the marketing function into perspective. There can be a lot of things to consider. That's why the *planning* or Business Model Management side is so important. It serves as a foundation – ensuring our marketing actions are focused, cohesive and sensical and that the perception of our business in the minds of both current and potential customers is clear, positive and strong.

Business Building

To sum up the SSB marketing function, imagine a building.

The business model is the foundation on which everything is constructed. It determines the potential size and scope of the entity being built.

Customer perception is the building itself. The size, scope and composition of the structure as well as the floorplan, fittings and furniture. With poor customer perception, the structure won't be fit for purpose. It won't be functional or comfortable, let alone a talking point that cultivates a trickle-feed of future visitors.

Market perception is the building's street appeal. It's the exterior aesthetics, landscaping, stepping stones and stairs – the elements that make it easy and inviting to enter. With no marketing activity, an SSB will have no street appeal. It'll be a wasteland of tumbleweeds and trash cans.

Figure 9: The Secret Service Business Building

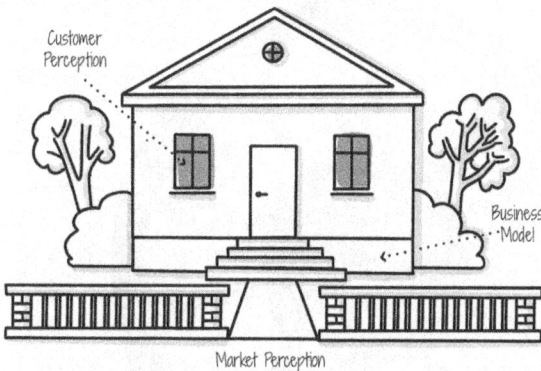

The blueprint for standing the test of time as an SSB owner: a strong but malleable business model, underpinning the active management of market and customer perception.

By the end of this book, you'll have all of the insight you need to create a successful, sustainable SSB; a business built on strong foundations, impressive in both form and function, with excellent market appeal. In the meantime, let's give some structure to the side of Perception Management that causes the most confusion, frustration and expense for SSB owners – Market Perception Management (aka the acquisition of new customers).

The Wheel of Business Fortune

The *Secret Service Marketing Wheel* is a framework outlining the marketing mechanisms and options available for SSB owners to attract new customers. It identifies 10 spokes of marketing activity, connecting the *rim* (our target market) to the *axle* (our business) via a *central hub* of possible interactions which, when activated successfully, generate *momentum* (a series of service transactions).

Figure 10: The Secret Service Marketing Wheel

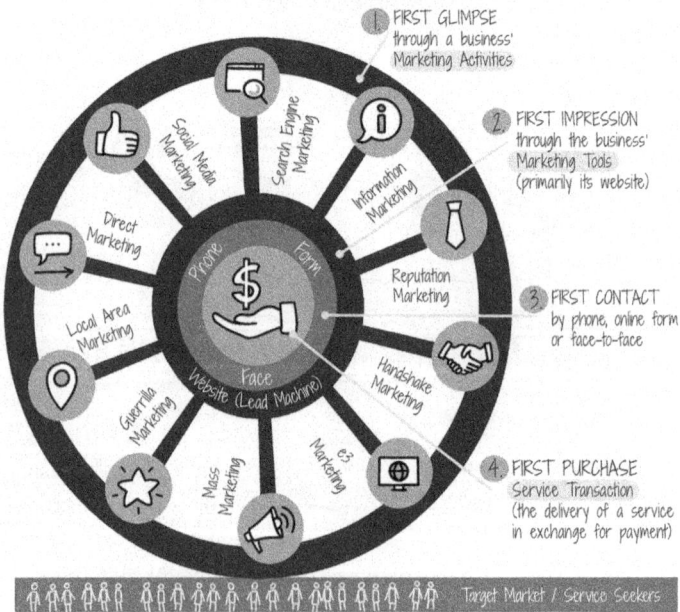

We'll look at the Marketing Wheel in detail later, and even more in *The Modern Marketing Arsenal*, but in the meantime, there are a couple of crucial points to note.

A Website – The Hub of the Wheel

An integral aspect to recognise about the Marketing Wheel is that a website is not one of the 10 spokes of marketing activity but a vital component in and of itself. Taking the Secret Service approach, a website is at the hub of all marketing activities and, when carefully geared as a *Lead Machine* (a website designed to convert visitors into sales leads), it is a core component from which business momentum is possible.

A website is central to SSB marketing. While marketing activities can drive leads directly (via phone, email or face-to-face introductions/enquiries), gearing them to funnel enquiries through a Lead Machine website (where possible) makes them dramatically more effective. That's because most people seeking out a skill-or-service business – referred to from here as *service seekers* – are information addicts and the internet is their dealer. Not only do they want to know more about SSBs they consider engaging, thanks to the internet, they *expect* to find it. If they can't find a hub of information about our services online, or aren't satisfied by what they do find, most won't bother to phone or email – they'll reject us in a heartbeat, no matter how many thousands of dollars we may have spent on letterbox drops, promotional pens or fandangled fridge magnets.

So, if you've been avoiding internet marketing, praying for a cyber-catastrophe to restore the world to pre-internet normality... it's time to wake up and smell the digital roses. As far back as 2010, research showed that 97% of people used the internet to *shop locally*.[7] Since then, the trend of using the internet to find and select businesses within the local geographic area has not only increased, it's become embedded in our culture. The internet is the lake that hungry fish (our potential customers) are swimming in. If we're not fishing in that lake, we'll starve. It's that simple.

The internet is here to stay. That means internet marketing is here to stay and SSB owners must embrace it. Creating a Lead Machine – equipped to convert website visitors into leads – is the cornerstone of doing just that. Without a Lead Machine as the hub of our marketing efforts, we can't expect to realise the business growth, longevity or profitability that we're capable of.

AN INTERNET MARKETING AMBUSH

The term internet marketing doesn't appear on the Marketing Wheel for good reason – it's been stretched beyond recognition and become too overwhelming a concept.

When first introduced, internet marketing meant having a website... then it expanded to include email marketing, search engine optimisation (SEO) and pay per click advertising, then social media marketing – all the while being proclaimed as a somewhat magical way to make money with little-to-no work through the automated sale of information products. No wonder we're confused.

But avoiding internet marketing is not the answer. That would be the business equivalent of looking a gift horse in the mouth. Instead, we just need to

break it down into bite-sized chunks - identifying the individual methods of online marketing
of most benefit to SSBs, then integrating them into
our new normal, alongside offline methods that can
still pack a punch. This is what the Secret Service
Marketing Wheel does, and one of the reasons it's
such a handy point of reference.

The Spokes

Just as a wheel can't have less than one thick spoke (as its axle
would need to defy the laws of physics), Secret Service Marketing
requires at least one marketing activity, in conjunction with
the hub, to work. A great website with no marketing activity
is of little benefit – it's expecting the marketing wheel to move
forward, with no connection between the hub and the rim.

With Secret Service Marketing, everything other than the
central hub and a couple spokes is optional, depending how much
momentum is needed. This means the more time-consuming
strategies, such as social media marketing, are entirely optional.
If you don't have the time or willpower to invest in social media,
that's fine. Without feeling it, it's near impossible to stick with it.
There's no need to rack yourself with guilt – just own your decision and move on to the next spoke of the wheel. If all else fails or
you change your mind, you can always revisit it later.

As Secret Service Marketers, we have the freedom to choose
the marketing activities (spokes) we do and don't use. We need
enough marketing activity to generate a consistent flow of traffic
to our website but, with a Lead Machine website built in accordance with *The Secret Service Website Formula*, this can be far
less than the activity that's typically required to sustain or grow

a business. With a Lead Machine, even a small, steady stream of high-quality traffic can be enough to keep leads rolling in. It picks up where our marketing activity leaves off – engaging and impressing potential customers and creating an organic in-flow of pre-qualified leads to our inbox and phone. If a website works well but isn't getting enough traffic to generate sufficient leads, it's a matter of adding another spoke to the wheel and doing so until it gains adequate momentum.

Before We Get Carried Away...

Although attracting new customers is important, it can also be dangerous. Prioritising the attraction of new customers over the strength of our business model or the satisfaction and retention of current customers is like prioritising the street appeal of a building over its fitness for purpose, strength or safety. It might look okay from the outside but, sooner or later, the word on the street will slow the flow of people prepared to step inside, or worse... the building will collapse without warning, taking hundreds of unsuspecting visitors down with it. So, before we attract too many new customers, let's shift our focus closer to home, to the heart and soul of our business – the service we exist to provide.

RECOVERY MISSION 1

What is a Recovery Mission?

Throughout the course of this book you'll find five Recovery Missions; each one a summary of recommended actions for that part of the book. Think of them as a set of instructions to systematically recover from the Big 4 Frustrations and the Busy/Slow Cycle.

Chapter 1 - The Modern Marketing Minefield

- **Confirm your status** – Use the definition of a small skill-or-service business on page 10 to confirm that the Secret Service approach is suitable for your business.

Chapter 2 - The Big 4 & the Busy/Slow Cycle

- **Access Unlocked** – Download the *Plot It to Spot It* spreadsheet file from *www.secretservice.biz/downloads* then perform the Step Back Analysis on page 23 to spot the Busy/Slow Cycle at play in your business.
- **Take command** – Accept responsibility for the Busy/Slow Cycle, its financial impact and any stress and struggle it's caused.
- **Mission control** – Commit to actioning Secret Service Marketing as a means to take control of your business.

- **Call a truce** – Let go of any preconceived ideas or interpretations of what marketing is, as well as any emotional associations you have with it.
- **Terms of engagement** – Familiarise yourself with the terms *Business Model Management* as the *planning* side of marketing and *Perception Management* as the *action* side.
- **Situation digital** – Accept the fact that, for SSBs, a website is no longer an optional marketing activity. It's a fundamental marketing tool and the key to driving leads and sales.

PART TWO

A 'FIRST FIX' CHECKLIST

When business is slow, it hurts. We can become anxious and stressed and turn to marketing – in some form or other – to relieve the pain and pressure, much like we turn to medication when we're unwell. As we get busy again, the symptoms subside so we stop the medication... until the next flare-up.

Just as the symptoms of many medical conditions can be alleviated or overcome through proactive measures and self-care, so too can business frustrations. The SSB equivalent of a healthy diet and regular exercise is the creation of a positive customer perception and a strong community of existing clients and contacts. With these as our priority, we can generate a consistent baseline of awareness and sales (marketing health) and reduce our toxic reliance on 'medication marketing'.

The Inside Out Overhaul

The most cost effective and sustainable way to get our marketing on track is to start from deep inside our business and work our way out, towards the attainment of new customers. This means working with the resources we *have* and controlling what we *can* control to create an immediate impact.

Working from the inside out not only gives a business an immediate energy boost, it ensures marketing activities implemented down the track aren't in vain. Marketing without laying the right foundations might win a few new customers but it won't retain them. We'd need a constant stream of new customers just to make ends meet, which is expensive, stressful and unsustainable. An ***Inside Out Business Overhaul*** flips that script, giving us the power to retain customers *and* set the stage for attracting new ones, while feeling calm and in control.

Figure 11: The Inside Out Business Overhaul

Listed in the diagram above are the five phases of the Inside Out Business Overhaul. The first may come as a surprise but the beating heart of a business is its owner. And sometimes, all it takes to get everything else on track is a bit of a jolt, so let's start there.

CHAPTER 4.

JUMPSTART THE HEART OF YOUR BUSINESS

As an SSB owner, the energy and attitude we bring to work sets the tone for the entire business. We can't expect customers to want to come back, or staff to consistently put their best foot forward, if we exist in a state of negativity, anger, scarcity, misery or fatigue. If we want vibrant, proactive staff who are committed to customer satisfaction and happy, appreciative customers who value the services we provide, we must lead by example, bringing that same energy with us, each and every day.

The only way staff and customers can possibly feel the love for our business is if *we* do.

Handling the Tough Times

It's easy to feel upbeat when things are going well – after making a big sale, for example. But when any of the Big 4 Frustrations kick in, our energy and attitude can take a nosedive. That's not to say we can't ever feel down – we are human after all – but one of the things that sets successful business people apart from those in an eternal life struggle, is their response to negative emotions.

When most of us feel a negative emotion – anger, frustration or helplessness, for example – we go into self-protection mode, using a combination of ego-fuelled *offence* and *defence* tactics to hold onto the emotion. These can include blame, excuses, justification, self-righteousness, martyrdom, self-sabotage, drama and aggression (passive, verbal and/or physical).

All these self-protection tactics do is keep us stuck where we are – as sad, sorry victims of an underlying problem, blinded by erratic thought and emotion. As long as we use them, we remain blind to a solution.

Truly successful people take a higher, but harder, path. Although they might deviate through 'Victimville' every now and then, they don't linger there for long. At the point in time when most of us kick into self-protection mode, successful people flick a mental switch, much like the line switch mechanism on a railway track. This switch sends them down a different, more productive path. It doesn't mean they avoid the emotion. In fact, they embrace it, allowing themselves to feel what they need to feel, as a means to work through it. Successful people know that negative emotions are fuel for self awareness and personal growth; each one is an opportunity to become happier, stronger and wiser... if you know how to work through it.

Picking ourselves up after an emotional blow is not easy, but it's much easier if we take a methodical approach. Having a step-by-step process helps. It harnesses and guides our thoughts which, in turn, reins in the emotion.

The process I use was developed at a time when I was desperate for change, having realised I'd been stuck in victim mode my entire adult life. After a long period of self-reflection, it dawned on me that I alone was the reason I hadn't achieved the success I was capable of. More specifically, I realised my constant feelings of dread and drudgery were the root of the problem. They were like a ball and chain, hindering my every move. If I wanted different results, I had to do something different. This led to the *Jumpstart Thought Process* – five sequential steps to overcome negative emotions.

Figure 12: The Jumpstart Thought Process

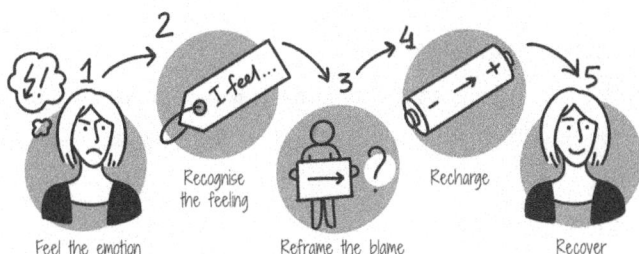

Feel the emotion   Recognise the feeling   Reframe the blame   Recharge   Recover

Step 1. Feel the Emotion

In order to heal it, we've got to feel it. So, after a stressful incident, or if you're in a long-standing 'funk', take some time out away from other people to allow the negative emotions to surface. Welcome them. Feel them. Cry or swear if you need to. Whatever comes out, appreciate the humanness of it. It's not weak and it does not define who you are. It's just being true to yourself – giving your emotions some airtime, so your inner self feels heard and acknowledged.

This step might take an hour or more to begin with – and may require an emotionally intelligent friend or partner to help unpack the emotion – but with practice, it can be condensed to a matter of moments (depending on the gravity of the situation, of course).

Note: For those of us with seemingly insurmountable problems or the tendency to bottle up our feelings, a few sessions with a counsellor or psychologist can be invaluable. Anything that helps us gain perspective and understand ourselves better is not only an investment in ourselves, it's an investment in our business – one which will pay dividends for the rest of our lives.

Step 2. Recognise the Feeling

Once we've experienced the negative emotion, we can examine it more impartially; identifying what the feelings are and why they're there.

Start by labelling them. Are you feeling angry, frustrated, disappointed, overwhelmed, guilty, etc, or a combination thereof? Then, articulate exactly why you feel this way, e.g. 'I feel angry because Shane didn't consult with me before dealing with a customer complaint. He handled it badly, resulting in the loss of a loyal customer who I now have no way of contacting.'

Identifying the 'why' isn't always easy, especially if the feelings we're experiencing are associated with a complex or long-ignored issue (such as disappointment at our business' lack of progress or profitability to date). But with conscious reflection (and a good counsellor, if need be), the root cause of the emotion will rise to the surface.

Step 3. Reframe the Blame

Next, we need to shift the emotion by looking for a way to *hold ourselves accountable* for the problem. This requires us to dig deep and get really honest with ourselves, to identify *our* mistakes, *our* misjudgements or *our* mismanagement. If you're ever stuck thinking a problem is all someone or something else's fault, such as your staff, customers, competitors, the tax man, God or the economy, then you're not there yet; you're still in victim mode. In order to move forward and overcome the problem, the blame must be reframed.

In the case of the poorly-handled complaint, it may be that we didn't have a procedure in place to empower staff to handle complaints, or that we hadn't run a refresher training session for three years. If that's not the case and the staff member is just a bad fit for the business, we need to take responsibility for that too. We made a bad hiring decision. And perhaps the reason we have no way to contact the customer to rectify the situation is because we never got around to choosing (let alone implementing) a customer relationship management (CRM) system.

It doesn't feel good to admit we've stuffed up, but feeling responsible and owning the problem is key to finding a good solution.

Step 4. Recharge

By this point in the process, you might be beating yourself up, reflecting on what you should have done, but guilt-based 'should haves' do nothing except compound the negativity, making things worse.

To ensure we don't stay and stew in a state of self-blame (a slippery slope to self-sabotage or even self-loathing) we need to counteract it using the power of thought. Interrupting our negative thoughts with positive ones is key to jolting ourselves out of the self-blame game, recharging our energy and creating the mental ambience required to find a solution.

I find the best way to interrupt my negative thoughts is with my favourite sayings. As clichéd as they may sound, my go-to quotes are: 'It's all meant to be' and 'I am exactly where I'm supposed to be'. Being quite philosophical, these statements – along with some big, deep breaths – ground, reassure and invigorate me, providing a sense of faith and reason. If you don't have a favourite quote, make it a priority to find one, or some, that resonate with you.

From there, build yourself up, reflecting on the reason you started your business and the feeling of excitement you had at the prospect of going out on your own. Think about how you felt when you received incredible feedback from a customer, or the feeling of satisfaction at finishing a project. Reflect on the impact you've had on the lives of staff members – teaching them, moulding them, remunerating them. Tap into the stream of positive emotions. When you begin to feel the love for your business or your customers (even a little glimmer of it), you're recharged and ready to recover.

Step 5. Recover

The last step in the Jumpstart Thought Process is to decide on a course of action, asking ourselves, 'What action/s can I take, starting now, to show I hold myself accountable for this problem and to help my business, staff and customers recover from my mistake/s?'

In the case of the poorly-handled complaint, we could:

1. Write a complaints procedure.
2. Apologise to the staff member for not having a complaints procedure in place.
3. Start researching and trialling CRM systems – commit to selecting one by the end of the month.
4. Set a date for a training session to introduce the new procedure to staff.

In business, verbal communication is an essential part of taking the higher, harder path. Speaking to those involved in a problematic situation with a blend of authority, humility and compassion, taking responsibility for our contribution to the problem, apologising and (if relevant) explaining the action/s we'll take to ensure the same situation doesn't happen again, is infinitely more powerful than blaming, shaming or sweeping issues under the carpet. Without accountability and open lines of communication, swept issues build up and, sooner or later, cause us to trip and fall.

A carefully considered, meaningful apology is a particularly powerful tool in an SSB owners' management toolkit. Not only can it diffuse a situation, clearing the air and setting a tone of honesty and openness, it can transform relationships, improving others' perception of us, while garnering their support and respect. Apologising also serves a strategic purpose – to highlight the person's character. If, upon receiving our apology, they are not compelled to apologise for their part in the problem (if relevant), it's a strong sign they're not a healthy fit for our business.

The ultimate recovery is threefold:

1. Acting with accountability;
2. Drawing meaning from the experience – i.e. 'What lesson did I learn from this?'; and
3. Being grateful for the lesson and thankful to the person who brought it to a head.

Apply the Jumpstart Thought Process enough times and it becomes second nature. You'll reprogram your brain to use negative emotions as fuel for productivity and progress.

The Wristband Rewire

You could read the last section a thousand times and commit to using the Jumpstart Thought Process to keep your emotions in check but chances are – you won't. That's because it's probably not your default setting. Most brains are wired to submit to negative emotions, not to use them as fuel to reach our full potential.

A great way to overcome this default setting is an always-present physical trigger; a tool to act as the line-switch mechanism for the neural pathways of our brain, prompting us to change course before being railroaded by emotion.

A silicone wristband (the variety popular for fundraising initiatives) is the ideal tool. While a hair tie or loose rubber-band will do the job, a silicone wristband or stretchy bracelet looks and feels better, making us more inclined to wear it.

This wristband can serve a dual purpose:

1. **To snap yourself out of it** – When a negative or self-defeating emotion creeps in, pull the band tight and feel it snap back against your wrist. Let the little sting be the

trigger to change course – to recognise the feeling, reframe the blame, recharge and recover – rather than falling victim to the emotion. If work is too frantic to go through the full process there and then, use the snap of the band as a pause mechanism – making a conscious decision to put the negative emotion on hold until you have time to work through it properly, later in the day. Once you've hit pause, skip to the positive thoughts of the recharge step (your favourite sayings, the reason you went into business, the feedback of happy customers, etc). Use these positive thoughts to 'feel the love' for your business and customers in the present, frantic moment – like changing the frequency of a radio to tune in to a different, more upbeat channel.

2. **To serve as an ever-present reminder** – The mere presence of a wristband can prompt the maintenance of an optimum emotional state. While working, our wrist is almost always in our field of vision, which not only makes it the ideal, easily accessible location for a 'line-switch' but for a visual stimulus. Every inadvertent glance of the band provides a visual cue to keep our energy high and our emotions in check.

Another handy aspect of silicone wristbands is the ability to feature words on them. While custom printed bands can be ordered online, it's better for the environment to repurpose one you've already got; punching holes in it with a 1mm hole punch to form a short but meaningful phrase, such as *FEEL THE LOVE*. Words with deep, personal meaning can make a wristband more effective as a brain rewiring tool by textually prompting the Jumpstart Thought Process and, therefore, a quicker, healthier response to emotional setbacks.

Are your old silicone wristbands cheesy promotional tools – stuck in your junk drawer and destined for landfill – or are they state-of-the-art tools to retrain your business brain? The choice is yours.

CHAPTER 5.

RALLY THE TROOPS TO THRILL CURRENT CUSTOMERS

Once we've become conscious of our energy, attitude and response to tough times, we can embark on the next phase of the Inside Out Overhaul, concerned with getting our staff and current customers on track. This is done through Customer Perception Management – introduced in Chapter 3.

Customer Perception Management involves the monitoring and improvement of two often-neglected aspects of business: *customer cringe-points* and *customer service*. With a bit of focused attention in these areas, customer perception – the experience and resultant feelings of recent and current customers – can instantly improve, having an organic flow-on effect on sales, profits, repeat patronage and word of mouth.

Customer Cringe-Points

Customer cringe-points are the physical aspects of a business' operations (beyond human interactions) that make sensitive customers cringe and less sensitive customers feel under-whelmed. They're the negative things they notice (see, hear, touch, taste or smell) while transacting with our business, which subtly detract from the overall experience.

It's easy to become blind to the finer details of the customer experience when working in a business day in, day out. Little things can be overlooked, such as wear and tear on fixtures and fittings, furniture that's grubby, uncomfortable or outdated, a lack of ambience, un-ironed uniforms, dog-eared menus, a plumber trampling through customers' homes with filthy work boots, an accountant with a messy office, dead flies scattered beneath dirty windows, grimey grout and broken door locks in the restrooms. Every little oversight does our business a disservice.

The first step to reducing customer cringe-points is identifying them. To help with this, a checklist is available to download from *www.secretservice.biz/downloads.*

Use the checklist as a guide to brainstorm a list of factors that could impact a current customer's perception of your business. Once the list is made, refine it. Do a 'walk around' of your premises or worksite, putting yourself in the shoes of customers; experiencing the business from their perspective to notice things you previously hadn't. As you go, score how well you're doing for each one on a scale from 0 to 10 (terrible to outstanding).

Some cringe-points can't be predicted – they'll only become evident through observation and conversation. So start paying attention. Notice customers' reactions before, during and after the delivery of a service. Watch where their eyes are drawn while waiting for their appointment or order to be filled, and open a meaningful dialogue with them – both in person and via feedback forms or online surveys.

Once a comprehensive list of customer cringe-points has been compiled, commit to improving three of these points per week. To begin with, this could be as simple as: 1) wiping the handprints and scuff-marks off the reception desk, 2) sourcing disposable medical shoe covers for technicians to slip over their work boots before entering customers' homes, and 3) finally replacing that broken lock on the toilet door.

Customer Service

Customer service is the humanity of a business transaction. It's how we interact with customers in the process of meeting their needs.

Despite the incredible tools and tactics available to small businesses today, *excellent customer service is still the best form of marketing we can do*. In fact, it's more important today than ever, due to the ability of customers to share their opinions and experiences with others via online reviews and social media.

Customer service can make or break our business. That's because, for the majority of customers, it determines: a) whether they will transact with us again, providing **repeat sales**, and b) whether they will recommend our business to others, providing **positive word of mouth**. These two factors underpin the survival of most SSBs, which means excellent customer service should be a given. Unfortunately though, it's not. Just as common sense, ironically, is not very common, many service businesses don't know how to serve. All too often, we make customers feel like an inconvenience instead of the gift that they are.

So let's cut to the chase – a practical approach to get your customer service on track.

Think & Work Like a Performer

There's a saying in big business that's used to try to motivate frontline employees: 'Customer service is not a department... it's an attitude'. This is absolutely true. However, a more useful approach for SSBs is to think of customer service not as an attitude, but as a 'performance'.

High-end actors, musicians, dancers, comedians and professional speakers are examples of finely-tuned performers. They are paid to play a role; to entertain and delight their audience, almost without fail. To meet the high expectations of their audience, they must block everything else out of their minds and focus solely on the task at hand for as long as they're on set or stage. If they were to let the worries of their personal lives impact their performance (if an actor were to slump onto the stage, for example, complaining about how busy and tired they are and delivering the wrong lines from start to finish), there would be outrage, mass audience walkouts and career-jeopardising consequences.

For many performers, the role they are playing is far removed from their day-to-day character. A well-known example is singer Beyoncé. Naturally shy, Beyoncé created a performance persona, who she introduced to the world in 2008 through the title of her album *I Am... Sasha Fierce,* to give her the confidence to be more assertive, free and sexy in her performances. Over time, she became comfortable and confident enough within herself to no longer need her alias, reportedly saying, 'I don't need Sasha Fierce anymore, because I've grown. Now I'm able to merge the two.'[8]

Providing excellent customer service is no different to a musical or theatrical performance. It's a role we must learn and play, with the floor of our premises or worksite as our stage and our customers as our audience. The performance begins at the start of each workday and concludes at the day's end until, one day, we realise our 'performance persona' is no longer an alias… it's just who we are.

Finding Your Performance Persona

Our **performance persona** is merely *us* on our best day. It's the most sprightly, personable and attentive version of ourselves, existing to anticipate and fulfil the needs of each customer with passion and purpose – to make their life (or a moment in their life) better, easier or more enjoyable. Switching on our performance persona is intrinsically linked with our emotional energy and attitude. If we feel happy within ourselves, we are much more likely to make our customers happy too.

Engaging your performance persona may feel a little fake or forced at first, particularly if you don't regard yourself as much of a 'people person' but practice makes perfect – with an ongoing, side-serving of profits as incentive.

Customer Service Killers

For SSBs, the three biggest killers of customer service are:

- **Self-sabotage** – Not serving customers the way we know they should be served, due to a lack of confidence in, or clarity about, our product or service. This is common among startups and young skill-or-service businesses with no clear precedent as to how to package and price certain offerings. It's rife among web designers, aspiring consultants and coaches but can strike anyone undertaking any business pursuit without a clearly defined business model.

- **Inconsistency** – Allowing unmanaged, fluctuating emotions to impact the customer experience, or assuming staff share our high standards of service, without communicating and enforcing them through policies, procedures and staff training. As the saying goes, 'You are only as good as your worst employee.'

- **Complacency** – Taking customers for granted or thinking of them as an inconvenience. This is a common mindset in established businesses and among mismanaged staff. It stems from a failure to recognise that each and every customer (including the challenging ones) deserves respect, gratitude and attentive service because without them, we wouldn't have jobs.

Overcoming Self-Sabotage

There is no magic cure for customer service self-sabotage. It's a matter of evolving our operations over time, trying different approaches to presenting, pricing and delivering our service, until we find the sweet spot of demand and supply. Once we reach a consistently high standard of operation and performance, self-sabotage will have morphed into self-belief. In the meantime, remember that you are your own harshest critic and that excellent customer service has the ability to offset many operational and personal deficiencies.

Controlling Inconsistency

While a little self-awareness works wonders for creating consistency in a sole trader scenario, it's not enough to rally the troops in a growing business. To get staff on the same page, and keep them there, a deliberate, structured approach is needed – one which unites the team while setting enforceable customer service standards.

Licence to Thrill: A Customer Service Policy with a Difference

Overcoming inconsistency requires leadership, not tyranny. Instead of dictating customer service protocols to staff and expecting them to comply, it's far more effective to take a collaborative approach; consulting with them to define their role in the performance. The key is to come together to define the ideal customer experience – a performance worthy of a standing ovation and rave reviews.

A meaningful, effective and enforceable **Customer Service Policy** (or **Performance Policy)** can be developed collaboratively, in three steps:

1. **Schedule a meeting** – Schedule a compulsory paid team meeting, requiring the attendance of every staff member.
2. **Meet and entreat** – When everyone is present, introduce the need for more consistent customer service and the concept of thinking and working like a performer. Explain

that you'd like to work together to reverse-engineer the ideal customer experience, in order to reveal each individual's performance persona and work towards the creation of an overarching Customer Service Policy.

This might sound like a lot but it all rests on a single, leading question: *'How do we want customers to feel when they/we leave (or when the job/project finishes)?'* This question is powerful as it invokes empathy. The only way staff can answer is if they put themselves in the shoes of the customers they serve, stretching their minds to find a deeper, emotive purpose to their work.

Once the ideal customer feeling has been articulated, there are several other questions to consider: *'How can we make sure customers feel this way? What attitude and level of energy do we need? What must we do? What must we say?'* The answers to these questions will help to define each staff member's performance persona and form the basis of the Customer Service Policy.

The final question to raise is *'Hypothetically, what other things could we do, going above and beyond the call of duty, to delight our customers?'* This opens the door to a higher level of possibility, ideas and insight. Be sure to reiterate that there are no wrong answers or bad ideas and no judgement.

To help guide the discussions, a bonus download – *The 5 Cs of Customer Service* – is available online via *www.secretservice.biz/downloads*. This file outlines points to consider under the topics of Courtesy, Communication, Connection, Consideration and Consistency.

3. **Document** – After the first customer service staff meeting, write up a Customer Service Policy, plus two or three initial customer service procedures in a growing document of Standard Operating Procedures (aka 'the SOP') for quick access by all staff. Involve high-performing employees in the process of writing procedures by asking them to jot down the steps required to complete a specific task to a high standard (e.g. 'How to greet a customer', 'How to answer the phone', 'What to do if a customer needs to wait for a table', etc). By involving staff in the development of customer service standards and procedures, they will be more likely to embrace and embody them and less likely to dismiss them as non-essential niceties.

4. **Introduce and inspire** – When the policy and initial procedures are ready, hold a second meeting to introduce them and address any questions or concerns.

   If you found the 'Jumpstart Wristband Rewire' helpful, use it with staff too. Give each member a wristband as a temporary addition to their uniform, explaining that it is to serve as a constant reminder to keep their performance persona switched on.

   The wristband strategy could be taken to the next level by introducing a reward system, much like the belt grading system in martial arts. If a staff member demonstrates consistently high standards of customer service, they are acknowledged in front of their colleagues and 'graduated' to the next colour level, with a token wristband. Although it would require careful management to ensure good deeds didn't continually go unnoticed, a ***Wristband Reward***

System could inject an element of healthy competition into the delivery of excellent customer service.

Overcoming Complacency

A colour-code reward system may sound like a childish way to encourage high standards but our brains respond incredibly well to simple, social rewards. Financial incentives tend to be our go-to method for motivating staff; however, research in the field of 'social cognitive neuroscience' shows that alternative, non-monetary motivators are far more effective.

In his book *Social: Why our brains are wired to connect*, Professor Matthew Lieberman outlines hundreds of facts and findings about the social 'wiring' of human beings. One fascinating section details the work of Professor David Rock of the Neuroleadership Institute, who has dedicated much of his career to persuading businesses that our social makeup matters – particularly in terms of how we motivate employees.[9] While monetary incentives have their place (commissions and bonuses in sales roles, for example), studies show they produce little to no improvement in employee performance.

The best way to improve performance and overcome complacency is to meet employees' social needs, not their perceived financial ones. This is done by using five 'non-monetary drivers of behaviour' which Professor Rock presents via the acronym *SCARF*; Status, Certainty, Autonomy, Relatedness (or connection) and Fairness.

Status is the position of importance or authority a person holds, relative to others in a group. Status carries a lot of social meaning, as it signifies an individual is valued by others. In business, status is usually communicated through job titles, however the Wristband Reward System is an example of using status as a motivator without promoting everyone.

Certainty relates to the fundamental needs for safety, stability of employment and a sense of order and purpose. Whinging to our staff about the cost of safety equipment or the state of the economy is enough to cast doubt over the certainty of their employment and spark an instant drop in motivation and productivity – all the more reason to keep our negativity in check.

Autonomy is the ability to make decisions and execute tasks independently of others. We are hardwired to crave autonomy. Without it, we feel stifled and suppressed. This is not to say that employees should be given free rein – rather, they will be more motivated if given opportunities for self-regulation and expression.

Relatedness is the level of social connection an employee feels towards their colleagues. With a strong sense of belonging and inclusion, employees are more productive – they feel more comfortable working as a team to achieve common goals, reaching out for advice or assistance and offering and providing help to others. An employee who feels socially secure is also more likely to communicate any workplace concerns, enabling them to be dealt with before they impede motivation. For these reasons and more, we must encourage social connection within our businesses, striving to create a sense of family.

Fairness relates to the perceived equitability of decisions in the workplace. If employees feel a decision is unfair they are likely to take a passive aggressive stand, such as slacking off or taking unnecessary sick days. Employee perception of fairness in the workplace can account for 20% of the differences in their productivity. Closely related to employees' desire for fairness is their desire for a better boss. Faced with the choice between a payrise and a better boss, around 65% of employees will choose the latter.[10] With a stronger, fairer manager, employee productivity, satisfaction and retention rates increase, and toxic workplace politics subsides. This supports the 'Inside Out' approach, in that getting ourselves on track (as the owner and human heart of the business) is integral to boosting productivity and profitability.

In addition to Rock's SCARF model, there's another non-monetary tool we can use to get the best out of our staff, which we'll call 'observed benefits'.

Observed benefits is the extent to which an employee understands how their work benefits others. Research by Professor Adam Grant shows employees who are given the opportunity to hear or read testimonials from those people who benefit directly from their work are astoundingly more productive.

In one case, workers at a university had the tough job of phoning old-scholars to raise money to fund undergraduate scholarships. Grant surprised a few of the workers with a 5-minute visit from a person who had received a scholarship in the past; a person who had benefited directly from the team's work. Their manager then told them to remember the meeting while they were on the phone. The result? Donation pledges increased by a whopping 171%.[11] Even when Grant replaced face-to-face meetings with written letters from scholarship recipients, donations still increased by 153%.

Observed benefits are equally as powerful for small business employees. Hearing or reading testimonials from those who've benefited from their work proves that what they're doing is worthwhile. It legitimises and gives meaning to it, filling them with a sense of belief in the product or service they're delivering. If employees believe in what they do, they are more inclined to take their work seriously and approach it with diligence and passion, knowing the business they represent not only has substance, but makes a real difference in people's lives. They are liberated to work hard through a feeling of purpose and authenticity.

An example of the observed benefits motivator in an SSB context would be a builder taking his/her employees (an apprentice builder and a personal assistant) on an excursion to a home built for a client, giving them the chance to hear how much the homeowner loves their house and how thrilled they are with the last-minute design changes. Once the visit is over, the builder then draws a connection between the visit and the employees day-to-day work, saying, 'Remember this when you're working – we are not just building houses, we are building homes. We want to make the experience of building a new home as relaxed and enjoyable as possible for each client and build them a home they'll love to live in, as much as this family does.'

The SCARF and observed benefits drivers of behaviour are powerful management tools for SSB owners. Making decisions and designing motivational strategies with these in mind, gives us the ability to reduce customer service complacency, increase productivity, transform the social dynamic of our business and substantially boost its bottom line. And the best part is... none of it costs a cent.

CHAPTER 6.

LAY THE GROUNDWORK FOR GROWTH

*** WARNING! DETAIL AHEAD ***
This chapter contains detailed instructions that
may be overwhelming at first. If you get bogged
down in it, switch to skim reading and return
to each section as it becomes applicable.

We've all heard the saying 'it takes a village to raise a child'. This sentiment holds true for human and business babies alike. Neither can survive in isolation. Both must be nurtured.

Our network of past customers and contacts is our business community or 'base'. Without a strong base – a supportive business community – it is virtually impossible for an SSB to grow into a thriving pillar of society. Despite this, few SSB owners actively nurture these relationships. Most of us are so preoccupied with operational activities (serving today's customers) or customer acquisition (finding tomorrow's customers), that we forget about customers and contacts from *yesterday* – to our own detriment.

Community Roots

Communication is the foundation of community... literally. Both words stem from the Latin root word 'communis', which means 'common, communiality or sharing'. Without communication, there can be no sense of caring and without caring, there can be no sense of community.

For SSB owners this boils down to a simple rule:

Communication = Community.

If we demonstrate that we remember, care about and value our past customers and contacts through communication, they will remember, care about and value us as a community. This means they will be a reliable base from which to draw support and sales.

Without a strong community, business is a battle. There's no baseline of sales to rely on, which puts us under constant pressure to find new customers. This is not only stressful, it's expensive. Attracting a new customer is speculated to cost around 15 times more than retaining an existing one. Beyond the cost, there's often a time lag in acquiring new customers. By the time we decide what marketing action to take, find the cash flow and contacts to make it happen, implement it, wait for a lead to roll in, quote if necessary and await the 'yay or nay' response, it may well be too late.

With a strong community, a certain baseline of sales can be prompted and expected from month to month. These sales flow in organically through repeat customers (regulars), word of mouth and alliance or referral partners. While new customers are still needed to grow the business, they are not necessary to sustain it. Having a strong community relieves the day-to-day pressures of having to find new customers to make ends meet.

Lay the Lines for Communication

While there are many ways to communicate with past customers and contacts, two simple tools are all we really need – email and a phone. With these, we have the power to revive past relationships and retain them into the future through a careful blend of *scheduled* and *spontaneous* communications. Accessing this power takes a bit of work – much like establishing a physical base of communication (a 'comms base' in military terms). We need strong foundations, the right combination of wiring and electrical connections and some manual groundwork.

Email for Marketing... Money for Jam

With the right infrastructure in place, email marketing is the quickest, cheapest means of maintaining connections and boosting sales. It becomes possible for leads or bookings to materialise out of thin air.

Email marketing is:

- **Cost-effective** – Emailing in bulk is free or low-cost, depending on the size of the mailing list, how frequently emails are sent and the email marketing software (often called *autoresponder software*) in use.
- **Personal** – Email is a form of direct marketing (as distinct from mass marketing) that allows us to communicate directly to the individuals on our list. With the right software, we can divide our list of past customers and

contacts into subgroups and create highly targeted, tailored communications (campaigns) for each group. This gives us the ability to maximise engagement through relevance and personalisation. A restaurant owner who notices booking numbers are surprisingly low for an upcoming evening, for example, could use email to promote a 'Rewarding our Regulars' Meal Deal to a subgroup of loyal customers. All that's needed is a personalised email in a short letter format, containing an enticing offer and a photo of the chef presenting a mouth-watering culinary creation and, voilà, bookings will begin to roll in.

- **Timely and transparent** – Both email and snail mail (traditional, posted mail) are opened at the discretion of the recipient, but with email, the sender has more control. With traditional mail, we relinquish control the second our mail hits the postbox. There's no way of knowing who's received it and – unless it's marked 'Return to Sender' – we can go on sending mail to obsolete addressees for years. Email is infinitely more transparent, due to its digital nature. Being online, our communications are delivered instantaneously, with no lag time. This gives us the ability to control when they land in recipients' inboxes; scheduling the most appropriate transmission time, down to the minute, to increase the chances of our messages being seen and read.
- **Trackable** – With the right email marketing software, we can see how many recipients are opening their messages, how many are taking action, which campaigns are the most effective and much more.

- **Auto-cleaned** – Email marketing software enables individuals to update their own details and subscription preferences instantaneously. Not only is this beneficial for them, it helps keep our list of customers and contacts 'clean' and up to date. This saves time and money at our end, while helping to retain the value of the list as a business asset.

In preparation to harness these benefits, however, there are two pieces of infrastructure we need... *email marketing software* (optional but preferable, as explained in Chapter 4 of *The Modern Marketing Arsenal*) and a *mailing list*.

The Gist of a Mailing List

Of all the SSB owners I've had the pleasure to meet, it's rare to come across one who retains the contact details of past customers, leads and contacts in a central list or database. It's rarer still to see them actively use this list as a marketing tool. Those who do, however, are less susceptible to the troughs of the Busy/Slow Cycle and experience far greater levels of optimism, growth and success. These are the businesses that tend to grow into pillars of society – the ones giving equal consideration to past, present and future relationships and revenue streams.

A well-maintained mailing list is one of the most valuable assets an SSB owner can possess. It is usually the missing link between a struggling SSB and an untapped reservoir of potential sales. The individuals on a business' list have already established a connection with that business – whether they've met the owner, engaged in a transaction, or shown an interest in doing so by enquiring or subscribing. This pre-existing connection makes a business' list a pool of warm leads by default.

A well-maintained list is an asset that can be leveraged to generate cash flow today and increase the value of the business as a saleable asset tomorrow.

List or Lost?

Although most of us use email, there are four main reasons SSB owners don't have a mailing list or aren't using email as a marketing tool.

1. We don't want to seem pushy;
2. We forget to ask customers for their contact details;
3. We don't want to get in trouble for spamming; and
4. Our computers and IT technicians, quite frankly, confuse the crap out of us.

So, let's set the record straight.

Email Marketing: Proactive or Pushy?

Once we've delivered a service, many of us make assumptions that hinder our business' growth. Commonly, we assume that if a customer needs our services again, they will contact us. Not wanting to seem pushy or desperate, we leave them to their own devices. From their perspective, however, we go missing in action – dropping off the radar through lack of communication. Before long, they move on with another service provider and we're left wondering what went wrong.

The secret to retaining past customers is to never assume their loyalty. While some customers will call if a need arises or when a service falls due, the majority won't. It's up to us, not them, to keep the lines of communication open. Without doing so, we relinquish control of the relationship and can leave tens of thousands of dollars on the table each and every year.

We have a responsibility to our business to build a strong community, which means we have a responsibility to communicate with past customers and contacts. At the very least, this means sending an occasional email, so they know we still exist, and prompting them when a periodic service falls due. Doing this, everybody wins – our community feels informed and valued (without feeling harassed) and we stay top of mind, making the most of our opportunity to generate recurring income through repeat patronage or periodic servicing. As long as we communicate with consideration and confidence, we will be seen as proactive and professional, not pushy.

The Winner's Way to Build a List

Some businesses collect customer details and build a basic list as a matter of course, but most need to get a little more strategic.

The trick to building a list is to incentivise the exchange; providing something of high perceived value in exchange for the customer's (or potential customer's) details. Incentives can take the form of:

- **Rewards** – Gifts and bonuses for demonstrating loyalty or spending a certain amount;
- **Education** – Access to information-based products or resources;
- **Exclusivity** – Special privileges or opportunities that aren't available to everyone;
- **Inclusivity** – A sense of belonging to a group, community or social movement;
- **Insight** – The opportunity to stay informed or be one of the first to know;

- **Savings** – Monetary benefits in the form of one-off specials or ongoing discounts.

Offering ongoing savings can be tempting but they eat directly into an SSB's bottom line. While a 10% discount may not sound like much, over time it adds up. An extra 10% gross profit means far more to us and our business than an ongoing 10% discount means to our customers. They might appreciate it initially but, before long, they'll assume we've factored it into our pricing and take the discount for granted.

So, before devaluing your services through discounting, it's worth considering what your customers *really* value and set out to unlock a combination of non-monetary incentives (rewards, education, exclusivity, inclusivity and insight) that works more effectively.

Once an incentive has been selected it's time to choose a mechanism to grow your list. This could be a:

- **New customer details form** such as those used by medical professionals – these are appropriate in an array of industries including health and fitness, beauty, trade services, finance, professional services and many more;
- **Membership form** providing membership to a club or loyalty program;
- **Loyalty/rewards card** e.g. 'Collect a stamp with each coffee purchase and receive your sixth coffee free (making name and email fields mandatory upon redemption);
- **Feedback form** with an email opt-in box offering occasional email updates about special offers and upcoming events;

- **Competition entry form or business card draw** with an in-house voucher as the weekly or monthly prize, redeemable for certain stipulated services;
- **Invitations** for selected regulars to attend special events or join an exclusive VIP rewards club, with access to last minute deals and discounts;
- **Website subscription form** offering a free information product such as an ebook, online training course or checklist (e.g. '5 things you must check before choosing a builder').

No matter what mechanism you choose to collect customer details, the customer service procedures surrounding it (the distribution and collection of forms, for example) must become integrated into day-to-day operations. Without consistency and commitment, your list will not grow.

Other ways to increase your collection rate are to:

- **Combine two or more collection mechanisms** – e.g. A feedback form incentivised by entry into a monthly draw.
- **Reconsider the wording** – As explained in detail in *The Secret Service Website Formula*, the way we ask a customer to take action (known as the ***call-to-action***) has an enormous impact on its effectiveness. By reconsidering the wording of a call-to-action, we have the ability to boost the perceived value of the exchange, thereby generating a stronger emotional response. 'Subscribe to our newsletter' is an example of a weakly-worded call-to-action that provides little incentive to act. With a little consideration, it can be reframed into one that provides a strong incentive of real benefit to our ideal customer.

For example, 'Subscribe below to be one of the first to see and sample our new menus, as soon as they're released.' The incentive won't appeal to everyone, but that's a good thing. As long as it appeals to our ideal customer, it will enable our list to grow while remaining clean and strong.

- **Put a dollar value on the incentive** where possible – e.g. 'Instant access to *The Little Book of Business* valued at $29', or 'Win a $50 voucher towards the beauty treatment of your choice'. Adding a dollar figure helps customers appreciate the value of the incentive.

- **Keep forms short and sweet** – Unless the circumstances justify asking for more, only collect the customer's most basic contact details to avoid scaring them off. Requesting their name, email address, mobile number and postcode is ideal when collecting data in-store using a paper form or mobile device (such as an iPad). For website subscription forms, name and email address is the generally-accepted norm. Any more fields and the conversion rate will likely take a nosedive.

Email Marketing to the Letter of the Law

Many SSB owners are afraid to build or email their list – concerned about being prosecuted for spamming. In my home country of Australia, the Spam Act 2003 (enforced by the Australian Communications and Media Authority) sets out the rules and regulations for sending messages by email, SMS, MMS and instant messaging with the intent to offer, advertise or promote goods, services or opportunities. While full, current details of the regulations are available online, they essentially boil down to three rules.[12]

1. **Get consent** – The recipient must be expecting (or have reasonable cause to expect) marketing emails from your business. This consent can be 'expressed' or 'inferred'. Expressed consent means that the recipient has checked a box to opt in to a mailing list, usually via an online or paper-based form. Inferred consent allows us to presume that a recipient would be interested in receiving our communications, due to a pre-existing relationship.

2. **Identify yourself** – Marketing emails must clearly identify the business by name and provide accurate contact details that can be used to reach you if necessary. Contact details should include an email address, phone number, physical and/or postal address and website address. Providing clear identification is important both practically and figuratively. The more transparent we are, the more legitimate our business seems.

3. **Give them a way out** – Every marketing email must give recipients the ability to opt out of future communications via an unsubscribe facility or system. This is easier than it sounds. If using email marketing software, email templates include an Unsubscribe link in the footer as standard. If not using email marketing software, this requirement can be met by providing a manual instruction, such as, 'To unsubscribe, reply to this email with 'unsubscribe' in the subject line.'

Bear these three rules in mind and remain aware of similar spam laws in your country and you'll have no cause for email marketing concern.

The Ups & Downs of Emailing IT

One of the main reasons SSB owners don't have a mailing list or make use of email marketing is that it's deemed too hard, from a technical standpoint. In most small businesses, customer and contact details need to be entered and maintained across multiple computer applications, for the purposes of accounting, operations management, project management, relationship management or email marketing to name a few. If these applications can't talk to each other, it creates excess work and undue frustration. Eventually, something or someone snaps... and the applications that are least critical to daily operations (usually email marketing or customer relationship management software, or both), fall by the wayside. This doesn't mean the software has failed; it means our IT infrastructure has failed.

If our comms base is built on rocky foundations, with old-school infrastructure, there'll be constant obstacles and frustrations. Things will never work as they should.

If built with state-of-the-art infrastructure, things just work – emails, contacts, calendars and documents synchronise beautifully and are accessible from anywhere on any device, applications play nicely together (sharing data where necessary) and systems can be streamlined in ways we'd once never thought possible. Now, it's not only possible, it's actually quite easy, as you'll discover in the next chapter. With Chapter 7 as your guide, you'll be navigating your way from computer chaos to control and ready to start email marketing in no time.

Hit the Phones, Jack

While email is an incredible marketing tool, it's no substitute for phone communication. Email may facilitate one-way, visual engagement but phones enable two-way, verbal communication in real-time. Writing an email instead of making a phone call can often squander an opportunity to strengthen a relationship through real-time conversation.

The Phone Phobia Phenomenon

There is a sense of safety in email and text messaging that causes many of us (usually the more introverted) to gravitate to it as our preferred means of communication. Many of us have wasted hours perfecting an email about a matter we could have handled in a couple of minutes by phone. And most of us have said something by email or text that we daren't say in person – fuelled by ego, emotion or alcohol. Camouflaged by our computers, it's common to present a more or less filtered version of our authentic self, which can stand in the way of building stronger relationships. While email can be personalised, a phone call is always more personal... but it's not always easy.

For phone phobics, making or taking a business call is the epitome of social pressure – we have a small window of time in which to say what we need to say. If we don't say it exactly right, we might look silly or make the other person angry or upset. Unlike a face-to-face meeting, there's little room for small talk and no ability to use or read body language or social cues. There's also an underlying pressure to respond immediately to avoid imposing awkward silence on the other person, stopping us from taking the time we'd usually take to think before we speak. Scary stuff.

But there's a reason it's scary.

Engaging in a phone conversation is unnatural. From the dawn of civilisation until the phone was invented in 1876, real-time communication was only possible if we were in another person's physical presence. From then until the late 1990s, there was no choice for business owners but to accept the phone as their primary means of communication. Now, armed with email, we are no longer forced to pick up the phone – limiting the growth of our businesses, our relationships and ourselves.

The underlying cause of phone phobia is not a fear of one-on-one communication, nor the phone itself – it's the combination of the two. As humans, we are hardwired to communicate face-to-face, with an estimated 55% of what we communicate being conveyed through our body language. Phone communication puts a 100% emphasis on the remaining 45%, which is purely verbal. For those of us who are introverted or sensitive, having the social spotlight shining solely on what we say can make us feel vulnerable, anxious and out of control. It gives rise to social fears of failure, conflict, rejection, judgement, inferiority, inadequacy, embarrassment, humiliation and more. We worry we won't be able to articulate what we feel or want, and how the other person will react if we do.

As handy as email is, it has given us an easy out; a means to avoid facing and overcoming our fear the hard (but surefire) way – through practice, perseverance and personal growth.

Tips to Conquer Phone Fear

- **Recognise that you are your harshest critic** – Most social anxieties experienced by SSB owners (the two most common being phone phobia and fear of public speaking) stem from a subconscious belief that people are judging us as harshly as we judge ourselves. For the record, they are not. You are, by far, your harshest critic. Rest assured, others are too wrapped up in their own lives to give you the same level of consideration they give themselves.

- **Rationalise your fear** – An effective way to rationalise the fear of making a phone call is to ask questions, such as: 'Of all the phone calls I've made, how many were worth this anxiety?', 'Will I remember this phone call in 10 years time?' or 'What's the worst that can happen and, if it did, would it kill me?' If there's no risk of death, it can't be that bad.

- **Write a list** – Jot down the key points to be conveyed. This helps establish a sense of focus and control. Note though, that these should be prompting words, not sentences. Read down a phone line, scripted sentences can be technically perfect but devoid of soul. They can also make it difficult to respond to unexpected questions or handle deviations in the conversation. So trust yourself enough to say what you need to say prompted by a few dot points. However it comes out is how it's supposed to come out. It will be a reflection of who you are in that moment, therefore perfectly imperfect.

- **Feel the fear and dial anyway** – Fear is just another fleeting emotion. Don't try to convince yourself you're not scared or that you're being silly. Feel and acknowledge it like any other negative emotion, knowing that it's not wrong and won't last long.

- **Let your fingers do the walking** – Just as working yourself up to jump is the hardest part of bungee-jumping (so I'm told), working yourself up to dial the phone number is the hardest part of making a call. Once you've dialled, there's a flicker of surrender and acceptance. From that point, the conversation is what it is. Before a call, remember that feeling of surrender, trying not to think about what your finger is doing. Just *jump*.

- **Get moving** – Make phone calls using headphones so you can stand, pace up and down and use body language like you usually would. Movement provides an outlet for nervous energy that can help words flow more easily.

- **Ask for more time** – There is no obligation to answer every question the second it's asked. If feeling stumped or backed into a corner, it's perfectly reasonable to ask for time to consider or research your response, e.g. 'Hmmm... Let me think about that for a moment' or 'That's a really good question. I need to look into that/give it some thought. Can I get back to you tomorrow?'

- **Negativity says more about them** – If the person becomes hostile in response to what you're saying (when explaining that the completion date for a project has been set back, for example), know that their negativity says more about them and their insecurities than it does about you – as long as you're being *honest*, *open* and *accountable*. Most rational people will respond to bad news such as a delay or anticipated budget blow-out in a calm, understanding way, as long as the bearer of the news takes responsibility for the problem, rather than trying to pass the buck.

Resuscitating Relationships

For bringing relationships with past customers and contacts back from the brink, nothing beats a personal phone call. The phone provides a means of spontaneous communication with real social impact.

Imagine this phone call: 'Hi Jo, it's Shannon here, your hair-dresser from MIA Hair & Beauty. I'm just calling because we haven't seen you in a few months. I just wanted to check you're okay and that you were happy with your last hair treatment? ... Oh, that's a relief! Don't worry, I understand. Time flies, doesn't it? Would you like to book an appointment now?'

Phoning customers who haven't transacted with us for a while does several things. It:

- **Shows care and concern** for the customer's wellbeing;
- **Shows courage and depth of character** by openly inviting criticism;
- **Demonstrates empathy and vulnerability**, which strengthen relationships;
- **Draws out honest feedback**, crucial for improving and growing a business;
- **Makes the customer feel valued** as a client and as a friend;
- **Gives us the chance to take accountability** for any mistakes and do what's necessary to retain the relationship (such as offering the service again, free of charge);
- **May result in a booking/sale** – if so, everybody wins. We feel like a magician, having created a booking out of thin air, and the customer feels a sense of satisfaction, having unexpectedly ticked an item off their to do list;

- **May *not* result in a booking/sale** – in which case, everybody still wins. We know where we stand and the customer has had the chance to air any grievances. This ends the relationship on a positive note and reduces the risk of negative word of mouth.

Whether we're calling a past customer or an old contact, they will be surprised to hear from us, and may even be standoffish or defensive at first. The best way to handle this is to exude a sense of warmth and calmness – resisting the urge to use small talk to break the ice – then be upfront about the purpose of the call, as in the above example. With the right introduction (a couple of carefully considered, pre-prepared points) we can offset any initial abrasiveness and see where the rabbit hole of telephone conversation takes us.

Face Facts

Despite our ability to use technology to communicate from a distance, the strongest human bonds will always be formed, solidified and strengthened through face-to-face contact. That's why, although we may initiate contact via phone or computer, the first real step in developing a relationship of substance is to meet in person.

The ability to interact and socialise meaningfully during a face-to-face meeting is the quickest way to build *trust*. Trust is as important in business relationships as it is in personal ones, because time, money and reputations are at stake – the three things that underpin our livelihood.

Face-to-face interactions set a foundation for trust, trust is essential to build a strong business community, and a strong community is essential for SSB success. It's therefore vital to prioritise face-to-face meetings with our contacts, each and every week... no matter how busy we are with other things.

Somewhat ironically, it's best to meet with contacts when we *are* busy, not when we're desperate to line up a sale. Meeting when we're busy shifts the dynamic of the meeting from desperation and victimhood to confidence and contentment, which are infinitely more attractive.

Community Rules

Building a business community is no different from cultivating a circle of friends. If we apply the same social etiquette when communicating with customers and contacts as we do in our friendship circle, our community will naturally flourish. Business relationships can be more fickle than personal relationships but by following five fundamental principles of friendship, outlined below, they can develop into incredibly rewarding lifelong bonds.

1. **Be present** – Communicate regularly and attentively with past customers and contacts, embracing opportunities to speak on the phone and meet face-to-face.

2. **Keep your word** – Do what you say you'll do. If promising subscribers special offers and discounts, give them special offers and discounts. If promoting 'family friendly' dining, go the extra mile to make it really family friendly. There's nothing more important than delivering on our promises.

3. **Keep secrets a secret** – Never breach privacy or confidentiality and never share or sell your list.

4. **Respect yourself and others** – Recognise that your time, money and needs are no more or less important than those of your customers and contacts. We can respect their time by not barraging them with constant communications (the social equivalent of overstaying our welcome) or relentlessly talking about ourselves or our business. We can respect their money by never promoting a product or service that we don't genuinely believe in, can't deliver on or haven't used ourselves. And we can respect their needs by recognising that it's rude to contact a past customer or contact only to push for a sale, just as it's rude to reach out to an old friend only to ask a favour.

5. **Be generous** – Give information, insights and opportunities without any expectation of return (within reason).

Essentially, these boil down to one golden rule: 'Do unto past customers and contacts as you would have service providers do unto you.'

Ready... Set... Grow

With all the marketing communication options available to SSB owners today, we have a tendency to overthink and underact. By narrowing our focus to the use of a core suite of communication tools to grow our community of pre-existing customers and contacts, it becomes easier to stop thinking and start doing. You don't need to launch into email marketing right now, just get used to the idea while you reacquaint yourself with the phone and face-to-face meetings, review your IT infrastructure and start growing your list. Before you know it, you'll not only have laid the groundwork for growth... you'll be living and breathing it.

CHAPTER 7.

FROM CHAOS TO CONTROL: IT FOR SSBS

Over the last few decades, IT (information technology) has come a long, long way. It has become integral to all business support functions, including marketing. The trouble is, identifying the right infrastructure can seem impossible. All too often we receive conflicting advice about the hardware and software we need and end up in an IT quagmire, with similar sets of customer data needing to be manually entered across several applications, because 'this' application won't talk to 'that' software and 'that' software doesn't allow for functions X, Y and Z. Once upon a time, this frustration was unavoidable. Now, we have a choice.

The Scoop on In-House Servers

A few years ago, storing our business software, files and emails on central, on-site servers was the epitome of SSB IT. A central server gave us the ability to share files, rather than having to store and access individual files on individual computers. It was important for business growth but also expensive and risky. To this day, a decent in-house server costs an exorbitant amount of money. On top of that, peripheral hardware such as a UPS (uninterruptible power supply), server cooling cabinet and off-site backup system are required to mitigate the risks of data-loss through electrical surges, fire and other disasters... and the expense doesn't stop there. The assistance of IT professionals is usually needed to implement, maintain and update the delicate system. Even the smallest of changes, such as creating an email account for a new employee, will come at a price.

But, thankfully, the days of the expensive in-house server are coming to an end. Where once a sophisticated $40,000 setup may have been the best option for a growing SSB, it is no more. For the vast majority of SSB owners, investing in an in-house server is not only overkill – it's a backward step. Today, we have access to far superior, smarter infrastructure at a fraction of the cost.

Cloud and Proud

Once upon a time, the primary purpose of the internet for SSB owners was to access and share information publicly via websites. Since then, there's been a monumental advancement. We can now use the internet not only to access and share data beyond the confines of our business but to operate, create and collaborate within it. This is possible via online platforms and services collectively known as *the cloud*.

Most of us have dabbled in one or more cloud-based applications, such as Xero for bookkeeping, Dropbox for file storage or

Gmail for email. Although that's a good first step, having one or two cloud-based applications doesn't allow us to tap into the life-changing benefits of a predominantly cloud-based system. When fully embracing the cloud for email, calendars, applications, file creation, file storage and more... everything just works. We can scrap our in-house servers and suspend our IT support. It doesn't matter what combination of desktop computers, laptops, tablets or phones we have, or where they are located. As long as we have an internet connection, we can access anything from anywhere.

A cloud-based IT system is far more flexible than a server-based system. Most of the major cloud applications are built to integrate with each other, allowing data to be shared between them. This means the frustration of entering the same data multiple times can be overcome. For those applications that don't integrate automatically, bridges called 'add-ons' and 'extensions' can be installed to connect one to another, enhancing our system's functionality and versatility.

And that's just the tip of the iceberg. There's a long list of other reasons to move to a cloud-based system, for example:

- **It's kind on your cash flow** – Cloud services are usually billed per user, per month or year. This is ideal for SSBs as it means our IT costs become predictable from one period to the next. If we have one user, we pay for one user. If we have 20 users, we pay for 20. It's all relative, with no nasty surprises.

- **An internet browser is all you need** – Working in the cloud, most applications are accessed and operated in an internet browser (such as Chrome, Firefox, Edge or Safari). With a username and password, they (and all our data) can be accessed on any device, with no requirement to download and store files locally. This helps keep local file storage to a minimum, while preserving the memory capacity and processing speed of our computers.

- **It's good to grow** – A cloud-based system grows organically, as a business does. As soon as it's set up, it's ready and able to support the business' expansion, without the interruption or expense of further IT overhauls.

- **Perfect harmony is finally possible** – Emails, contacts and calendars synchronise across multiple devices, without the drama that most SSB owners have come to expect.

- **Improved time management** – Events and meetings can be scheduled for individuals and groups. RSVPs can be requested, calendars updated and reminders sent automatically, boosting productivity and reducing human error and oversights.

- **Proactive IT support** – With cloud-based applications, updates and bug fixes happen automatically. Where once SSBs were left out in the cold by software providers – desperately seeking support for buggy software – it's in the best interest of modern cloud-based providers to stay at the top of their game and keep us happy. Without providing a high-quality platform and excellent customer support, they'd be crippled by bad ratings and reviews. To avoid this fate, they tend to go above and beyond, performing updates regularly and fixing bugs before most of us even notice them – a far cry from the software support of old.

- **Reduced risk of data loss** – With cloud file storage applications such as Google Drive or Dropbox, our computers can be set to mirror what's saved in the cloud. This means we have full, up-to-date copies of files at all times – accessible if our internet connection drops out, for example. These files can be backed up as normal, giving us several layers of protection. If we lose our laptop or our hard drive dies, there's no need to panic. We can simply replace it, log in to our cloud services and pick up where we left off.

- **Use the right file every time** – Gone are the days of saving documents to a USB drive to work remotely, or emailing drafts to ourselves or colleagues as attachments, creating confusion, unwanted copies and extra work. With files stored in the cloud, we can kiss the USB collection goodbye; working on the latest version of any document wherever we may be, and collaborating with others in real time, without duplicating a single file.

- **The ability to embrace remote staffing** – A cloud-based IT system makes it much easier and more feasible to engage the services of a virtual assistant (VA) or give employees the flexibility to work from home.

A Productivity Suite: Your Springboard to the Cloud

The often missing link between dabbling in the cloud and diving into it, is the selection and installation of a *cloud-based productivity suite*. A productivity suite is a set of online tools that takes care of a business' IT essentials – email, calendars, internal communication, file creation and storage. With this as a foundation, other cloud-based applications can be 'plugged in' to work happily around it, sharing data where need be.

There are several cloud-based productivity suites to choose from. The main ones are provided by the giants of IT infrastructure: Google, with Google Workspace (previously G Suite) and Microsoft, with Microsoft 365. Lesser known options, such as Zoho, are also growing in popularity.

Each suite has distinct advantages and special features. Google Workspace for example, is incredibly flexible – its ability to facilitate collaboration and create custom applications to systemise and streamline workflow is second to none. Microsoft 365 includes access to the popular Microsoft Office suite, which is appealing to software traditionalists. And Zoho has a range of applications that are ideal for small businesses, including an excellent bookkeeping application called Zoho Books, a fully-featured CRM tool and an HR management app called Zoho Recruit.

Of these three platforms, I typically recommend Google Workspace. At the most basic level of implementation, this means using:

- **Gmail** instead of Outlook;
- **Google Docs**, **Sheets** and **Slides** instead of Word, Excel and PowerPoint;
- **Google Drive** for file storage;
- **Google Forms, AppSheet and other add-ons** for digital data collection, the creation of custom apps to streamline business-specific processes and much more.

With a productivity suite in place, choosing applications for the various functions in our business (bookkeeping and email marketing, for example) becomes easier. We can seek out and select applications based on their compatibility with our productivity suite, budget and business needs, creating a state-of-the-art IT environment from the comfort of our home computer.

Is a Cloud-Based System Safe?

The major concern about switching from a server-based system to a cloud-based system is a perceived lack of security. While shifting to a cloud-based system does mean placing a high level of trust in the cloud service providers we choose, it's important to retain a sense of perspective.

Businesses of all shapes, sizes and budgets are flocking to the cloud, from sole traders to global corporations. Without having confidence in Google and Microsoft's incredible infrastructure and security-centric approach to operations, these organisations would never have made the transition.

Could Google or Microsoft steal our data? Probably. But would they? No... not without jeopardising their reputations and respective market shares. It just wouldn't be worth it to them.

The top three causes of data loss for SSBs are human error, hardware failure and data corruption.[13] Examples of human error include losing a laptop which is not backed up, theft of a device with inadequate password protection, or clicking a link in a spam email that activates malware. The second cause, hardware failure, occurs when a component of our physical infrastructure (such as a hard drive or server) fails irreparably and the data is irrecoverable. The third cause, data corruption, is when a glitch occurs that breaks a computer programme or file, making it unusable.

None of these causes of data loss involve the cloud.

In fact, with a cloud-based system, the risks associated with these three vulnerabilities are significantly reduced. Using

Gmail, for example, spam protection technology is so comprehensive that spam is almost obsolete. Less spam means there's less of a chance of inadvertently installing a virus. If a hardware failure occurs, or a device is stolen, the original data will be waiting patiently for its owner, in the cloud, mitigating what would otherwise be a disaster. And as for data corruption, cloud service providers have far greater lines of defence and recovery than we ever could with an in-house setup.

It's important to note that the cloud is not a substitute for regular in-house backups and virus protection. A passionate advocate for Mac (Apple) computers, I use and recommend Time Machine (which comes standard on a Mac) to perform daily backups on an external hard drive. If your business doesn't use Apple computers, you'll need to find a suitable method for performing daily backups. You'll also need to work with an IT professional to ensure adequate security infrastructure is in place, such as antivirus software and firewalls, as non-Mac computers are more vulnerable to viruses and other outside threats.

Cloud Comfort

Cloud-based technology is a game-changer for SSBs. With very little upfront investment, your business can become more streamlined than ever before, requiring less human capital to achieve the same or better standard of work. In turn, it will be easier to manage, cheaper to run, more profitable and professional. The comforts of the cloud can't be enjoyed without taking a leap of faith, however. It might feel a little scary but once you've made the move to a cloud-based productivity suite and start exploring applications to integrate with it, you'll wonder how you ever lived without it.

RECOVERY MISSION 2

Chapter 4 – Jumpstart the Heart of Your Business

- **Mind your mantras** – Identify and print out quotes or phrases that give you a sense of hope and reassurance; whether they ground you, inspire you or put things in perspective. For example, 'It's all meant to be' or 'I'm exactly where I'm supposed to be'. Stick them where you're sure to see them – on the fridge, near your computer or the back of a door.

- **Special ops assignment** – Dig out a silicone wristband to use for the Wristband Rewire on page 62 and commit to wearing it everyday for at least two months. Let it serve as a reminder to keep your performance persona activated; thinking and working like a performer as much of the time as possible. Whenever negativity creeps in, flick the band against your wrist. Let the snap trigger you to change course: to *recognise* the feeling, *reframe* the blame, *recharge* and *recover*.

Chapter 5 – Rally the Troops to Thrill Current Customers

- **Access Unlocked** – Download and print the *Customer Cringe-Points Checklist* and *5 Cs of Customer Service* files from *www.secretservice.biz/downloads*.

- **Collect evidence** – Work your way through the Customer Cringe-Points Checklist. Take the opportunity to talk with customers (both past and present) to identify unspoken cringe-points.

- **Take remediating action** – Select two cringe-points to fix by the end of the week, then create a schedule to fix the rest. Decide how often you'll complete the Cringe-Points Checklist: quarterly, half yearly or annually, and set a reminder in your calendar.
- **Clarify your cover** – Consider your performance persona. What does your best self look, feel, act and communicate like? Write down how you would like to be perceived by customers and by staff (if applicable).
- **Make it official** – Develop a Customer Service or Performance Policy. If the 5 Cs of Customer Service resonate with you, incorporate them into your policy and ensure staff are trained to prioritise them.
- **Avoid bribes** – Consider ways to motivate staff based on the *SCARF* model and *observed benefits* research (page 74) rather than purely financial incentives.

Chapter 6 – Lay the Groundwork for Growth

- **Keep your friends close** – Using a spreadsheet, bring the details of past and present customers and contacts together in one place to form a mailing list. Fields can include first and last name, business name (if relevant), email address, phone number, post code, any applicable subgroups (e.g. VIPs) and more if desired.
- **Cultivate contacts** – Decide on an offline strategy to legally grow your mailing list, then design a form (be it a customer details form, membership form or feedback form) to implement it. Start using the form to collect

customer details, making sure there's a process in place to promptly transfer the information to the mailing list.

- **Strengthen the signal** – Aim to phone three past customers or contacts per week with no expectation or underlying agenda. Simply re-open the lines of communication and, where relevant, suggest catching up face-to-face for a coffee.
- **Be email aware** – Whenever you sit down to write an email, stop and consider whether email is really the best way to communicate the message. If addressing a complex problem or anticipating a negative reaction, pick up the phone instead.

Chapter 7 – From Chaos to Control: IT for SSBs

- **Spell IT out** – Write a list of what you like and dislike about your current IT setup as a starting point for change. Consider what's working, what's costing you time and money and what an ideal IT setup would achieve.
- **Secure a digital base** – Research, select and implement a cloud-based productivity suite; the first and most pivotal step in an IT overhaul.

PART THREE

SURVIVAL OF THE FITTEST

It's no secret that surviving in business requires hard work and dedication... but there's more to it than that.

Just like training for the armed forces, building our 'business muscle' requires an intense period of physical and mental conditioning, discipline, patience and persistence. It also requires the development of foresight and adaptability – a willingness to identify our strengths, weaknesses, opportunities and threats, to assess them, make decisions and take action – constantly evolving and improving, in order to enjoy the SSB equivalent of 'advancing rank'.

Of the SSB owners who don't survive in business, it's rarely through lack of physical effort. Small business owners tend to work longer hours than most other professions and take less time off. 60 to 80 hour work-weeks are common... as is going years without a proper holiday.

We are clearly working hard – but are we working smart? The incredibly high small business failure rate suggests not. With approximately 50% of sole traders in any given year ceasing to exist a mere four years later, it goes to show that all the extra hours we're working aren't doing us a whole lot of good.

Working smart is the equivalent of taking time to 'work *on* your business, not *in* your business'. It means taking time away from (or in addition to) our operational activities to assess our results to date, consider options for improvement, make decisions and adjust our actions accordingly. It means separating ourselves (physically and emotionally) from our day-to-day problems to make room for solutions. It means asking the right questions (of ourselves and others) to get positive, productive and ultimately profitable answers.

If we only work *in* our business, we are training for physical strength alone – not developing the mental strength to survive, let alone advance rank. Physical strength might have kept Indiana Jones one step ahead of the giant boulder chasing him out of a temple but, without the foresight and adaptability to know when to leap out of its way, his adventures would have been cut short. He'd have plunged to a quick death or slowly had the life crushed out of him; either way, a tragic and untimely demise (not fit for daytime TV let alone blockbuster status).

Business owners run a similar gauntlet each and every day. Without a balance of hard work and smart work, our business' fate is virtually sealed... a quick and dramatic demise, upon realising there's simply not enough money to pay the bills, or an excruciatingly slow one, with the Big 4 Frustrations drawing our suffering out for years, if not decades.

Working *on* our business is an ongoing process of envisioning, planning, painting, moulding and maintaining the 'big picture' of our business. Most SSBs start out with little more than a basic business plan – a big picture equivalent to a rough pencil sketch. Over time, with a blend of practice, patience and persistence – working in and on the business – the picture should evolve in depth and detail, until it's as clear and sharp as a photograph.

The trouble is, when many of us sit down to create or update our business plan, we hit a brick wall. We end up with a slightly rehashed version of the same document and little to action or implement. A year later, our business looks the same as it always did... with the same frustrations, the same financial situation and the same feeling of impending failure.

There's a saying that sums up this phenomenon: 'If you always do what you've always done, you'll always get what you've always got.' When we endeavour to work on our business without any direction or guidelines, we inadvertently do what we've always done and continue to produce the same result. This is unsustainable. Eventually, the boulder of business doom will come bearing down on us, causing a quick business death or years of semi-entrepreneurial agony.

Sustainable success and satisfaction – the alternatives to doom and destruction – are achieved by working smarter not harder. This part of the book is geared to equip you to do just that. Over the next four chapters, you will see what foresight and adaptability looked like for me, with tips and techniques to discover and implement them for yourself – making the hours you spend working *on* your business, the best, most productive use of time possible.

CHAPTER 8.

'SO... WHAT DO YOU DO?'

Our ability to succeed as an SSB owner rests largely on our ability to communicate what we do; to use words that attract and entice people to support our business and engage our services. However, without having a clear understanding of what it is we actually do, it's near impossible to convey it in an effective, engaging way – whether we're speaking to a friend or reaching out to potential customers through some form of marketing activity.

So let's strip 'what we do' back to bare bones and flesh it out from there.

The Bare Bones of Service

There are four types of service, as shown in the matrix below. Which of these types a service falls into is determined by the perceptions of potential customers, about: 1) the necessity of the service, and 2) the level of risk associated with it.

Figure 13: The Service Skeleton – A matrix to determine the type of service you sell

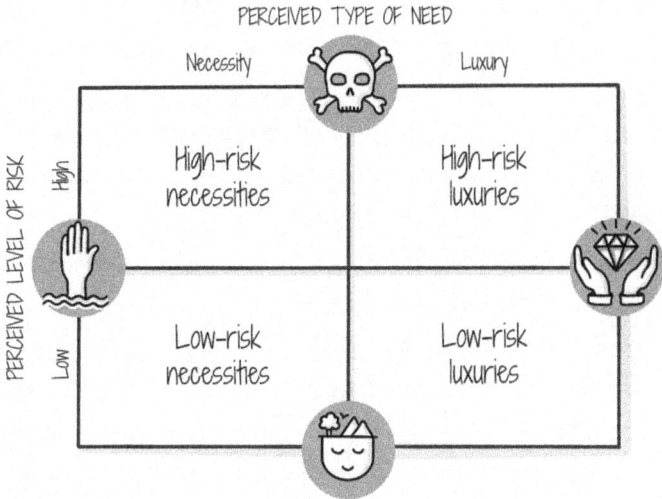

Necessity or Luxury?

A **necessary service** helps us attain or maintain what we believe to be an acceptable, modern standard of living. This includes services to sustain or improve (for practical reasons) our lives, health, lifestyle, assets/amenities and livelihood. The services of general practice doctors, lawyers, tradespeople, most business-to-business (B2B) professionals and low/mid-range eateries are examples of necessities. We engage a necessary service if and when we feel it's essential. The decision is not whether or not to buy, but who to buy from.

In contrast, a service is a **luxury** if we pursue it for the sake of personal enjoyment, satisfaction or reward, prestige or social acknowledgement. The demand for luxury goods increases as income rises and decreases as it falls, in line with our disposable income. Beauty services (beyond basic haircuts), custom jewellery and garment design, premium hospitality services and high-end residential design/construction services are luxuries to most people. With luxuries, the decision of which provider to choose can be made long before the customer is ready or willing to purchase, through 'aspirational planning'. For example, 'When I finish my thesis, I'm going to have a pamper day at Life of Luxury Day Spa,' or, 'When I get married, I want Isle of White Couture to design my dream dress.'

While some services are obviously a necessity or a luxury, others aren't so clearcut. Perception is subjective. What one person perceives as a luxury (takeaway meals, in-home cleaning or the design/construction of a swimming pool), another may perceive as an absolute necessity. It pays to determine whether our most loyal and profitable customers view our services as a luxury or necessity so we can attract more of the same; planning, writing and designing our marketing communications and sales materials accordingly. Making this distinction and subtly framing our services as either a luxury or necessity can have a big impact on the effectiveness of our marketing and, in turn, our bottom line.

Risky Business

Perceived level of risk is how much a potential customer feels they stand to lose, should the delivery of the service go wrong. Purchasing a meal at a café is low-risk – we might feel disappointed with our experience but in the grand scheme of things, we know we haven't lost much: a few dollars and the opportunity to have had a better experience elsewhere. In comparison, booking a venue for a large wedding reception is high-risk.

It's a substantial commitment with a lot to lose. More money is at stake, as well as the physical comfort of guests and, often, the perceived social standing or reputation of the bride, groom and their families.

There are six key indicators of a service's perceived risk:

- **Price** – Generally, the higher the price, the higher the perceived risk. Where low-risk stops and high-risk begins is impossible to say, as each person's perception of price is unique to their own financial situation and beliefs surrounding value for money. As a rule of thumb, however, a one off purchase in the *hundreds* of dollars or less is likely to be considered low-risk by the majority of the market, while a one-off purchase or ongoing commitment amounting to *thousands* of dollars or more is likely to be considered high-risk. Beyond the amount itself, the way in which price is communicated can have a big impact on a service's perceived risk. Generally, preset pricing (in the form of standardised consult fees, price lists or packages) is associated with lower risk services, while 'post-op pricing' (custom quotes, proposals and tenders – explained further in Chapter 10) is associated with higher risk services.

- **Urgency** – The urgency of a need can outweigh the perceived risk of a service. Emergency services such as general dentistry or plumbing are classic examples. If we find ourselves without something that we've become accustomed to or reliant on (such as health or hot water), we experience a sense of suffering and are driven to relieve the pain as quickly as possible, largely ignoring any perceived risk.

- **Commitment** – The level of commitment involved in a service transaction plays an important part in a customer's determination of perceived risk. It can be influenced by:
  - The size and scope of the project (including the degree of technical skill and customisation required);
  - The duration or frequency of service delivery;
  - Barriers to exit (financial, physical, emotional and social costs of ending the relationship early, if need be);
  - Contractual obligations (including the formality, fairness, length and substance of a written service contract); and
  - The amount of input/action required of the customer to attain the desired result (providing access to certain assets, information or systems or following a certain self-improvement regime, for example).

    The bigger the commitment, or more daunting it seems to the customer, the higher the perceived risk.

- **Presence** – Whether or not customers are physically present during the delivery of a service contributes to their perception of the risk involved. Many services, such as beauty, health and hospitality, can't occur without the active participation of the customer. If they're physically present and actively involved, customers naturally retain a sense of control over the service transaction – keeping its perceived risk to a minimum. At the other end of the 'presence' spectrum are services involving technically complex or customised projects, such as website or building design. With time-consuming projects such as these, most of the heavy lifting occurs behind-the-scenes. It's simply not practical for customers to be present throughout the entire process, so, by default, the perceived risk of these services is higher.

- **Social care factor** – The potential for social reward or repercussion is important to consider when analysing a service's perceived level of risk. When making certain purchases, it's natural for customers to take the opinions or judgements of others into consideration, e.g. 'How would this make me look?' or 'What would people say?' This line of thinking can heavily sway the purchase of goods or services to those more likely to garner social acceptance, approval or admiration. While some people's social care factor is higher than others, certain services give rise to greater social consideration, such as the wedding venue example. The higher the potential for social scrutiny, the higher the perceived risk.

- **Connection** – The energy, attitude and general likability of the person selling a service is one of the most important factors determining a potential customer's perception of risk. Those of us who demonstrate confidence, passion, authenticity and empathy (identifying with prospects' thoughts, feelings and circumstances) will sell more at higher prices than those who seem nervous, disinterested, detached or self-concerned. Feeling a strong connection with the SSB owner or salesperson can cause service seekers to overlook or justify things that may have otherwise put them off, including a price that's significantly higher than comparable alternatives.

Identifying the perceived risks associated with our service is important for two reasons. Firstly, it makes us better sales-people. It gives us the insight required to spot inklings of insecurity in comments or cues from our sales prospects and address them with empathy and understanding, before they manifest into deal-breakers. Secondly, it's an important step in determining which lead-to-sale strategy is best for our business (explored in Chapter 17), paving the way to higher conversion rates, sales and profits.

Fleshing Out the Detail

Getting to grips with the basics of our offering is one thing, but moulding flesh onto the bones – giving substance to our service and being able to talk about it in an engaging way – is quite another. This comes to light when we're asked that inevitable question by past friends or new acquaintances – 'So... what do you do?' If our service has substance and scalability, we'll welcome this question. If it doesn't, it sends chills down our spine.

Another word for substance is **value**: the perceived worth of a good or service. Value has a huge impact on the effectiveness of our marketing and sales efforts. When we don't incorporate and communicate enough value, we lose customers to the businesses that do.

Most of us leave our customers' perception of value to chance, when we could be actively influencing it and reaping the rewards of doing so. In such a fast-paced world, SSB owners no longer have the luxury of letting potential customers join the dots about the value of our services. We've got to draw the picture for them through the use of a strong **value proposition**.

The All-Important Value Proposition (VP)

A value proposition or VP is a verbal or written spiel which communicates how a business adds value to (impacts, improves or enhances) a customer's life or bank balance.

The delivery of a VP exists on a spectrum, from a snippet or 'canapé' version to an unabridged or 'banquet' version. A ***canapé VP*** is a small, well-presented and tasty teaser, often wheeled out at networking events. It's a sentence or two that concisely communicates *what* is possible; the impact or improvement our business can have on/in the lives of our customers. Essentially, the canapé version of a VP is a juicy carrot, dangled to attract the interest of potential customers. It should cause them to become so curious about *how* such an outcome is possible that they can't resist taking a bite (asking a follow-up question to extract more information).

At the other end of the VP spectrum is the banquet version. The ***banquet VP*** is a longer, more formal and detailed proposition, appropriate for a sales meeting. It goes beyond a teaser of *what* outcome is possible, to a comprehensive explanation of *how* that outcome is possible, reinforced by calculations, diagrams and other visual proof. The banquet version of a VP is most relevant for SSBs selling high-risk services, faced with the challenge of building a high enough perception of value for potential customers to justify the risk that comes with signing on the dotted line.

A strong VP doesn't write itself. It takes careful consideration and refinement – often over many years. High-performing salespeople often have three or more versions of the one VP (the equivalent of a canapé, light meal and full banquet) to suit different occasions. But unless we're born with the innate ability to sell ice to eskimos (a skill that isn't all it's cracked up to be) this doesn't happen overnight. It takes time and conscious effort to craft, trial and tweak a strong VP to the point where the appropriate version can roll off our tongue at the appropriate time.

Which version of the VP to create first (short or long) depends on our personal strengths. If detail-focused, start with the long version and consider hiring an experienced copywriter to help scale it back. If more focused on the big picture, start with the short VP and consider engaging a business consultant or accountant to help flesh it out.

VPs fall into two categories: ***monetary*** and ***emotive***.

The Monetary (Solid) VP

The strongest VP is one that can be defined and presented in dollar ($) terms, giving the potential customer a solid monetary value to compare against the proposed price. A ***monetary VP*** allows sales prospects to see, consider and appreciate the *full value of the service itself, or the possible value of the service outcome*, to help them put the price into context.

Monetary VPs are most relevant to SSBs selling *high-risk necessities*. They are particularly useful for those delivering a measurable outcome or result, such as builders, landscapers, business coaches or web designers.

Three of the most powerful monetary VPs are:

1. ***Slash and Dash VP*** – This is commonly used by platform speakers selling entrepreneurial coaching packages. With it, the inclusions of the package are listed one by one along with their full retail price to build the perception of value. The grand total is then calculated (to the dismay of the audience, who can't justify tens of thousands of dollars)

but then crossed out, and an amazing, limited-time-only offer revealed (often around one tenth of the package's total value). This presents a massive saving and, possibly, an incredible opportunity (depending on the integrity of the seller).

The Slash and Dash approach can be very effective as a supporting sales tactic but dangerous if used as the primary VP. It is not conducive to building a business of substance and sustainability, as it can make us look desperate, cheap, unsophisticated, or 'too good to be true'. Using a Slash and Dash VP as the primary VP can also have catastrophic consequences down the track if the listed value of package inclusions is not a legitimate representation of their actual value. If prices are falsified for the sake of boosting perceived value, karma will kick in – through scathing online reviews and scam reports – and, sooner or later, the business will collapse like a house of cards.

2. *Past Proof VP* – This leverages the value of the results attained by past customers, as proof of the possibility of a certain monetary outcome for the sales prospect. Using the Past Proof approach we could present, for example, a major increase in sales experienced by a particular client, as proof of the monetary impact our services can have, if given the opportunity.

   For the Past Proof VP to work well, the past customer needs to be sufficiently similar to the potential customer, for the scenario to be relatable. If the prospect comes from a completely different industry or walk of life, the VP won't engage them and the value may be disregarded due to a perceived lack of relevance.

3. ***Dollars and Sense VP*** – This is the most sophisticated and arguably the most powerful of all VPs. Both the Past Proof and Dollars and Sense approach highlight the possible value of the outcome of a service but the Dollars and Sense VP does so in a more effective way. Instead of drawing value from past customer experience, it's drawn from a hypothetical scenario which applies a 'big picture' trend, fact or statistic of relevance (such as the Busy/Slow Cycle) to demonstrate the potential monetary impact of the service on offer.

For example, a builder specialising in home renovations, could – by crunching a few numbers with a local real estate agent – determine that, in a given location, a home with recently renovated wet areas sells for 15% more on average, than a home with outdated ones. This can then be presented as a monetary story, e.g. a $450,000 home, pre-makeover, can sell for as much as $517,500 with a renovated kitchen and bathroom. That's an increase in sales price of $67,500... and suddenly, a $35,000 kitchen and bathroom makeover seems like a cash cow.

Such is the power of a great VP.

The right monetary VP can change the course of a sales meeting in a matter of moments, making the price seem more reasonable – even generous. A Dollars and Sense VP has the added advantage of being grounded in fact, yet not specific to any one person, making the value proposition seem reliable, relevant and highly relatable. No matter what approach (or combination of approaches) we use, a good monetary VP can shift the perception of a service transaction from an expense or unnecessary outlay to a saving or investment, making the decision to engage our services a no-brainer.

Monetary VPs work because 'money talks' but, that said, it doesn't always speak the right language. As powerful as it can be for high-risk necessities, presenting the monetary value of our services is not always enough and, in the case of luxury services, it can be completely irrelevant. In these instances, we need to build a sense of non-monetary or *emotive* value.

The Emotive (Soft) VP

An **emotive VP** builds the perceived value of a service by tapping into the personal or social needs, values or priorities of potential customers. Instead of money and calculations (processed by the logical left brain), a series of words, non-monetary concepts and/or images (mostly processed by the emotional right brain) are used as an emotional hook to induce a feeling of desire for the service outcome.

The Busy/Slow Cycle began life as an emotive VP; a simple model with a memorised spiel:

'SmartStart websites make it possible for trade service business owners to even out the peaks and troughs in the Busy/Slow Cycle by driving more leads, more often. That means – instead of worrying about where the next dollar is coming from and constantly competing on price – you can start cherry-picking the customers or projects you want and charge what you're actually worth.'

This in itself was a highly effective VP, however, when taken a step further – demonstrated using a fictional before/after financial scenario – it morphed into a hybrid 'no-brainer' or **double whammy VP**. While a monetary VP is processed by the logical left brain and an emotive VP by the emotional right brain, a double whammy VP appeals to both sides. This amplifies perceived value, preventing fewer potential customers from slipping through the cracks.

How to Create a Strong VP

The VP is the single-most important aspect of marketing communications for an SSB but it can also be the most difficult to articulate. Activities to help find a good angle for a VP include:

- **Trend-spotting** – Researching trends, statistics and ratios pertaining to your industry or target market.
- **Shape-shifting** – Using visualisation or physical immersion (through work experience, interviews, etc) to put yourself in the shoes of your target market. In what ways are they suffering or lacking? How does your service reduce this suffering or sense of lack? Answer these questions for maximum monetary and emotional impact in a concise, matter-of-fact way and you'll have the substance required for a powerful VP.
- **Brain-picking** – Booking a paid consultation with an experienced marketer, copywriter, business advisor or accountant to get objective insights from an expert.
- **Number-crunching** – Identifying a relevant, truthful, number-based fact or feature (such as a statistic, ratio or other quantifiable element) to serve as a point of comparison against the industry standard or other offerings in the market. For example, '30% faster...' or '5 times stronger...'
- **Benefit-extraction** – Using the joining phrase 'which means' or 'what that means is' after a number-based

fact or feature (as in the above example) to extract the benefit for potential customers; how proceeding with the service will make their life easier or better. This is a handy copywriting technique, presented in more detail in Chapter 10 of *The Secret Service Website Formula*.

The funny thing about a strong VP is that its effect on us – as an SSB owner and salesperson – can be as powerful as its effect on our sales prospects, if not more. A strong VP gives us confidence in the value of our service. This, in turn, gives us confidence in ourselves, making us less inclined to sell ourselves short. Feeling confident that the value of what we're selling exceeds its price provides a sense of certainty and reassurance. It can shift the dynamic of business communications from 'desperate selling' to 'empowered advising', boosting sales conversions and making our role as SSB owner infinitely more satisfying.

Pitch Imperfect

Many business coaches and trainers assert that a pre-prepared VP or 'elevator pitch' is the optimum response to the question 'What do you do?' For the record, it's not... at least, not for SSB owners.

Elevator pitch training differs from VP preparation in a couple of ways. Firstly, it endeavours to prepare business owners for situations where we have 20–60 seconds (the length of a hypothetical elevator ride) to pitch our business or business idea to an ideal customer or potential investor. This means preparing for a one-way, uninterrupted monologue in which we dominate the conversation. Secondly, in extreme cases, we're taught to avoid mentioning the service we provide (website design, for example) to avoid being judged on that basis, instead stating what we *really* do, e.g. 'I help business owners explore online marketing opportunities.'

This sounds good in theory. However, if you're an SSB owner who's mustered up the courage to give it a go at a social gathering or networking event, you'd know that for us, it's about as effective as cold-calling homeowners at dinner time. If you're lucky, the victim of your pitch responds politely, as they silently plan their escape. If not, your carefully crafted elevator pitch is met with awkward silence, a furrowed brow and the words 'But... what do you actually *do*?' (as if you didn't quite hear right, the first time).

Ditch the Elevator Pitch

To be clear, the process of writing an elevator pitch is invaluable. It forces us to consider the service we provide, beyond its technical label (accountant, builder, etc), as well as the problem we solve and the benefits we provide – two essential ingredients of a good VP. However, for many SSB owners, taking the next step as prescribed by the experts (delivering the pitch to peers and prospects until we perfect it) can be detrimental and, in some cases, damaging.

In most unstructured scenarios, elevator pitching defies social convention and intuition. Launching into a problem/benefits monologue, instead of clearly stating what we do, is like trying to sell a multi-level marketing opportunity without using the name of the program itself. The lack of transparency invokes suspicion and pushes people away – at least, those people who are savvy, streetsmart and/or successful – the kind of people most of us want to attract, not repel.

Delivering an elevator pitch to someone who has not asked to hear it, is not only awkward for us, it's invasive for them. Interpersonal communication is much like a dance; one person may lead but the energy and input (generated through speaking, listening and the use of body language) needs to feel balanced, natural and comfortable on both sides, in order to create a connection and foster a relationship. An elevator pitch is an unnatural, one-way 'overshare' that makes us look desperate and interrupts the flow of the dance, pushing the other person away.

The social impact of the elevator pitch is more important for the owners of SSBs to understand than any other business type. Unlike an off-the-shelf product-based business, which can avoid any trace of humanity in its marketing (names, faces, first-person communications, etc), an SSB can't exist without it. By leading with an elevator pitch, we sabotage the very thing we need to survive: the ability to create emotional connections with others.

For us, the far easier and more effective alternative to leading with an elevator pitch, is to relax, be ourselves and engage in natural conversation... with a twist.

From Elevator Pitch to Response Rich

Questions and answers are critical to the discussion 'dance'. A question engages the other person and leads the conversation. Without questions posed from both sides, communication becomes uncomfortably one-sided or stilted. From there, it dissolves... connection lost.

While asking questions is crucial, so too is the ability to respond without upsetting the conversation's energetic balance. If our answers are too short (if we're shy, for example), the conversation will be hard work for the other person. They'll struggle to explore points of interest or identify common ground and, before long, communication will fizzle. If our answers are too long (as with elevator pitching), the other person will feel irrelevant, as if we're more interested in ourselves, our sales script and our agenda than in them as a person. They'll come away feeling frustrated that they wasted their time, trapped by a narcissistic steamroller.

The Rope Swing Response

Answering a question is an opportunity to not only fuel the conversation, but to create 'invited air-time' in which to get our full message across. The *rope swing response* is a technique to do just that; unknowingly used by great communicators and conversationalists in the world of business and beyond.

When a question such as 'What do you do?' is asked upon meeting someone new, a conversational void opens up. Where a short response such as 'I'm an accountant' usually lands dead in the water – providing no context and little conversational stimulus – and a long-winded response (such as a banquet VP or elevator pitch) gets stuck in the trees on the other side, a rope swing response is just right.

A rope swing response is a short answer bolstered by an extra snippet of relatable information, to spark a mutual point of understanding and interest. For SSB owners answering the inevitable question 'What do you do?', all that's needed to trans-form a conversation-killing answer into a rope swing response is a few extra words, e.g. 'I'm an accountant for local medical practices – GPs, chiropractors and dentists.'

As in this example, the best extra snippet for SSB owners to include in an initial rope swing response is our target market... but not just any target market – a highly specific *niche* market, articulated clearly and concisely, using jargon-free, easily recog-nisable language. This gives the rope swing enough momentum for the other person to catch it and confidently swing back, landing energetically closer to us.

A carefully crafted niche provides the substance SSB owners tend to lack when articulating what we do. With a niche in our initial rope swing response, new conversational partners tend to become curious or even excited to learn more; wanting to know why we chose that segment of the market to the exclusion of all others. This can lead them to ask deeper questions, giving us social permission to voice the problem our service solves, e.g. 'Yeah, well, I noticed that small medical practices really struggled when it came to...'. Before we know it, we've presented the longer, 'light meal' version of our VP, they've given us the name of a friend who runs a local medical practice who needs to speak to us... and we haven't forced a thing.

To have the greatest impact, an SSB's target market needs to be unusually specific. If the market is too broad – such as 'women' (50% of the population) or 'small businesses' (97% of the business population), the rope swing will fall short, unless we've had such success that we've been able to scale up to a large market and have another fascinating point of interest to hang our hat on. If you're reading this book however, chances are, you're yet to earn the stripes of success necessary to take on a big target market and win. In which case... It's time to unleash the niche.

CHAPTER 9.

UNLEASH THE NICHE

*** WARNING! DETAIL AHEAD ***

This chapter contains detailed instructions that
may be overwhelming at first. If you get bogged
down in it, switch to skim reading and return
to each section as it becomes applicable.

After years of frustration, floundering and impending doom,
I had an epiphany; one that resulted in my struggling business
transforming into a profitable and purposeful pursuit.

As far back as my university studies and in scores of books
and business courses since, I'd heard about the power of niching:
tailoring a product or service around the needs of a specific
segment of the market. Although I'd recommended it to clients
time and time again, I had always dismissed its relevance to my
own business. Then one morning, sitting at my desk, I asked
myself a crucial question...

'If I were to niche, what would I niche to?'

I started scouring client records, looking for a common thread between those I'd most enjoyed working with and generated the best results. Within a matter of minutes, I had my answer – trade services. And, just like that, Cyberstart Tradie was born.

The Business of Niching

Cyberstart Tradie is an example of niching at a business level. *Business level niching* involves overhauling a business to clearly communicate a highly targeted direction, through core elements of its brand, marketing materials, the customer experience and the service itself.

Given the competitive nature and poor reputation of the web design industry, I felt that for us, a complete brand overhaul was necessary to stand out. I took the trademarked word 'Cyberstart' from the cheap website package I'd developed for micro-business years earlier, upgraded it to our new trading name, added the word 'Tradie' to the logo, crafted a crystal clear subline and slogan, organised new business cards and brochures and we were off and running in our new direction.

Although a brand overhaul can be incredibly beneficial, it's not essential. In less competitive industries, a partial rebrand – adding a carefully considered subline and slogan (covered in Chapter 12) – can be just as effective, as long as the existing business name and logo doesn't contradict or confuse the new niche.

When NOT to Niche

As a rule of thumb, business level niching is a national or 'big city' growth strategy. The niche market must be big enough, accessible enough, wealthy enough and 'hungry' enough, to sustain the entire business. This is more likely in densely populated areas, or if services can be sold and delivered nationally or globally without increasing costs (which I realised, almost by accident, that ours could).

For this reason, business level niching can be *irrelevant* or *risky* for an SSB that:

1. Is located in a *regional area*, has a *limited geographic reach* and primarily exists to provide necessary services to the local community (such as a café or plumber in a rural town); or

2. Is located in a *metropolitan area*, delivers *on-premise services from a brick-and-mortar building* and primarily exists to provide necessary services to the local, urban community (such as a hotel, general practice doctor or hairdressing salon).

If your business falls into one of these two categories, limiting yourself to a small niche market can do more harm than good by repelling the available local market. In these cases, niching at a *service level* can be more beneficial.

Service Level Niching

Service level niching is the creation of a tailored offering, package or deal for one or more niche markets, while continuing to provide general services to other customers. This allows us to tap into a niche but minimise the risk of a complete business overhaul, through market diversification.

For businesses providing on-premise necessities, service level niching is best used to boost bookings for days or times that are not consistently busy enough. This is done by creating a packaged service for a niche market, restricted to certain times. Examples include a 'Seniors Lunch Deal', or a 'Business Function Package' catering to the weekday meeting and training needs of local businesses.

The Clout & Contradiction of Niching

Other than the two scenarios in which business level niching is riskier than service level niching, most SSBs stand to reap extraordinary benefits from the former. Adopting a business level niche implies a far greater understanding of – and commitment to – the distinct needs and wants of a target market. To service seekers in that market, this makes the business stand out like a lighthouse in a stormy sea of equivalent providers.

For me, business level niching was like a breath of fresh air. I was liberated to:

- **Highlight a big problem in desperate need of a solution** – In examining the real-world struggles of trade service business owners, the Busy/Slow Cycle model came to light. At first it was just a theory based on casual observation but it resonated with potential clients so strongly that it became a crucial element of our marketing and sales materials. I used it to educate and inform our target market at group training seminars, while clearly communicating the potential value and impact of our services in dollar terms.
- **Create services with substance** – Having identified a big problem – as well as myriad other challenges trade service business owners face day-to-day – I was able to tailor precise, all-encompassing solutions. Every feature

or inclusion of our website and marketing packages either contributed to the generation of leads for trade service clients, or saved them time and frustration. No corners were cut to keep prices down. If a feature helped solve a problem, it was included. If it was merely superficial... it was scrapped.

- **Attract better clients and more of them** – One of my biggest concerns about niching was that finding new clients would become even harder, as I'd be restricting the size of our target market. But once I bit the bullet, I found it had the opposite effect. We began attracting clients who appreciated our service as an investment, not just another hope-fuelled marketing expense. My business became a magnet for great clients – and plenty of them.

- **Put prices up... and up... and up** – Because we were able to demonstrate the value of our services (through the Busy/Slow Cycle model and proof of the hundreds of leads and millions of dollars in revenue generated by our clients as a result of our intervention), the perceived risk of our services dropped and our customers became less sensitive to price. Over time, our most popular package became more than double the average price of other local, small business focused web design services.

- **Stop stressing about the competition** – Where once the mere mention of another website or marketing agency made me anxious or envious, they were no longer on my radar. I stopped worrying about what competitors were doing, wished them well and focused on providing services of value to our niche market.

- **Open doors** – Organisations and industry associations who shared our target market were keen to collaborate, providing direct access to potential clients.
- **Get noticed** – After establishing my personal brand, *Laura de Lacy – The Tradie Marketing Lady*, I was invited interstate to provide group training to rooms full of trade service business owners. Niching meant I was no longer invisible.
- **Sell with pride and confidence** – Our service provided incredible value for money and I knew it. This confidence shifted the dynamic of sales meetings, removing any trace of desperation. There was a mutual understanding that our service was exactly what their business needed. It just came down to whether they were ready to invest in themselves as a business person, or not. Many were not... and that was okay. As long as we had a stream of delighted clients, it was clear that the 'thanks but no thanks' responses weren't a reflection of our offering, price or value.
- **Get real-world results** – The results I'd so desperately craved came flooding in. Websites were set up so I was notified when a lead was received. To this day, scores of leads roll in from our Cyberstart Tradie websites and the feedback we receive from our clients is beyond anything I could have hoped for.
- **Stay self-employed** – Prior to niching, I took on any project – profitable or not – just to feel busy. Wrapping myself up in 'busy work' was a temporary escape from the shame of not achieving the career success or income-earning potential I was capable of, had I just gotten a job. However, as a natural effect of focusing on

the services created for our niche market, the dead wood of random, unprofitable projects fell away. I started turning down projects that didn't fit our new focus and website projects developed a familiar rhythm and consistency. Suddenly, it became possible to standardise and streamline operational processes, train others to do what I previously thought only I could do and delegate core operational functions to staff, freeing me up to focus on sales and strategy. For the first time ever, we were making a predictable profit with each and every website project and business started to make sense.

For a struggling SSB owner like I was, tapping into a juicy niche feels somewhat miraculous. It brings with it a refreshing form of drive and determination, grounded in strategy and reality instead of hope and wishful thinking. For me, niching made business measurable and determinable. I suddenly realised how 'proper' businesses were able to forecast and budget – things I'd tried but failed at time and time again due to the unpredictable nature of my 'one stop shop' business model.

Despite its benefits, few SSB owners niche because niching is a contradiction. It involves scaling down our target market, with a long-term vision to scale it back up – if and when the time is right. For most of us, this is counterintuitive and a relinquishment of control. It feels like a backwards step, away from our dream business. The thing is, by holding on too tightly to that initial dream, wanting it here and now, instead of humbly working up to it through mastery of service in a small market, our ego circumvents the attainment of sustainable success. Subconsciously, we don't feel worthy of success and as long as we don't feel worthy of it, it simply cannot be.

Overcoming this self-imposed barrier to niching success not only takes foresight and adaptability, but depth of character. Niching takes an open mind, courage, humility, integrity and most of all, empathy – the ability to put ourselves in the shoes of our customers to identify their needs and feel their pain. Niching also requires a sense of faith and trust, knowing that if we're meant to achieve our original business vision, it will come full circle, and by then, we'll have earned every skerrick of the success we achieve.

5 Steps to Find & Carve Your Niche

Niching at a business level can be one of the most rewarding breakthroughs an SSB owner can make, but it must be a well-considered, strategic decision. The process of finding and carving a niche must be undertaken mindfully. This can be broken down into five steps:

Step 1 – Narrow the Field

The first step towards identifying a suitable niche, is to decide whether our business is B2B (business-to-business) or B2C (business-to-consumer), thus narrowing our field of vision. For some of us, this is an easy distinction. For others – trade service contractors offering industrial, commercial and residential services, for example – it can be tricky. Not committing to a business or consumer market spreads most SSBs too thin; it makes marketing – and other business functions – more difficult than they need to be. So, take some time to reflect on your past experience and ideal customer, then decide: are you B2B or B2C?

Step 2 – Open to the Options

Niching effectively requires us to spot the common threads linking a juicy subgroup of potential customers in our already narrowed B2B or B2C market – and that can be easier said than done. Without an awareness of the threads to look for, it can be hard to recognise a good niching opportunity, even when it's staring us in the face.

To assist with this, an assortment of possible niching opportunities are listed below – the first list for B2B service providers and the second for B2C.

Business-to-business market niches

B2B service providers may be able to niche by:

- **Business sector** – Servicing trade service businesses, mortgage brokerage firms, Not For Profit (NFP) organisations, primary schools, music teachers, real estate agents, department stores, cabinet makers, petrol stations... The options are endless.
- **Business model** – Servicing only wholesalers, exporters, franchises or ecommerce stores, for example.
- **End customer or user** – Businesses that target a particular market, e.g. those targeting mechanics or parents of toddlers.
- **Ownership of an asset** – Businesses that own a factory, boat or crane, for example.
- **Use of a particular resource** – Businesses that use a certain piece of software, hire apprentices or lease fleet vehicles, for example.
- **Use of a system or formula to multiply production** – Businesses whose needs for certain services arise in

multiples, or repeatedly over time, as a byproduct of their business model, e.g. property developers (requiring multiple roofs, fences, etc for the many dwellings in a development), or franchisors (fitting out one store after another).

- **Location** – Businesses within a specific geographic area.
- **Business structure** – Sole traders, partnerships or Pty Ltd companies.
- **Business size** – Micro-businesses, small businesses or organisations with a quantifiable number of employees or level of turnover.

Business-to-consumer market niches

B2C service providers may be able to niche by:

- **Career or occupation** – Individuals with a particular job or profession, such as accountants, authors, professional athletes, self-employed builders or teachers.
- **Workplace or educational institution** – Those who frequent a particular place for work or study purposes, such as employees in CBD office towers or parents of children who attend certain schools.
- **Age group or life stage** – Individuals in a similar phase of life, such as parents of teenagers, or retirees.
- **Marital/family status** – People with a particular relationship or family structure – single, partnered, engaged, married with multiple children, single parents, etc.
- **Gender or sexual identity** – Those who identify as male, female or with one or more streams of the LGBTIQA+ spectrum.

- **Culture or religion** – Individuals of a certain culture or faith, such as Italian, Muslim, 'spiritual but not religious'.
- **Health or physical condition** – Sufferers of a certain ailment, such as infertility, asthma, hay fever or sciatic nerve pain, or those with a particular impairment, diagnosis or disability.
- **Body size or shape** – Those who may be short or tall, petite or of size, curvy, slim or athletic, or aspirations to change their shape in some way.
- **Event or trauma** – Individuals who have had a particular life experience – Immigrants or expatriates, victims of a vehicle or workplace accident, or returned soldiers, for example.
- **Ownership** – Those who own a particular asset, item or animal, be it a family home, investment property, Porsche, Thermomix, horse or a brood of backyard hens.
- **Passion or pursuit** – People with a certain hobby, interest or pursuit, such as tennis, fine wine, chocolate or mixed martial arts.
- **Location** – Individuals living or working in a certain geographic area.

It is important to note that a B2C niche should be a means to meet the unmet needs of a specific group of consumers, not a means to exclude others. If a group's needs are no different than those of other consumers, e.g. plumbing services for Catholics only, this is *not* niching; it is discrimination, which is not only morally inept but illegal in most countries.

Note too that niching *solely* by location, business structure, business size, gender, age group or life stage is *not* niching. It doesn't have the personal relevance or specificity required to make an emotional impact on potential customers. What *does* make an impact is niching by at least two of the above characteristics (such as business sector *and* business size, or health condition *and* gender). The needle-sharp focus and attention to detail this requires, packs a real punch when networking and marketing – cutting through the noise of mundane offerings in the market.

Niching around obligation and opportunity

Some of the best niching opportunities arise out of government rulings. When legislation changes (with an amendment to work health and safety compliance laws or energy efficiency standards in the national building code, for example), the administrative obligations of businesses or consumers can take a sharp and unwelcome increase. In order to tick the box of compliance, outside assistance can become necessary – a situation that a savvy SSB owner can benefit from; positioning their business to receive an obligatory flow of work from a niche with an unavoidable need.

Government incentives and investments provide a similar opportunity. When the government implements a new socio-economic or environmental policy (such as reduced tariffs in the vehicle manufacturing industry or rebates for the installation of solar energy systems), opportunistic SSBs can win big – leveraging government funding to acquire new customers and contracts. Sometimes – as was the case with solar in Australia – new players jump on board in droves, but many lack the substance to hold on when the going gets tough. They gradually fall off as the money dries up, leaving those with stamina and substance (including the tightly niched) to thrive as dominant forces in a fledgling industry.

Niching to maximise recurring income

One of the biggest niching opportunities for SSBs lies in the opportunity to generate recurring income through periodic servicing. Whether it's cleaning solar panels, maintaining gardens, servicing vehicles, cutting/colouring hair, performing dental check-ups or any number of other services that gradually 'expire', opportunities to create streams of recurring revenue exist for most SSBs, but in some niche markets more than others. This is important to bear in mind when selecting a niche, as an ongoing service opportunity – be it ongoing service or maintenance agreements, retainer based contracts or a more casual arrangement based on periodic 'prompting' – can make a big difference to the viability of a business.

Step 3 - Look Back to Move Forward

Some say we should 'leave the past in the past', but reflecting on the past can be the key to a healthy, happy, productive future – and this certainly holds true for niching. Reflecting on past business, career and personal experiences is (in my opinion) the single best way to identify a suitable niche market. It gives us a pool of pre-existing insights to draw upon and, therefore, a shortcut to a viable business model.

To recall experiences with niching potential, set some time aside and take a deep-dive into:

1. **Your customer records**

   If you've been in business for a while, print a list of your top 20 customers or simply delve into your database or filing cabinet, pulling out the files for your easiest, most satisfied and/or most profitable customers, with a view to identifying the common threads between them. Study each customer, one by one, in conjunction with the potential niches listed from page 142. Prompted by the customer's name and any notes in their file, visualise each one, reflecting on their key characteristics and the needs and concerns they revealed during the sales process. Cast your mind back to what they said, what they did, the service transaction that took place and any feedback since. Google them and their business. Read through their website and any social media profiles.

Sooner or later, a trend should start to emerge. If/when it does, keep digging... there may be better options or stronger threads hidden just beneath the surface.

2. **Your resumé**

If you are new to business or find yourself lacking a quality client base, the perfect niche may be hiding between the lines of an old resumé. Often, it's not until we deliberately reflect on our pool of past experiences with employers and their customers, that chunks of highly specific knowledge – accumulated almost without realising it – float to the surface; for example, an electrician's extensive knowledge of the water processing sector, acquired while working for a large commercial contractor many years earlier.

To look for potential niches in your resumé, start by reflecting on the jobs you've had, individually and as a collective history. Any experience working in or for a particular industry, or solving a specific problem for a certain type of client, is a niching opportunity worthy of further investigation.

Before closing your resumé, be sure to reflect on the *education* and *interests* sections. Consider any unpaid work experience, subjects, projects, extra curricular activities or outside interests you once enjoyed. Personal, social and voluntary experiences can be as valuable and niche-worthy as paid employment.

3. **The book of life**

Many niches are inspired through personal struggle – problems, traumas, health challenges or diagnoses – things that happen to us or someone we know that highlight the need for particular services or solutions. Personal challenges can light a spark of desire to help others resolve, overcome or manage similar circumstances.

With business level niching, any experience working in or with a niche, or even better, having a history of *belonging* to that niche, puts marrow in a business' bones. It not only justifies the decision to niche, it injects a sense of purpose and meaning into a commercial venture – giving rise to a fascinating business story.

Although it's possible to choose a niche without drawing on past experience, it's not ideal. It means having to start from scratch to develop the basic pool of knowledge required to adequately serve the market. Instead of forcing a completely unfamiliar niche, it can be better to power through for six months or so, taking on an array of customers or projects, keeping your options open and eyes peeled for niche opportunities that genuinely pique your interest.

Then, with a clear concept, it's time to test the waters.

Step 4 – Investigate & Validate

Without taking the time to investigate and validate a potential niche, we revert back to hope as a strategy, which defeats the purpose of niching. With that in mind, there are three questions to answer before committing to a niche.

Question 1. Can it afford to pay? There's no point pursuing a niche if the price of the proposed service is too high for the niche market to bear. New mothers might seem like the ideal niche for a personal stylist, for example, but if preliminary research suggests that new mums tend to cut back on low-risk, luxury services for themselves, then it'll be a tough slog.

Asking this question upfront may seem crass but it can save a lot of time, energy and anguish, helping us find our path to success sooner rather than later.

Question 2. Is it physically viable? A viable niche is not only small and exclusive enough to provide a striking point of difference, but large and accessible enough to sustain a business. Researching the size and accessibility of a potential niche is key to striking this balance.

- **Size** – The size of a potential niche market can often be determined by analysing publicly available data provided online by the national bureau of statistics (the ABS in Australia), relevant industry associations, organisations, educational institutions or other peak bodies.

  Alternatively, we can analyse our customer database to determine a percentage of total customers who fall into the niche, or conduct our own independent survey. An estimate (based on a relatively small, unbiased sample) is all we really need to get a feel for the size of the niche as a proportion of the full B2B or B2C population.

- **Ease of access** – A niche is accessible if it's easy to find and communicate with, for the purpose of marketing. This is important, because the easier it is to reach (independent of mainstream media), the lower our marketing costs will be.
- Society's reliance on the internet makes researching the accessibility of a niche easier than ever before. In less than an hour of online research, it's possible to build a solid profile for a potential niche by considering:

  1. **If/where niche members gather** – Do places or organisations exist to bring members of the niche together, such as industry associations, educational institutions, care facilities, clubs, programmes, online forums or discussion pages on social media? If so, it's a good sign that the niche is active and accessible.

  2. **What niche members read** – The existence of specialty magazines, books, blogs, email subscriptions and other resources created to educate or entertain the niche, is another indication that it could be a viable market. Note that resources such as these are not only handy for determining the viability of a niche, but as a resource for investigating key problems and frustrations within it.

  3. **What other businesses target the niche** – Another sign that a niche market may be a worthy pursuit is if other businesses (in your industry or beyond) exist to service it. If businesses in other industries are successfully targeting the niche, there may be opportunities to establish alliances or joint ventures down the track, cultivating an organic inflow of leads and sales.

If other businesses in your industry are already targeting the niche you're considering, don't write it off without closer investigation. When researching the small trade service niche for my business, I stumbled across several website agencies targeting tradies. My heart sunk... until I looked at their offerings more closely and realised their solutions were stock-standard and, in my opinion, not what the niche needed. Thankfully, I decided to trust my gut on this and you should too.

Question 3. How hungry is it? Although the physical viability of a niche is crucial, it's virtually useless without the context of 'demand'. A niche could be quite large but if it has no driving need for your services or no real problem to solve, demand will be low and your business will struggle; you'll only be able to lure customers in by dangling a price-based carrot, which is never ideal. In contrast, a niche could be small but in desperate need of a solution to a highly specific, very painful problem. The higher the demand or 'hunger' for a solution, the higher the price a market will bear, eradicating the need for price-based carrot dangling.

An easy way to get an indication of how hungry a niche market is, is to use a free online tool called Google Keyword Planner. Accessed via Google AdWords, the Keyword Planner tool is very handy; allowing users to research the monthly volume of searches for particular keywords or phrases, within a defined geographic location. Generally, the more people searching for a particular keyword or phrase, the bigger and hungrier the market.

While quantitative hunger research like this is helpful, it can't be used in isolation. That's because, often, potential customers will only recognise the physical symptom, frustration or 'pain point' of an underlying problem, not the problem itself. They'll Google a diagnosis or quick fix for the symptom or frustration (e.g. 'adult acne treatment'), not a solution for the underlying problem ('naturopathy for dairy intolerance') because they don't know what the problem or solution is yet. Once we identify our niche market's pain points, the Keyword Planner tool can be used more effectively, not only to measure searches conducted by individuals in our target market who know what solution they need but also those who *don't know* the solution yet; those who are 'symptom searching' to self-educate and find relief.

Pinning down pain points

Identifying pain points is a crucial aspect of finding a worthy niche but unlike other parts of the niching process, it can't be done at our desk. Without first-hand experience working with the niche market, no amount of thinking or contemplation will make the pain points present themselves. It's only in working with, speaking to and studying individuals within the niche (and others who've done the same) that we can identify and explore the symptoms and frustrations that plague them.

Exploring pain points requires deliberate effort and interaction with our proposed niche market; whether it's carrying out a survey, conducting interviews or total immersion through unpaid work experience. Pain points rarely float to the surface – we've got to dig for them, by asking carefully worded questions, listening to the answers and reading between the lines.

Much like a medical examination, preliminary questions for those in our niche market should be geared to determine:

- What pains or frustrations trouble them (pertaining to our field of service, as well as more generally, at an individual or business level);
- How these pains and frustrations affect their day to day life;
- When the pains and frustrations started;
- What approaches or treatments they've tried in an effort to alleviate them;
- Their history or experience with businesses in our field of service.

Qualitative human research is the purest way to extract, embody and articulate the frustrations of a group. What's more, it builds the insight, passion and tenacity required to diagnose, treat and overcome the underlying problem.

Once you've investigated the wealth, physical viability and hunger of a niche, you'll know if it's worth pursuing. If it's not, simply return to Step 3 and try again. There's always another way to niche.

Step 5 – Problem-Solve

Piecing together the jigsaw puzzle of symptoms and frustrations creates a complete picture of a niche's pain points. The deep thinking and contemplation (which in my case, morphed into passionate obsession) starts there.

With a full view of the big picture, we have everything we need to answer the following questions:

1. **What is the most striking trend or common frustration?** and/or **is one of these pain points causing the others?** (For Cyberstart Tradie clients, the common frustration was the physical, mental and financial pain of constant fluctuations in customer demand.)

2. **How can I communicate this most painful problem simply and succinctly, with the use of a model or concept?** (This question led to the creation of the Busy/Slow Cycle.)

3. **What is causing the problem?** (For my niche, the cause was confusion and overwhelm about the marketing function since the internet changed the game, resulting in a lack of business direction and an unreliable, inconsistent flow of leads.)

4. **What is needed to overcome this problem?** (Tradies needed a website that could act as a stand-alone marketing tool, geared to consistently generate high-quality leads.)

5. **What is the formula for this solution?** (Over time, the answer to this question became clearer and evolved into *The Secret Service Website Formula*).

Note: It can help to write or type out these questions and answer them as if writing a report.

Asking deeper questions activates our intuition. It helps us think and feel beyond our day-to-day responsibilities and frustrations, to articulate, unravel and overcome problems – including the most painful problem experienced by a niche market. Asking the right questions shifts our perspective; it transports us from being *in* the problem, looking out, to being *outside* the problem, looking in.

Solving a niche's most painful problem may involve:

- Changing **trading times** to make a service more accessible (as with 24-hour gyms);
- Providing a **mobile service** – As with on-site corporate massage or a mobile dog wash;
- Providing a **pick-up or delivery service** – As with home meal delivery or door-to-door dry-cleaning;

- Offering **supporting services** – Child care or recycling for example;
- **Innovating** through the adoption or creation of new technologies;
- Undertaking in-depth **research and development**;
- **Changing pricing strategies** – The focus of the next chapter;
- **Rebranding** – Changing business name, logo, subline and/or slogan;
- **Bucking tradition** – Expanding a business' capabilities and overhauling processes to include an aspect of planning, design or 'grunt work' typically handled by clients themselves or a third party (such as the writing of website content for web design projects or the lodgement of development applications for building projects);
- **Culling certain offerings** – Scrapping services that are superfluous to (or not in the best interest of) the selected niche market.

Niching can be difficult to get your head around, particularly if you're used to providing services that are superfluous to the new niche. In my case, niching meant I would no longer need to write marketing plans for clients. Even though (try as I might) I could not do it profitably, my love of strategic planning and writing had stopped me from niching in the past. The self-concerned thought, 'But where would strategy writing fit in?', had always stopped me in my tracks. When niching to Cyberstart Tradie however, I realised strategy writing didn't fit in and that was okay... because it wasn't about me or what I wanted, it was about our niche market and *what they needed*. And, as it turned out, my flair for strategy and writing came into play in far more satisfying ways; ways which have allowed me to help more people, provide more personal satisfaction and actually make ends meet.

Developing a solution to a niche market's most painful problem does not happen overnight. It takes time, tenacity, trial and error and a whole lot of tweaking. When you've found the optimum solution, you know, simply by talking to – and obtaining testimonials from – customers. A pattern of success emerges, evidenced by the evaporation of their original symptoms and frustrations.

When building a business around the successful alleviation of a niche market's pain points, a funny thing happens. The satisfaction you get from making money takes a back seat to the satisfaction you get from delivering services of value and making a real difference in people's lives. When money is no longer our main focus or reward, it's like a blockage cleared from a pipe – money can finally start to flow.

Niching Is For Now... Not Forever

Occasionally, an SSB owner will start out in business with a strong, clear niche – one identified through prior engagement in a highly specialised field of service. But, for most of us, it doesn't happen that way. We tend to start out with a strong grasp of our capabilities but not the needs of our target market. We create 'one stop shops', endeavouring to boost our chances of business survival by being all things to all people. A few thrive with this approach. Most struggle. Many surrender. In a last-ditch effort to avoid defeat, I took a different path. As the unstable ground of self-employment was crumbling beneath me, I took what felt like an enormous leap of faith (on an ironically solid foundation of researched facts and findings) and landed on solid ground. And if I can land that jump, you can too.

But before you do, it's important to recognise that your niche probably won't define your SSB forever... nor should it. Businesses should continue to evolve over time, just as we do.

Once you've 'cracked' a niche, opportunities abound. You might expand geographically, broaden your niche to encompass another segment of the market, or change the niche entirely; perhaps teaching fellow service providers (those once regarded as competitors) how to achieve what you've achieved by following a formula. This can be done through franchising, creating an accreditation system or launching an information-based product such as a book or online course. Business models such as these use niche success as a stepping stone to greater success. Implemented well, and for the right reasons, they expand our reach while amplifying our impact on the world, through the empowerment of others.

Building a business is like climbing a steep mountain. Below us is the slippery slope to failure. Above us is the summit of success, hidden from view by rocky terrain and layer upon layer of low-lying cloud. It's only through the application of foresight and adaptability, by using the right equipment to make the right moves at the right time, that we can ascend through the layers of fog, inching our way towards the peak.

Niching is like switching from free climbing to aided climbing, halfway up the mountain. Although it's safer, it *feels* scarier because it's a transition from self-reliance to an unfamiliar system of extrinsic tools and techniques. But push through the discomfort. Follow the steps to find your niche and not only will the summit of success appear sooner, its views of thousands of delighted customers will be more spectacular than you could ever have imagined.

CHAPTER 10.

THE PRICE IS RIGHT... OR IS IT?

For some SSB owners, pricing is a piece of cake. In property management or dentistry for example, generally accepted industry standards or customer expectations dictate the structure of rates and charges. With this as a reference point, many of us can simply use *comparative pricing* – researching and comparing the prices of competitors, then positioning ourselves as a premium, budget or middle-ground provider, relative to them.

SSB owners in other industries (usually those with a physical end product) have a pricing 'rule of thumb', such as a suggested gross profit margin, sometimes expressed as a formula. This rule serves as a benchmark for pricing, taking the guesswork out of an otherwise ambiguous process. In hospitality for example, the rule of thumb chefs use to determine the price of a meal is the cost of its ingredients, multiplied by three: one third for the direct costs of the dish, one third as a contribution to overheads (including labour) and one third for profit.

It sounds straightforward but, when faced with 'costing out' an entire menu, plus daily specials, it can be an arduous, time-consuming process until years of experience and familiarity with the cost of ingredients make it possible to set prices largely on instinct.

Then there are industries like web design, consultancy and coaching, in which SSB owners have no pricing standard or rule of thumb. We are left to our own devices on a painstaking quest to find a method of pricing that works for us, and it can be a tough slog.

The Time-Trading Trap

When starting out in business, many SSB owners fall into the trap of trading time for money, through *rate-based pricing* or 'charging by the hour'. This is counterproductive for several reasons.

1. **It restricts revenue** – Selling our time at an hourly rate puts a cap on our business' earning potential. That's because the hours we can work, and subsequently charge for, are limited to the number of hours in a day, week or year.

2. **It's a slippery slope to minimum wage (or less)** – It's human nature to underestimate the amount of time needed to achieve a given result. For SSB owners, underestimating hours in a fixed quote causes our actual hourly rate to drop very quickly. At the extreme, this can mean earning less from a project requiring a high degree of skill and knowledge than we could earn on public assistance or unemployment benefits (aka 'the dole').

3. **It devalues the solution** – Charging by the hour places the value on the human hours required to deliver a service,

not the outcome or result it produces for the customer – and most customers can't comprehend, let alone value, our hourly input. Our time has no emotional meaning to them, so, for those of us providing solution-based services, charging by the hour can reduce the chances of converting leads to sales, stand in the way of receiving full credit for the results of our projects and leave thousands of dollars on the table.

4. **It can stifle efficiency** – Charging by the hour gives us no incentive to become more efficient at what we do. As we get quicker, we quote for fewer hours and can end up earning less money per hour for delivering the same result.

5. **It can stifle growth** – By quoting on and selling time, clients tend to expect that we, the owner and most experienced technician, will do the work. This expectation can make it difficult to scale the business by inhibiting the delegation of operational tasks to staff.

For SSB owners in complex industries, or those with no set pricing formula, pricing can be a relentless burden; a ball and chain preventing us from moving forward with any real momentum. It certainly was for me.

As you'll read in *The Secret Service Website Formula*, quoting was once the bane of my existence. I was so desperate for sales that I would quote on any marketing, design or web development opportunity that came my way – good, bad or indifferent. Initially, my quote documents were pretty standard: a description of each task, the number of hours required to complete them (an overthought stab in the dark), an hourly rate and a grand total. Our conversion rates were so low, however, I felt I had to give more. So my quotes morphed into lengthy proposals detailing intricate marketing strategies specific to each prospective customer – all before they'd paid a cent. In hindsight, it was ridiculous. I'd spend days developing a proposal and take it personally if the prospect chose not to proceed – assuming the quote had been too high or my strategy poorly communicated. I felt used and rejected but, most of all, frustrated and angry that doing all I could to win work was not enough. In reality, it was more than enough. Too much. I didn't need to try harder, just work smarter: get out of my own head, define my ideal customer and put their needs first, starting with a different approach to pricing.

While there's no magic formula for setting prices in industries without clear-cut pricing rules or standards, awareness of one simple concept can make it a whole lot easier.

Pricing by Rote or by Quote

Every SSB's pricing approach fits into one of two overarching categories: 'preset' and 'post-op' pricing.

Preset Pricing

With *preset pricing*, prices are set prior to a lead or enquiry coming in. They're calculated in advance and minimal (if any) financial allowances are made for any one customer. They are what they are, whether they take the form of consult fees (typical of medical services), prices on a menu, a price list, or a range of set packages. No matter what form they take, preset prices are communicated transparently from one potential customer to the next. As such, they can be quickly and easily supplied upon request, making the provision of a quote or indicative pricing a breeze.

Post-Op Pricing

With ***post-op pricing***, prices hinge upon the specific requirements of each individual prospect, so they can't be set in
advance. Not until a lead is received and an investigative 'operation' carried out, can the prospect's needs be extracted and a
course of action recommended. Only then can a price be calculated and provided for consideration, in the form of a variable
estimate or fixed quote.

Post-op pricing is common in complex, project-based industries where each customer has highly specific needs requiring a
customised solution. In large-scale commercial construction for
example, there can be hundreds of thousands of variables in a
single project – far too many to itemise in a price list.

The Mainstream Methods of Post-Op Pricing

The most common methods for calculating post-op prices, are:

- **Rate-based pricing** – Trading time for money, using an
  estimate of the hours we think it'll take to complete the
  job or project, in conjunction with a schedule of hourly
  rates (e.g. 6 hours at $120 per hour = $720).

- **Cost-plus pricing** – Adding together the direct cost of
  materials required to undertake the job or project, an
  estimate of our direct labour costs and a contribution for
  overheads, plus a markup percentage to build in a margin
  for profits.

- **Value-based pricing** – Estimating the perceived value of
  the proposed solution to the customer, then striking a
  balance between what the solution is worth to them and
  what we believe they'd be willing to pay.

- **Project-based pricing** – Calculating a price using one or more other methods (a blend of rate-based *and* value-based estimation, for example) and presenting the price as a 'flat fee'.

The common thread between these four methods is the need to *estimate* – to roughly calculate or judge the value, quantity or extent of one or more variables – in order to arrive at a price.

The Art of Estimation

Many SSB owners are gifted at estimation, priding themselves on their best-guesses. Each estimate is a blend of experience, intuition and self-confidence, compounded over time. These hardy individuals usually approach quoting quite philosophically, with a 'you win some, you lose some' attitude. In their minds, quoting isn't the most fun of jobs but it is what it is. They receive a lead, schedule and conduct a pre-quote analysis (usually a free measure and quote or consultation) and provide a quote. *Bam, bam, bam...* quote done. With this attitude, post-op pricing works just fine.

At the other end of the spectrum are those of us whose estimation skills don't serve us as well as we'd like them to. For us, quoting is agony. We often find ourselves leaving potential customers hanging, not because we've forgotten them but because we are paralysed by pricing indecision.

Post-Op Pricing Paralysis

Pricing paralysis occurs when our all-important estimation abilities are diluted by a flood of emotion. Faced with preparing a quote, our emotional floodgates open, preventing us from thinking, acting and pricing rationally.

Symptoms of pricing paralysis include:

- **Procrastination and avoidance** – Delaying the preparation of a quote for days or weeks;
- **Obsession** – Spending hours or days preparing a single quote, worrying that the estimated price will make us look too cheap or, if we don't adequately explain and justify it, too greedy;
- **Indecision** – Changing the quoted price multiple times before finally submitting it;
- **Post-quote paranoia** – Second-guessing the value of our services after sending the quote. Negative thoughts may be accompanied by a sinking feeling, amplified by not receiving a response from the potential customer within a matter of hours;
- **Hypersensitivity** – Taking the rejection of a quote personally, allowing it to impact our self-worth, the value of our services and future pricing decisions.

Pricing paralysis is not only incredibly stressful, it is completely counterproductive. It frustrates and often repels prospects who are keenly awaiting a quote, slows the sales cycle to a snail's pace and causes the underpricing of jobs or projects. This stifles sales and profits and is not sustainable.

The underlying causes of pricing paralysis are:

1. Lack of confidence
2. Perfectionism
3. Empathic sensitivity

Lack of confidence tends to resolve itself over time. Confidence is a natural byproduct of business experience and certainty about the quality and value of our service. It develops with patience, perseverance and a commitment to continual improvement (explored in Chapter 11). If you're feeling low on confidence right now, rest assured that if you had the confidence to *start* a business, you can develop the confidence required to *succeed* in it.

Perfectionism and empathic sensitivity are more complex. They are deeply ingrained personality traits, which won't remedy themselves over time, nor should they necessarily.

Perfectionism presents as a drive to do things perfectly and get things right. This can be problematic when setting prices, because estimating – by its very nature – is imperfect. In the eyes of a perfectionist, a price must be 'right', otherwise the entire foundation on which the price was estimated (namely, our best judgement), must be wrong. Every time a quote is rejected, our foundations are shaken to the core, reinforcing the belief that we cannot trust our own judgement. This lack of faith in ourselves gives rise to the anxiety and indecision of pricing paralysis.

Empathic sensitivity is the ability to tune into the emotions of other people and, unharnessed, it can make business incredibly challenging. Those of us with high empathic sensitivity tend to approach pricing from the perspective of the potential customer; we feel and prioritise the prospect's perceived emotional needs over and above the needs of our business. When preparing quotes, we anticipate the recipients' most extreme possible reactions to the price or service offering (such as disappointment or outrage) and allow these feelings to influence our pricing estimations. If using rate-based pricing, we tend to undercut ourselves and the value of our services because it feels wrong to inflate quoted hours (as a wise means to assure a project can be completed within the stated hours and proposed price). We literally feel the disappointment and betrayal of being lied to, inducing a heavy sense of guilt that influences the estimation of hours and, therefore, the price we put forward. Over time, we associate the pricing process with a feeling of dread and can become paralysed as a result.

Awareness of these two traits can make or break an SSB. Left unrecognised and unmanaged, perfectionism and empathic sensitivity will not only paralyse the pricing process, they can paralyse our business. Without making some changes, our work life will likely be a constant, painful and highly personal struggle until our business is forced to close. But, with a little foresight and adaptability, we can fight this fate... and win.

To be clear, perfectionism and empathic sensitivity should not be switched off in business. When we channel these traits effectively – working with them instead of fighting against them – they become the most highly prized professional qualities and invaluable business assets: **high standards** and **emotional-social intelligence (ESI)**. These pave the way for the creation of the most viable kind of business; one built on integrity, authenticity, innovation and a genuine desire to relieve the suffering of others, all while making a profit.

The Antidote for Pricing Paralysis

It's often said, 'doing the same thing over and over again, expecting a different result, is the definition of insanity.' By that token, persisting with post-op pricing, if it's causing us physical or emotional distress and inhibits the success of our business, is nothing short of madness. With post-op pricing, the anguish and drudgery of pricing projects is relentless; every job must be evaluated, costed and quoted separately, all before a single dollar of income is earned. Without the drive to manually and consistently turn these cogs, the machine of sales will grind to a halt. For post-op pricing to work, quoting needs to become an efficient and unemotional process (discussed further in Chapter 17).

If your personality prevents you from quoting efficiently or unemotionally, taking a different approach to pricing could be your business' saving grace – as it was for mine. This requires a change from post-op to preset pricing and, specifically, the creation of *packages*.

The Power of Preset Packages

A *preset package* is a bundle of goods or services that is marketed and sold together as a group. The package is given a flat price which does not deviate from one customer to another.

Switching from post-op pricing to preset packages transforms the lead-to-sale cycle. With packages, the hard work of costing and pricing is a 'one-off', not something we need to do for every prospect. Not only is it a less stressful approach to pricing, it is remarkably more efficient. With preset packages, time-consuming aspects of the traditional post-op pricing process (such as on-site 'measure and quotes', discovery meetings and quote preparation) become obsolete. This saves an immeasurable amount of time, money and human resources, minimising the work required to convert leads to sales.

What's more, the sale of our services as preset packages can dramatically reduce the perceived risk associated with them, making them easier to sell. The value of a packaged offering is typically much clearer, as is the fact that others have paid the same price for the same offering. This simplicity and transparency can come as a breath of fresh air to service seekers bombarded by complex alternatives, so they're more likely to accept the price, trust the sales process and proceed with the transaction.

About three years into business – when the pain of staying the same began to outweigh the pain of change – I dipped my toe into the waters of preset packages. I created two packaged services: MohJoh, an affordable message-on-hold solution for small businesses with a multi-line phone system and Cyberstart, a website package for micro-businesses on a tight budget. Both consisted of a base package with a menu of optional extras.

Introducing preset packages, meant:

- **A power shift in my favour** – With packages, inclusions and prices were set once and only reviewed occasionally. This resulted in an unexpected power shift. Instead of bending over backwards to mould our services to fit the customer's needs and budget, they moulded their needs and budget to fit the constraints of our packaged offerings. I was finally in the driver's seat and my pricing paralysis was left in the dust.

- **Selling became easy** – Converting leads into sales became a clearly defined, simple process devoid of negative emotion. A sales presentation folder was created to maximise perceived value and minimise perceived risk, while strategically guiding prospects through their purchasing decision. In comparison to post-op pricing, selling a preset package was a leisurely stroll in the park.

- **Conversions boomed** – With a clearly defined sales strategy, sales conversions increased from approximately 18% (for websites quoted on with post-op pricing) to 98% (for the

Cyberstart package). In the time we offered this original package, only one person I sat down with chose not to proceed and no one ever tried to negotiate the packaged price.

- **Increased productivity** – With preset packages, only one meeting was needed to connect with the client, outline the package and optional extras and get a signature on the dotted line. Meetings and associated travel time halved. Post-sale productivity increased exponentially too. Because we were delivering the same base website package to all customers, operational aspects such as the preparation of design briefs, front-end design and back-end development could be systemised and streamlined in a way that wasn't possible with custom projects. Simple, standardised checklists were used to guide the process through to completion. This saved time and money while making us look incredibly organised and efficient in the eyes of our clients.

- **Entrepreneurial insight** – Through the creation and sale of these first packages, I caught a glimpse of myself as a successful entrepreneur with a highly profitable, scalable venture that wasn't reliant on trading my time for money. Unfortunately, however, this glimpse was fleeting.

Problems with 'One Size Fits All' Packages

Despite the positive aspects of offering preset packages, I hadn't 'cracked it' by any means. Sure, I'd mastered the process of turning leads into sales but generating leads – in industries flooded with competition (message-on-hold and website design) – was no easy feat.

For both MohJoh and Cyberstart, my strategy was to deliver products that were equal to or better than those of the competition, at a budget-friendly price – making them more attainable for the small businesses who stood to benefit from them the most. But having done that, I was plagued by a nagging sense of dissatisfaction and inadequacy. MohJoh had a minor technical issue – an unexplained audible 'crackle' when the message played down the phone line. This took a long time to resolve and by then I was deflated by the lack of impact my marketing efforts were having, online and offline. Other than the odd lead here and there (from those who somehow found us on page 14 of a Google search), MohJoh fell by the wayside.

Generating leads for Cyberstart was almost as tough. One day, I went so far as to trudge through thick mud in high-heel boots – sheepishly placing flyers under the windscreen wipers of cars at a digital marketing conference in a desperate attempt to generate leads. But not a single enquiry came through. Other than referrals from the local small business centre, the only marketing that worked for us demanded my physical presence: face-to-face networking and the facilitation of small group workshops. The investment of time and energy I had to make to generate a single lead with these activities far exceeded the return made on them. The marketing of Cyberstart was unsustainable and definitely not scalable.

My problems were compounded by the fact that – when I honestly and accurately factored in my own time – Cyberstart wasn't profitable. Although I'd calculated the cost of both MohJoh and Cyberstart, I did so with a preconceived idea of what their prices needed to be to compete as budget offerings in their respective markets. To make these low prices possible (on paper at least), I understated the amount of time I would realistically need to manage each project. I devalued my time, so I'd have some price-based carrots to dangle. Deep down, I knew if the prices were to reflect the *actual* value of my time (taking my high standards into account), they would have to be much higher, leaving me with no way to make the packages stand out. After all, price was their only point of difference. This was a precarious and unfulfilling business strategy, and a hard thing for a self-proclaimed 'small business marketing specialist' to admit.

Although pricing our packages had been less emotional than my post-op pricing endeavours before that, the process was still heavily influenced by emotion; namely, by fear. I had created budget offerings under the noble guise of 'making them affordable for small businesses' but really, it was to make them as easy as possible for me to sell to minimise my chances of rejection and failure.

Although we were giving businesses what they wanted (cheap, functional websites), it wasn't sitting well with me. Our Cyberstart websites were little more than online flyers. In designing the website templates, I had worked with my designers to ensure they would be flexible enough for use by any micro-business – from cabinet makers to ecommerce stores and online directories.

This 'one size fits all' approach was backfiring because, in trying to please everyone, I felt like I was failing them – and myself. Although Cyberstart clients were happy with our service and pleased to have an online presence at a budget price, they didn't rave about the impact of their website on their business. If I'd been motivated by money instead of results, perhaps I could have pushed on and built a booming business... but I just couldn't. In my heart of hearts, I knew that although a cheap website package was what my target market thought they wanted, it was not what they needed.

Before long, my integrity won out and I was forced back to the drawing board. I'd learned that preset packages worked wonders to boost and streamline the lead-to-sale cycle but did nothing to generate leads. I'd also learned that competing on price was not a sustainable, satisfying or success-inducing strategy. But I had no idea what the alternative was.

Once again, I was lost.

The Dynamic Duo: Preset Packages for a Niche Market

It wasn't until several years later, while trying again to reformulate Cyberstart, that I had a revelation. As long as I kept taking on clients with special needs (those wanting online stores and directories, for example), I'd be unable to streamline operations and create a sustainable business. The only way forward was to niche to a small segment of the market and definitively rule the rest out.

When I finally mustered the courage to niche down to trade service businesses under the banner of Cyberstart Tradie, I drew on the lessons I'd learned about packages and pricing years earlier and everything fell into place. I created three website packages and two ongoing marketing support packages (the latter of which were far from perfect but that was okay – they evolved over time as we sold them, delivered them and tracked their results). Working out how to frame, price and present the Cyberstart Tradie packages took time, but it was time well spent.

Beyond the benefits of niching outlined in Chapter 9, the combination of niching with preset packages meant:

- **My personality had a purpose** – My perfectionism and empathy were channelled into the creation of solution-based packages of genuine service and value to our clients.

- **Pricing paralysis evaporated** – I was so confident in the value of our services and the positive impact they would have on the lives of our clients that I could detach emotionally from the pricing process. I was finally free to stop focusing and competing on price. The package prices took all costs into consideration, including my labour, and factored in an ample profit margin which continued to increase over time.

- **I took control** – Previously, I'd given Cyberstart customers a choice of five layouts and a menu of optional extras to choose from. In doing this, I'd given away my power to affect positive change on their businesses through results-focused design and content. With Cyberstart Tradie, I took back creative control. All functional features and design elements, specific to the needs of tradies, were bundled into our main solution-based package, SmartStart. With SmartStart, there was no choice of layout and no suite of optional extras. Instead, customers were given a choice of three packages – KickStart (a budget option, based on the original Cyberstart), SmartStart and PowerStart (a premium option). This had the desired effect of drawing prospects to the middle package.

- **Leads began to flow** – With our target market as a unique point of difference and confidence in the value of our packaged solutions, it was like someone turned on a tap. Leads started to flow... and they didn't stop.

Beyond these benefits, the combination of niching and preset packages did more for me personally, than I could have ever imagined. Through the implementation of this business model, I not only overcame my tendency to trade my time for less money than it was worth, I finally learned how to trust my gut. Most importantly though, it liberated me to embrace the parts of my personality that, I'd been told, 'had no place in business'. Never again would I accept that I needed to 'lower my standards' or 'toughen up' to survive in business. My perceived weaknesses were actually entrepreneurial superpowers.

For SSBs struggling with post-op pricing, niching with preset packages is a winning formulation. It changes the game of business by transferring the focus from money to results. This shifts a business' energetic vibration from 'surviving to thriving' and 'force to flow'. It can take time to find and validate a worthy niche, then articulate and refine solution-based packages around its needs but, once you do, it's like cracking the combination to a lock... the door of entrepreneurship creaks open.

CHAPTER 11.

AGILITY: USE IT OR LOSE IT

Most struggling SSB owners invest in business coaches or courses at some point – with high hopes of turning things around. We do as we're told and give it our all but, after a temporary upswing in motivation, productivity and sales, we peak, plateau and regress. We then beat ourselves up for not sustaining our input and effort or, worse still, blame our coach or course facilitator for not delivering on their side of the bargain.

But often, there's a legitimate reason why our investments in coaching and courses fail to pay off. It's simply that the content of most programs is geared for businesses that have 'found their feet', when ours hasn't. We're investing in tips, tools and techniques to help our business run faster, when it hasn't yet learned to walk.

To be clear, this is not the fault of our coaches or course facilitators, nor their responsibility. Just as a parent is responsible for monitoring and intervening in the delayed developmental progress of a baby, we are responsible for the developmental progress of our SSB. Until we accept and embrace this responsibility, our business will continue to crawl and much of the advice and tutelage we receive will feel like 'too much, too soon', if not completely irrelevant.

The Trifecta of Consistency

You know you've found your feet as an SSB owner, when **consistency outshines chaos** – when the business is **consistently breaking even**, when customers are **consistently delighted**, and when each order, job or project follows a **consistent rhythm and routine**.

This consistency trifecta is indicative of an SSB's long-term survivability. As with a stool or tripod, a weakness in any of the three legs of consistency will cause the business to come crashing down. All three need to be strong to sustain and support business growth. We've looked at the first two – the importance of breaking even (striking a balance between demand and supply) and delighting current customers – but the third, finding a sense of rhythm and routine in the day-to-day delivery of our service, is a new concept; a concept that's essential to grasp to strengthen a business' legs as quickly as possible.

For an SSB owner, finding a sense of rhythm and routine is like finding a soul mate – you don't realise you've been missing it, until you find it – then you can't imagine life any other way. Striking a semblance of consistency between jobs or projects changes the nature of business, providing a sense of relief, liberation and ease. Instead of having to consciously think 'Where do I start?' or 'What do I do now?' at every turn of every project, the steps are predetermined – they flow in a predictable, step-by-step sequence. When each order, job or project follows the same basic process like this, the operational side of the business settles into a familiar rhythm and routine; one which gets faster with time and experience and is essential to SSB success.

Before it finds rhythm and routine, an SSB operates at a mere fraction of its business potential. There's little consistency between orders, jobs or projects, so it's like starting from scratch every time. With each new customer comes new things to learn, special factors to consider and unexpected issues to overcome. Each order, job or project is reliant on the SSB owner's expertise and intuition to guide it from kick-off to completion, preventing the service process from being broken down into nice, neat steps for the purposes of streamlining systems and delegating to staff. This lack of consistency not only makes business much harder than it needs to be, it stands in the way of productivity, profitability and progress.

So how do we obtain the elusive trifecta of consistency?

The only way possible – through change.

The Power of Agility

Imagine businesses are boats; boats of all different shapes and sizes. SSBs are the sailboats – not big or flashy, nor equipped with expensive, powerful engines. But with their small size and structure comes agility – the ability to move quickly and nimbly in market waters. Unlike the corporate cruise liners and supertankers of big business, our little sailboats can change course quickly. In such close proximity to the water, we can assess our position and performance constantly, make decisions swiftly and act on them without the departmental delays of a corporate enterprise.

Agility is an incredible power that *must* be activated to achieve SSB success, and yet so many of us don't realise we wield it. If our business isn't tracking in the right direction, according to our original itinerary, we assume we can't or won't reach our desired destination and many of us abandon ship way too soon.

Continual Improvement-ship

While size, structure and a decent pair of sails make agility possible, it's the seamanship of the sailor that makes the boat move in the desired direction. The business equivalent to seamanship is *continual improvement-ship* – the conscious, ongoing effort of a business owner to improve customer perception, market perception and business performance, through change and innovation. Without an awareness of, and commitment to, continual improvement, an SSB nullifies its power of agility and, sooner or later, will run aground.

To me, the term *continual improvement* always implied 'subtle tweaks and changes, made incrementally over time – mainly relevant to big business'. When I delved deeper into it, I realised that continual improvement was more than an airy fairy corporate concept and it changed my approach to business forever.

Continual improvement is a critical consideration for businesses of all shapes and sizes, comprising two distinct, equally essential modes: *incremental adjustments* and *breakthrough improvements*. Making the most of our natural agility through incremental adjustments and breakthrough improvements – the equivalents of 'course corrections' and 'changing course' in sailing – is key to surviving, and ultimately thriving in, the stormy seas of business. It's particularly important for SSB owners traversing the seas in such tiny, vulnerable vessels.

Incremental Adjustments (Course Corrections)

Incremental adjustments are corrections we make to our business offering to *get back on course* when we're blown off it. They can include updating tired furniture, introducing staff procedures, switching to more reliable suppliers, upgrading software, or any other operational improvements to overcome customer cringe-points (as per Chapter 5). Without incremental adjustments, our customers and other stakeholders will become increasingly disappointed. The business will stagnate and eventually fail, just as a boat sinks if holes are not repaired – slowly at first, but faster and faster as water seeps in.

Breakthrough Improvements (Changing Course)

While incremental adjustments are corrections we make to stay on our initial course, breakthrough improvements are carefully considered deviations *away* from it. Changing course is necessary to explore opportunities – particularly those in niche waters too shallow for bigger boats to access – and to navigate around hazards and threats.

Figure 14: Spot the difference – An incremental adjustment and breakthrough improvement

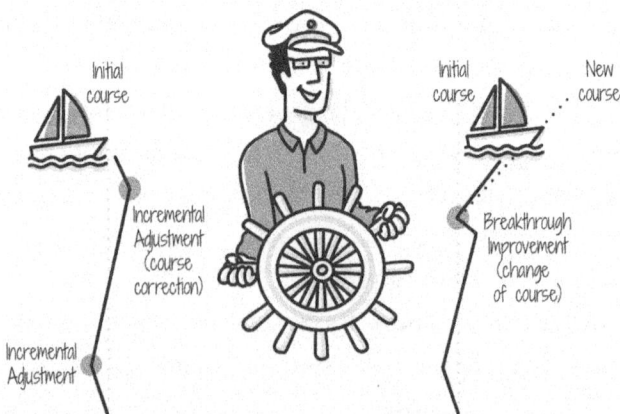

Breakthrough improvements are integral to an SSB's long-term survival. They give it substance and scalability and make the trifecta of consistency attainable. Without breakthrough improvements, the foundation on which our business is built (its business model), will eventually crumble – just as a sailboat that never changes course will eventually capsize or crash.

It's worth noting that breakthrough improvements don't necessarily change our vision or intended destination. They're what make our vision a clear and accessible reality, as opposed to a hazy, hope-fuelled mirage.

A Business Model Breakthrough

In Chapter 3, the two halves of the SSB marketing function were introduced – Business Model Management and Perception Management. We've explored the latter in detail but until this point, Business Model Management has remained an abstract concept. Having introduced the idea of breakthrough improvements though, it's time to change that.

Breakthrough improvements are central to Business Model Management. In fact, the two concepts are intrinsically linked. Breakthrough improvements are modifications to our business model that enable our SSB to be of greater service, provide more value and/or become a more viable enterprise by making better use of time and resources. They change our business' approach to market and, therefore, the course we set out to chart.

Building a Strong Business Model

Illustrated below is a framework to guide the Business Model Management or *planning* side of SSB marketing. It highlights the eight areas that determine an SSB's level of substance and scalability – the same eight areas to examine when the Big 4 Frustrations kick in.

Figure 15: The 8P Business Modelling Mix

Each of the 8Ps is explained below.

PROSPECT

Our business' ideal customer, identified by one or more distinguishing features or characteristics. Prospects en masse are our *target market*.

PRODUCT

The outcome or result we produce, which solves our target market's problems and/or satisfies their needs and wants. Products can be goods, services or a combination of the two.

PRICE

The pricing strategy we use to determine the amount customers pay in exchange for our goods and services and to make paying that price as appealing as possible. For example, preset or post-op pricing, packaging, the availability of payment plans, etc.

PLACE

The sites, locations, modes or platforms through which our goods and services are delivered – be it on-premise or mobile servicing, remote or digital delivery, or more outside-the-box forms of distribution such as licensing, franchising or print-on-demand (POD) publishing.

PROMOTION

The core elements of our brand and the primary marketing activities used to funnel new customers into our business.

PURPOSE

Comprised of two parts: 1) a *vision statement*, articulating our ambition for personal contribution – the big picture 'what' and 'why' of the change we want to see in the world, and 2) a *mission statement*, articulating the 'who' and 'how' of what we need to do right now to step towards the achievement of our vision.

PASSION

The energy and enthusiasm we have for our business model. This is the fuel that powers an SSB and activates its substance and scalability. Passion is felt, so it cannot be articulated – it's either present or not. If our business doesn't light us up, our energy isn't in alignment with our business model, so our model needs to change.

PERSONALITY

The human face, presence and voice of our business and the most valuable component of our brand. As an SSB owner, we must be prepared to fuse our human identity and image with that of our business, through physical, verbal and photographic means. If we're not, it's a sign that we don't have faith in our business model, or in ourselves – in which case, more business-modelling or self-development is required. Like passion, personality can't be articulated. It's either present (we're prepared to incorporate our personality into our marketing) or it isn't.

EXAMPLE: Cyberstart Tradie 8P Business Model

1. *PROSPECT* – Trade service businesses operating in Australia, with 0–5 employees.

2. *PRODUCT* – Website design and marketing support packages geared to overcome the Busy/Slow Cycle by driving a reliable flow of qualified leads to our clients' businesses.

3. *PRICE* – Package prices determined using a preset pricing strategy (cost and value-based), with a payment plan option for websites (facilitated by an independent finance company) and monthly billing for marketing support packages which can be cancelled at any time, beyond the first 6 months.

4. *PLACE* – Remote delivery using the phone, email and online infrastructure (Dropbox, WordPress, etc) as mediums of communication and exchange.

5. *PROMOTION* – Business to operate under the name Cyberstart Tradie with the slogan 'Smart Marketing for Time-Strapped Tradies'. Primary marketing activities to include strategic alliances with trade service industry associations and delivery of training workshops.

6. *PURPOSE* –

   Vision statement – To shift the balance of power in Australia's economy from big business to small business; increasing the annual small business survival rate (over 4 years) to 80% by 2030.

   Mission statement – To take the pain and guesswork out of marketing for trade services businesses Australia wide, empowering them with the tools and knowledge to capitalise on their size, cut through competition (without cutting prices) and create raving fans.

7. *PASSION* – Present (in abundance).

8. *PERSONALITY* – Present – solid sense of self. Note – owner to be promoted as 'The Tradie Marketing Lady'.

Note: When my passion for the Cyberstart Tradie business model dissolved, I knew it was time to make some big changes. Although it seemed counterintuitive to those close to me, I felt I had to scale the business back in order to move forward and stand a chance of achieving my vision. The prospect of writing books to help SSB owners en masse brought my passion flooding back – so that became the basis of my new model.

As with the Cyberstart Tradie example, a business model doesn't need to be complicated. It just needs to be well thought out and based around the needs of a well-defined target market. With a crystal clear vision of who we're serving and how they're suffering, the remaining Ps tend to fall into place.

The 8P Business Model vs the 4P Marketing Mix

If the 8P Business Model looks familiar, it's because it's an extension of the well-known ***marketing mix*** (commonly called ***the 4Ps***) – a model developed for big business.[14] Adding the Ps of *passion*, *purpose*, *personality* and *prospect* transforms the original model from a corporate concept into a useful small business planning tool. For SSBs, these four extra Ps are essential. Here's why:

Passion – Big businesses are fuelled by a collective muted energy of hundreds or thousands of employees, which churns the cogs of progress. SSBs, on the other hand, are powered by currents of energy from the owner; a blend of purpose, passion and personality. Without this energy, even the strongest of small business concepts will fall flat. Passion is included in the 8P Business Model as a vital reminder to check that our energy aligns with the direction of our business. If it doesn't, and we're radiating dread or dissatisfaction for example, our business model must change or, sooner or later, an external force will swoop in and change it for us.

Purpose – For SSBs, writing a vision and mission statement is paramount. It's how we stretch ourselves. My vision seemed so big and bold when I wrote it, I remember chuckling to myself, having no clue how I (or anyone) could possibly attain it. All I knew was that it felt right. It lit me up, made me stand a little taller and work a little faster. Then one day, I read my vision statement without laughing. I realised I could see a path to achieving it. A survival rate of 80% by 2030 may be unrealistic but what does it matter if my vision inspires and motivates me and, as a result, helps a few thousand businesses avoid failure? As the old saying goes, 'Shoot for the moon. If you miss, you'll land amongst the stars.'

Personality – Customers don't connect with an SSB's logo, they connect with its people – in particular, its owner. A willingness to make our personality a key element of our business' identity conveys a sense of authenticity, accountability and trustworthiness that's impossible to achieve, to the same extent, in any other way. Of course, it's possible for our SSB to survive without being the face and voice of our business, but it makes marketing a whole lot harder.

Prospect – In the original 4Ps, having a clear target market is more of an underlying assumption than a factor for careful consideration. Big businesses have a 'mass' mentality – mass marketing, mass production, mass distribution. Their target market has to be broad for the business to be sustainable at such a large scale. The needs of SSBs are different. For us, clearly defining a relatively narrow or niche target market (prospect) is key to a clear, cohesive and viable business model.

MIND YOUR Ps

It's worth noting that although the original 4P marketing mix grew to as many as eight in recent decades, those extra Ps – most commonly presented as People, Physical Evidence, Process and Performance – are superfluous to Business Model Management. As Secret Service Marketers, we are only concerned with elements that have a major bearing on an SSB's approach to market. People, Physical Evidence, Process and Performance fall under Perception Management and, as such, are covered elsewhere in this book.

Changing Your Business Model

When experiencing stress or strain in business, reviewing our business model is often the last thing on our minds. Most of us are quick to blame things outside our control – be it economic or political unrest, actions of competitors or the advertising medium we're using. This is akin to, and equally as effective as, barking up the wrong tree.

Relief from the stress and strain of SSB ownership is rarely found by looking outside of our business. It's found by examining and reinforcing its foundations; analysing and adapting the 8Ps of our business model.

To do this, start with *The Weak Link ID Chart* below. The chart lists some of the most common SSB stressors alongside the 8Ps. If a stressor strikes a chord with you, track along the row to see which Ps are ticked. This will highlight potential areas of weakness in your business model; areas requiring review and possible modification (breakthrough improvement).

Note that the Ps ticked for a particular stressor may come as a surprise. That's because the weakest link is rarely the most obvious. Having to compete on price to win jobs or projects, for example, doesn't necessarily mean Price is the problem. It's more likely to be a symptom of a deeper issue: not having a clear target market (Prospect), not solving a big enough problem or providing enough value (Product), or not communicating the value of the offering clearly enough (Promotion).

Figure 16: The Weak Link ID Chart - Common SSB stressors and the Ps likely to be causing them

Common Symptoms & Stressors	Possible Points of Weakness in Your Business Model							
	PROSPECT	PRODUCT	PRICE	PLACE	PROMOTION	PASSION	PURPOSE	PERSONALITY
You're unable to find a sense of rhythm and routine between jobs or projects	✓	✓			✓		✓	
You struggle to capture the attention of potential customers—almost as if your marketing is invisible.	✓	✓		✓	✓		✓	✓

Common Symptoms & Stressors	Possible Points of Weakness in Your Business Model							
	PROSPECT	PRODUCT	PRICE	PLACE	PROMOTION	PASSION	PURPOSE	PERSONALITY
You struggle to convert leads into sales (low conversion rate).	✓	✓			✓ (Poor lead-to-sale strategy)	✓	✓	✓
Customers are satisfied, but you don't get rave reviews or word of mouth.	✓	✓				✓	✓	✓
Potential customers are very price sensitive—you're constantly competing on price.	✓	✓			✓		✓	✓
The pricing process causes you stress and anxiety.	✓	✓	✓				✓	✓
You don't get enough "walk in" traffic.	✓			✓	✓		✓	
Your services are in high demand, but you struggle to make ends meet.	✓	✓	✓	✓			✓	
You struggle to break even from week to week	✓	✓	✓	✓	✓	✓	✓	✓

Once you've identified the weaknesses in your business model, download *The Weak Link Repair Guide* from *www.secretservice.biz/downloads*. This handy bonus provides ideas to strengthen your weak links through breakthrough improvements.

While incremental adjustments come quite naturally to most SSB owners, breakthrough improvements rarely do. Recognising that major change is necessary – let alone acting upon it – requires foresight, intuition, courage and a degree of humility. Strategic thinking and creativity are needed to plot a new course, then hard work, leadership and commitment are required to see it through.

In the world of SSB ownership, breakthrough improvements are the 'path less travelled' because change is uncomfortable. The mere prospect of change can give rise to all sorts of fears and insecurities... and fair enough. It's a rocky road; one that gets harder to traverse before it gets easier, as demonstrated in The Satir Change Model (aka The Change Process).[15]

Figure 17: The Change Process – An illustrated representation of Virginia Satir's Change Model

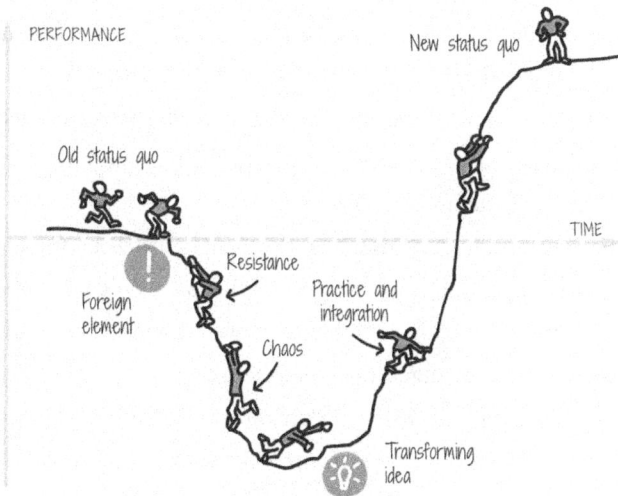

As the cartoon shows, change is no walk in the park. It can take us to chaotic new lows before a 'transforming idea' (an insight or revelation about how the change can be of benefit) leads to a new and improved 'normal', which supersedes the old status quo. No wonder change is scary. And no wonder that – in small business at least – breakthrough improvements tend to be few and far between. But this must change.

A willingness to change and innovate is what sets successful entrepreneurs apart from SSB owners caught in an eternal cycle of struggle. Business success is largely defined by the quality and quantity of breakthrough improvements we make. Entrepreneurial treasure troves don't exist along a straight line of navigation... changing course is needed to find them. It's part and parcel of becoming a strong, successful businessperson.

Some breakthrough improvements require demolishing a business (scaling it back or closing it down) to rebuild on stronger foundations. It can be hard to admit your business model is flawed, or that you're no longer feeling it. But quitting in order to regroup (be it the next day, year, decade or longer) is *not* failing. It's a feat of strength and resilience, and a story that will inevitably define our success.

No business owner gets everything right 100% of the time. Quite the opposite. Just as planes and boats are off course about 90% of the time, so too are we. Even if we were to get everything right every time, change is inevitable because our market environment – like the wind or sea – is constantly moving and changing. Without adjusting our sails to correct or change course, our sailboats would run aground, sink in stormy seas, or worse... never leave the jetty.

Successful entrepreneurs know this, which is why they covet change. They seek it out, looking for things to improve and problems to solve. They welcome the sour taste of change, knowing it will be negated by the sweetness of eventual success.

Building an SSB with strength, substance and scalability doesn't happen by accident. It requires a business model with the capacity to consistently break even, delight customers and enjoy a sense of rhythm and routine, all while aligning with who we are and what we feel. This takes conscious planning, action and reflection over time. Finding our business' feet rarely happens overnight but once we're there – once we're excited to answer the question 'So... what do you do?' – threats imposed by stormy economic seas, fellow sailboats or corporate cruise liners tend to quickly disappear over the horizon.

RECOVERY MISSION 3

Chapter 8 – 'So... What do you do?'

- **Read the room** – Using the Service Skeleton matrix (page 117) and the definitions that follow it, determine whether your goods or services would be perceived as necessities or luxuries with a low or high level of risk.
- **Assess the risks** – Carefully consider your goods and services from the perspective of potential customers, listing the risks that could be associated with them.
- **Prepare a proposition** – Determine whether a monetary, emotive or double whammy value proposition (VP) is most appropriate for your business. Then schedule time to write, practise and refine it.
- **Grip the rope** – Prepare a rope swing response for the question 'So what do you do?' Start using it in interactions with new acquaintances, noticing the reactions you receive.

Chapter 9 – Unleash the Niche

- **Size up the system** – Determine if business level niching is suitable for your business, using the identifiers under 'When NOT to Niche' on page 135.
- **Prepare to pivot** – Embark on the niching process with '5 Steps to Find & Carve Your Niche' on page 141 as your guide.

Chapter 10 - The Price Is Right... Or Is It?

- **Know your price** – Identify your current pricing strategy: preset or post-op pricing. Once known, outline your specific type and method of pricing.
- **Acknowledge the agony** – Identify any difficulties you have with pricing your goods or services. Is pricing easy or do you experience pricing paralysis?
- **Flip your flaws** – Acknowledge your perfectionism and empathic sensitivity (if applicable). Reframe them as 'high standards' and 'emotional-social intelligence'.
- **Get preset** – Consider preset packages for a niche market. Start thinking about goods or services you could bundle together to meet the niche's specific needs.

Chapter 11 - Agility: Use it or Lose it

- **Take the test** – Answer yes or no to the following questions:
  1. Does your business **consistently break even?**
  2. Are your customers **consistently delighted?**
  3. Does every order, job or project follow a **consistent rhythm and routine?**
- If you answered *no* to one or more questions, your business is yet to experience the flow and growth that stems from the trifecta of consistency. In other words, your business is yet to find its feet and will likely require changes to its business model.
- **Remember your training** – Identify any business coaching or courses you've invested in that haven't seemed beneficial. Take accountability for the lack of results derived from them, acknowledging (if applicable,

based on the trifecta of consistency test) that your business hadn't found its feet at the time, so it wasn't ready to reap the rewards of your education. Then, recognise that those investments weren't in vain. You attained valuable knowledge… it's just yet to be reflected in your bank account. So drop the resentment.

- **Map out your model** – On a whiteboard or large piece of paper, map out your current business model by writing the 8Ps as large headings with a sentence or two for each (like in the Cyberstart Tradie example on page 185).

- **Mull it over** – Position your business model somewhere you can see and reflect on it regularly. Take note of how it makes you feel… excited, motivated, anxious, sluggish, confused. Any negative feelings indicate your business model needs work.

- **Identify your weak links** – Refer to the Weak Link ID Chart on page 189. With this and your business model for reference, identify possible areas (Ps) of concern.

- **Access Unlocked** – Download and print The Weak Link Repair Guide from *www.secretservice.biz/downloads*. With this, look up the Ps you identified as weak links for ideas to inspire a breakthrough business improvement.

- **Be the change** – Modify your business model until you feel excited and energised by what's in front of you. Reinforce your excitement with facts and figures to make an informed decision, then implement the required changes and give it your all.

PART FOUR

FOR YOUR EYES ONLY

In 1992, the United Nations Development Programme (UNDP) published a groundbreaking report which showed, among other things, that the richest 20% of the world's population controlled 82.7% of the world's income.[16] This mind-blowing statistic was one of the most significant confirmations possible, of the validity of the *Pareto Principle* or *80/20 rule*, an economic rule of thumb developed by Management Consultant Joseph M. Juran (based on earlier observations of Vilfredo Pareto, an Italian economist).

The 80/20 rule states that, for many situations, approximately 80% of outcomes stem from 20% of causes.[17] The most well-known application of the 80/20 rule in business is that 80% of sales come from our top 20% of clients, while 80% of complaints come from our bottom 20%. Knowing this, we can refine our focus – nurturing our best clients and encouraging the more diffi-cult ones to go elsewhere (to become another business' concern).

An equally important application of the 80/20 rule relates to who generates the lion's share of income in a market or industry. Thanks to the Pareto Principle, we can conclude that 20% of service providers in any market or industry, earn approximately 80% of its total revenue. We'll call these domi-nant players the *rich kids* and *rockstars* of business; rich kids if they sell necessary goods or services and rockstars if they sell luxuries.

Rich Kids & Rockstars

Rich kids and rockstars are well-established businesses with the money to preserve or grow their market share through high-exposure advertising. Fast food giant McDonalds is an example of a rich kid in the low-risk necessity category. Service seekers are drawn to rich kids by default, as they're perceived to be an affordable, reliable option.

Rockstars are the rich kids of luxury goods and services, with a perceived level of prestige and exclusivity. The high-end, international hotel and resort chains Westin and Four Seasons are examples of rockstars. They attract 'groupies' through their premium branding, offerings and reputation. High prices contribute to the prestige, making their offerings exclusive to those with the disposable income to indulge in them.

80% of the revenue pie is gobbled up by the rich kid/rockstar minority, which leaves the rest of us (the 80% majority) battling it out over 20% – equivalent to a few crumbs. Although this may sound bleak, it's actually very exciting. The pie is bigger than most of us realise – we just need an effective way to ask for a bigger slice. The 80/20 rule may be the natural order of things but it's never set in stone. Just as global income distribution has changed dramatically in the last two decades, so too can our share of the revenue pie.

To flip the 80/20 rule on its head – staking our claim for a bigger slice of the pie – we need to shake up the natural order of things. This requires changing our attitude and approach to business (the focus of this book so far), as well as busting a few mainstream marketing myths.

For too long, generally accepted principles and practices of marketing have filtered down from our corporate cousins. They've muddied the waters of business, causing us to get snagged; spending time and money on things that have little bearing on our business' success. It's time to dispel these outdated instructions and replace them with ones that are not only of practical relevance to struggling SSB owners, but of a distinct advantage... starting with branding.

CHAPTER 12.

THE TRUTH ABOUT BRANDING

*** WARNING! DETAIL AHEAD ***

This chapter contains detailed instructions that
may be overwhelming at first. If you get bogged
down in it, switch to skim reading and return
to each section as it becomes applicable.

Our brand is usually the first 'packet' of sensory data processed by a potential customer. It influences their first impression and ongoing perception of our business… but not in the way we're conditioned to believe.

As it stands, most of us inadvertently sink the bulk of our branding budgets into elements that matter the least. This not only wastes money upfront, it can inhibit our business long into the future by failing to clearly communicate who we are and what we do in that all-important first instance. To buck this trend, let's set a few things straight.

The Logo Myth

We all know logos are a crucially important marketing investment and essential to business success... or are they?

The truth is, we could spend tens of thousands of dollars on an extraordinary logo but most of it would be a waste of money. That's not to say SSBs don't need a logo. A quality logo is important – it conveys a sense of professionalism, provides a pictorial element of interest (to catch and draw the eye) and makes our business easy to recognise. But a high-end logo won't make us any more successful than one designed on a shoestring.

For SSBs, a simple, clean, low-cost logo is as effective (sometimes more-so) than a highly creative or expensive one. So, forget what you've heard – your logo *won't* make or break your business. But more basic elements of your brand certainly can.

Brand Basics

Stripping it back, an SSB's brand is comprised of three essential elements:

1. **Business name**
2. **Subline and/or slogan**
3. **Contact details**

We've all seen businesses (often trade service businesses) cope just fine with little more than these basic text elements on their signage and advertisements. This goes to show that, for SSBs, a logo is *not* the most important aspect of a brand. Getting the business name, subline/slogan and contact details right is infinitely more important. These elements form a foundation of logic on which the suitability of our business is assessed by potential customers. If we specialise in commercial plumbing, for instance, but don't communicate that in the basics of our branding, potential customers will assume we don't do it. They'll pass us by, writing our business off as irrelevant, until our brand clearly communicates what we do.

So let's get our business' basic brand elements on track – first and foremost, its name.

Business Name

The name we give our SSB is a precious commodity. It's an opportunity to communicate something specific and meaningful about our business that will resonate with, and appeal to, our target market.

A name like Walters Commercial Plumbing, which might seem boring to corporate creatives or mainstream marketers, can be highly effective for an SSB. It's clear, meaningful and can be processed instantly; communicating what the business does (specialist plumbing) and for whom (commercial entities), while implying that customers receive personal service from a family business (via the name 'Walters').

A vague alternative, such as WCP Solutions, has none of these attributes. It contributes nothing positive to the perception of a business, sounding cold and detached and implying a lack of direction. Existing customers may know what WCP Solutions does but potential customers won't. They'd have to work harder to decipher what WCP Solutions does than they would for Walters Commercial Plumbing, and most won't bother.

You might be thinking 'What about Apple and Nike – their names don't say what they do?' The difference is, they are big businesses with established goods-based brands. Delving into their histories, even Apple and Nike started out as Apple Computer Inc and Blue Ribbon Sports. With time and growth, they earned the right to shorten their names to cooler, catchier brand names. We aren't there yet.

Business Names: The Good, The Bad & The Ugly

A business name is the most prominent feature of a brand. So, before committing to an initial or new name, it's wise to consider various naming strategies and their implications on market perception.

The most common strategies for naming an SSB include:

Personal names – As mentioned in the example above, marketers and creatives often think business names featuring the owner's personal name are bland or boring, or that the owner must lack originality and strategic vision. True or not, these opinions don't matter. The fact is, injecting a personal name into our business name can be a smart move. It gives our brand an instant sense of authenticity, accountability and warmth, which can be highly appealing to those seeking a service.

If contemplating a personal business name, following are some points for consideration.

1. **Technical involvement and expertise** – A personal business name is most appropriate if you have mastery in your field of service, are confident in your technical abilities and work hands-on in the business. Checking these three boxes gives depth and substance to a personal brand.

2. **First or last** – Whether you feature your first name, last name or both depends on the perception you want to create.

Using a first name gives a brand a relaxed, casual feeling. It also implies that the services will be delivered by the owner (not an employee or stand-in). This can suit certain industries – particularly those providing personal services (e.g. Jo's Personal Training, Ashley's Eyebrow Bar) and some low-risk trade services, like lawn mowing – but otherwise, it's not appropriate. For professional, B2B or high-risk services (architecture, legal services, accountancy, building, real estate, etc), the casual, fun feeling of a 'first-name name' would conflict with the perception we need to create to appeal to high-value customers, causing our business to struggle. For the majority of SSBs considering a personal business name, a last name or first/last combination (as long as it's not too wordy) is most appropriate.

3. **Can strangers spell it?** – If your name has silent letters or an unexpected or complex spelling, be cautious including it in your business name. Potential customers *will* misspell it. That's not the end of the world but is something to be mindful of; ensuring you optimise your website for common misspellings to ensure your business can be found online, no matter how it's spelt.

Place names – SSB owners who factor the name of the region they service into their business name can gain a distinct competitive advantage, particularly online, where users tend to search for services by location and type, e.g. 'Canberra crash repairs'. In this example, a business named Canberra Crash Repairs would likely rank well in search results due, in part, to the number of times the words Canberra Crash Repairs would appear on its website. A website littered with a certain phrase is likely to be deemed highly relevant to those searching for that phrase, and ranked accordingly in search results. This can be highly advantageous.

However, place names can deter some service seekers. Depending on the size and population of the city or region, potential customers may perceive that a business with a place name is bigger (and more expensive) than it actually is. This misconception will cause some to dismiss the business, assuming it won't provide the level of service or affordability they're seeking. Whether that's bad or not depends on the calibre of customer we want to appeal to.

Place names can also be off-putting if the size or scope of the referenced region is out of sync with other characteristics of the business. Naming a business Global Building Services, despite being a home-based sole trader, creates a contradiction between its brand and business model. Any subtle incongruence like this can cause streetwise customers to run a mile.

Acro-names – Some of the most successful entities in the world have acronym-based business names (acro-names for short): ANZ, SGIC, BHP, ING, KFC... the list goes on. Like Apple or Nike, these corporations have earned the right to shorten their names. A series of letters with no intrinsic meaning is fine for them – they have the marketing budget necessary to give it context through constant mass exposure. Small businesses don't have that luxury. In SSB branding, every word counts. Condensing a business name to three or four letters wastes a major opportunity to reach and connect with potential customers.

Quirky names – Quirky names are appropriate for some businesses and not others. Kinky Boots Coffee House might work well for a café, while Kinky Boots Accounting would create confusion and likely lead to damaging assumptions about the business' owner or target market.

A name can have multiple meanings, depending on which words we emphasise. For example, the **Crazy Cat** Café could be interpreted as the Crazy **Cat Café** – one will attract different clientele to the other. Potential misunderstandings or interpretations of our business name can severely impact our brand and the resultant success of our business, so it's important to consider them in advance. The best way to do this is to run the proposed name past people we trust – collecting first impressions and honest, objective opinions before making a final decision.

If opting for a quirky name, 'randomness' can be alleviated by rolling it out as a *theme*. In the case of a café, the name could inspire the fit-out, front façade, signage design, uniforms, background music, menu and more. A theme can give layers of meaning, character and context to a brand, not only making a business more appealing in the first instance, but more memorable; a place customers are likely to talk about and return to.

A strong theme has the power to turn a business' premises into a destination and its service into an experience. I once worked behind the scenes at a venue called New York Bar & Grill, not in New York, but in Adelaide, Australia. With an intricately crafted façade featuring scale replicas of the Empire State Building and Statue of Liberty, internal bar and dining areas depicting the lights and sights of Times Square and Manhattan, and floor staff dressed in NY Yankees inspired baseball uniforms, the New York theme was beautifully and thoroughly executed. Its innovative concept, attention to detail and unrivalled commitment to its theme, saw New York Bar & Grill quickly become an award-winning venue and a renowned, local landmark. Such is the power of a well-executed theme.

Clever cookie names – A clever cookie name is one with multiple layers of meaning, communicated in a succinct and memorable way. It can be a fusion of words, a play on words or a cheeky play on a cliché or saying. My favourite, local examples are Udder Delights (an Adelaide Hills cheese cellar) and Pane in the Glass (an Adelaide glazier) – SSB branding at its best. Clever cookie names are generally short, sweet and easy to recall. Although people may not be able to deduce what a business does from the name alone, it's clever and catchy enough to invoke the curiosity needed to read on and find out.

Note: If fusing words together to make a 'new word', avoid ending it in -*tec* or -*lec*, e.g. Comlec, Buildtec. This approach is overused, particularly in trade, industrial and IT services.

Business Naming Tips

1. **Keep it clear and concise** – The key to a great business name is to strike a balance between clearly communicating what you do and keeping the number of words in the name to a minimum, so it can roll off the tongue.

2. **Google it** – Before committing to a name, be sure to check what appears when you Google it. If another business exists with a similar name, in a similar industry, potential customers *will* be confused between the two. Some will contact the other business when they mean to contact you and vice versa. And if the other business has a bad reputation, it *will* taint yours.

It's also worth checking what displays under the 'Images' tab in the Google search results for your proposed name. My first trading name was Southern Xposure – a clever cookie name, expressed using a play on words (a twist on the name of a 90s TV show – *Northern Exposure*). It wasn't for about two years that a male client, grinning cheekily, suggested I Google the name and check the image listings. Turns out, Southern Xposure is a gentlemen's club in Utah, so the image search results were a little... revealing. Despite this, I stuck with the name until I had a clear business direction. It was the least of my concerns at the time, and made for an amusing talking point.

3. **Check availability** – It can be quite a challenge to come up with a suitable name that's available for registration, particularly now that, in Australia at least, business names are administered at a national level. Where once a name only needed to be unique to the business' state of operation, it must now be unique to the entire country.

What's more, a proposed business name must be available as a website domain name. Domain name registration is separate to business name registration so it's easy to overlook, but – due to the pivotal role a website plays in an SSB's marketing efforts – it is an equally important consideration.

If a seemingly perfect business name is not available as both a business name *and* domain name, it's not the perfect name. Try subtle variations of it (Southern Xposure instead of Southern Exposure, for example) being conscious of the potential consequences of spelling a business name in an unexpected way. Failing that, keep brainstorming and checking the availability of different options. An ideal alternative will come to you.

Subline & Slogan

A subline (pronounced sub-line) and slogan are not the same thing; they are two different brand elements that share a common purpose.

A **subline** is a line of text featured below, or in conjunction with, a business' name and logo, stating what services the business provides.

A **slogan** is a catchphrase or motto designed to communicate what's different or better about a business, in an engaging, relatable way. A great slogan gives the brand a sense of personality and/or induces an emotion, which makes potential customers more likely to take action.

Fictional Examples

Business name: Your Kitchen Rules
Subline: Kitchen Resurfacing & Renovations
Slogan: 'For bitchin' kitchens on a budget'

Business name: Wheely Delicious Pies & Snacks
Subline: Mobile Bakery & Coffee Bar
Slogan: 'The #1 choice for a well-deserved work break'

Together, a subline and slogan give us the chance to fill in any blanks left by a business name. They give us the opportunity to clearly, concisely and consistently communicate who we are, what we do, who we do it for and why we're worth considering.

Branding or rebranding an SSB is a rare opportunity – one

which is not fully exploited without engaging the services of an experienced copywriter to create or refine a subline and slogan. A **copywriter** is a person whose job it is to write enticing marketing materials, such as advertisements, website content and sales presentations. Where most people write to relay facts, copywriters write to relay facts while invoking emotion and inspiring action. Whether we have a natural flair for writing or not, drawing on the expertise and objective viewpoint of a copywriter is one of the best business investments we can make. It can transform a brand from bland to bold, and make a world of difference to the effectiveness of our marketing.

To create a strong brand (or any marketing communication, for that matter), the trick is to hire a copywriter *before* hiring a graphic designer. Working with a copywriter before getting caught up in visual aesthetics helps ensure that the vital brand basics – provided to the graphic designer as a design brief – are as clear, concise and enticing as possible. With a strong business name, subline and slogan, a designer is better equipped to produce a strong visual identity and make the most of a limited budget.

Contact Details

Contact details are a core component of branding because they make inbound communication possible. Without a phone number, customers can't phone us. Without a location, they won't know if we're in their area or where to visit us. Without a website address, they can't look us up online – at least not without further online exploration and the risk of getting side-tracked on a competitor's site along the way.

But there's more to it than that. Contact details aren't just important because of the facts they convey, but because of what they imply about our business and its operations. Understanding the possible interpretations of the contact details in our marketing materials is essential, as they can inadvertently repel potential customers through the power of assumption.

Phone Numbers

The phone is an incredibly important tool for SSBs. It's often the only means by which service seekers feel comfortable making contact with us, so the phone call-to-action on our marketing materials must be clear and concise. While it's fine to list all available phone numbers (landline, mobile, etc) on business cards, stationery and email signatures, one number must be chosen to serve as the ***promotional phone number***: the number used to encourage phone enquiries from new customers, in every public-facing marketing communication – from our website and social media pages to our storefront and vehicle signage.

The phone number we select as our promotional number is more than just a sequence of digits. It can imply certain things about our business, which can add to or detract from the perception we're trying to create.

- **Mobile** – Using a mobile (or cell) phone number as a business' promotional number, implies that the owner is a sole trader or 'one-man band'. This is appropriate if you are a sole trader but can be bad for business if you're not – sparking a perceived contradiction between your brand and business model.

  If a mobile promotional number is appropriate, be aware that a couple of stigmas are attached to it, which can stop potential customers from calling. The first is that phoning a mobile number will open a line of communication with the business owner directly. Some service seekers like the idea of this, while others are put off by it – assuming they'll have to leave a message, play a game of 'phone tag' or be rudely ignored. The second stigma is that it costs more to call mobile numbers. Thanks to capped phone plans, this stigma has largely died out, however service seekers on basic landline plans can still be deterred from calling a mobile number due to higher call rates. As such, it's worthy of consideration – particularly for those with an elderly customer base.

- **Landline** – The promotion of a landline number 'grounds' a business, by implying the existence of a solid base of operations. It also reaffirms our geographic location, as the area code and prefix will be familiar to those who live or work in the area. This is the best option for SSBs confined by geographic area, due to the need to serve customers on premise, in their homes or on-site.

  A landline promotional number is less appropriate for businesses operating remotely or servicing a broad geographic area. If promoting a landline, potential customers from interstate can assume a business' services are limited by state or region – writing it off as unsuitable before giving it any real consideration.

- **VOIP** – A VOIP number has the same effect as a landline, without the added benefit of geographic familiarity. To some, it can imply that the business is technologically savvy or (if no street address is listed) that it is run from home.

- **International** – The extended international version of a phone number (such as +61 for Australia) should only be used if marketing and selling internationally. Many SSBs add an international prefix to their promotional number in an effort to make the business appear bigger than it is, not realising that they're shooting themselves in the foot by complicating the calling process for locals – who need to consciously drop/add certain digits to convert it back to a local call.

- **Free call** – A toll free number (such as 1300 or 1800 in Australia) is an excellent marketing tool for growing businesses, especially those servicing a broad area. Not only does it make a business look highly professional, it allows the words 'free call' to be included in the phone call-to-action in marketing materials. This is a powerful, subconscious sweetener that increases the likelihood of potential customers taking action by phone.

No matter what number we choose as our promotional phone number, it's crucial to consider how our phone will be answered and by whom. To avoid losing leads in droves, it's critical to have some simple phone protocols in place – explained in Chapter 16.

Physical Addresses

As with phone numbers, the addresses listed (or not listed) on our marketing materials reveal a lot about our business operations.

- **Post office box** – A PO box address with no accompanying street address implies that a business operates from home and that 'drop-in' visitors are definitely not welcome.

- **Street address** – A street address indicates that a business has a commercial premises or brick-and-mortar store which welcomes foot-traffic.

Like a landline phone number, a physical address helps 'ground' a business, making it appear more stable and trustworthy. Home-based business owners can tap into this by promoting their physical address – be it a home address, a shared office space or the premises of an associate or supplier (with their consent) – followed by the words 'by appointment only'. This gives the benefit of a street address, without risking unwanted foot-traffic.

Online Addresses

Last but not least are our business' digital addresses, which guide potential customers to reach and connect with us online. In order of importance, these are listed below.

- **Website address** – With the Secret Service approach to marketing, a website is more than a website... It's the online face of our business and a gateway to connection, interaction and transaction. To help it serve this purpose, our website address must be promoted as our primary means of online contact. This is done by formatting our domain name in a bigger, bolder font than other contact details and making it easily recognisable as a website address via the inclusion of the prefix 'www'.

- **Social media** – Social media addresses are often long, ugly and difficult to remember. For this reason, it's best to avoid listing them in written form and instead display the graphic icons for each respective platform (subject to the platform's terms and conditions). Not only does this look cleaner and more professional, it prompts brand recognition for the social networks themselves – communicating that you have a social media presence without drawing attention away from your website address.

Note that only the icons of social media platforms your business is truly active on should be included in your marketing communications. Never include extra icons for the sake of looking 'cool'. Potential followers will only end up feeling underwhelmed or irritated.

- **Email address** – An email address should be included on business cards, stationery and email signatures but *never* on a website, in ads, signage or other marketing materials. It's an unnecessary extra detail which can sidetrack those who would otherwise happily phone or submit a website enquiry form. This is one of the most common branding mistakes SSB owners make, attracting unqualified leads, time wasters and – if your email address is accessible via your website – an influx of spam in your inbox.

  Another common mistake is the use of a 'third party' email address, such as abcaccounting@gmail.com or jonesythebuilder@hotmail.com. A third party email address makes a business look unprofessional, as if it's not built on solid foundations, so – if applicable to you – it's something to rectify immediately.

  Creating professional email addresses such as info@abcaccounting.com.au or jake@jonesbuilding. com.au is not difficult. All it takes is the registration of a domain name (e.g. www.abcaccounting.com.au) and an email service – setup through a web hosting account or, preferably, a cloud-based collaboration suite like Google Workspace (explained in Chapter 7).

Once a business name, subline/slogan and contact details have been finalised, it's time to create a ***visual identity*** (or VI) to tie the basic brand elements together, catch the eye and visually distinguish the brand from others in the market.

The Visual Identity of a Brand

While an SSB can survive with strong brand basics alone, an equally strong visual identity amplifies its impact and appeal.

For an SSB, a strong visual identity consists of the following elements.

- **Logo** – An icon designed to represent the business and display its name, for ease of recognition. Logos typically feature unique fonts or graphic elements to stand out, add visual interest and give context to the words.

  An ideal SSB logo is a simple one. It's easy to read, recognise and comprehend, without being overly artistic. Logos that contain gradients, shadows or intricate illustrated details tend to date quickly, so it's best to opt for a clean, two-dimensional (2D) design.

- **Colour palette** – A selection of colours used in marketing materials and other business applications (wall colours, fittings and furnishings, for example) to create a consistent look and feel. A brand's colour palette is usually inspired by, or determined in conjunction with, the logo.

Many theories exist about the subconscious meaning of certain brand colours: blue = professional, purple = premium, green = relaxed or natural, etc. However, as SSB owners, we are far more likely to lose leads because the basic, text elements of our brand fail to communicate what we do, than because of the colour of our logo. From my experience, the colour we choose has little, if any, bearing on an SSB's success. So, don't overthink it. Use your favourite colour as a starting point and let the designer take it from there.

- **Font palette** – The selection of typefaces to be used in marketing materials and business communications. A strong font selection is important – it paves the way for legible, consistently presented communications. When every sign, poster or flyer uses a different font, businesses look messy and unprofessional, even more so if the fonts are stock-standard fonts, such as Times New Roman or – the bane of every graphic designer's existence – Comic Sans.

  Before finalising your fonts, there are three things to check. Firstly, each one should be easy to read, both from a distance and when printed at the required size on a business card or small ad. Secondly, they must be free for commercial use, or if not, adequately licensed by the designer. Lastly, check if the fonts are 'web safe'. If they're not, that's okay – just be sure to ask the designer to stipulate alternative fonts for online use.

- **Extra design elements** – Strong brands often encompass extra design elements, such as shapes, graphics or illustrations, applied in conjunction with the logo for added impact or contrast. From a strategically placed line or block of colour to a series of graphics representing various services, extra design elements can help tie a brand together, giving it a more distinctive, professional finish.

For SSBs, extra design elements often come to be when a designer is tasked with creating a business card, sign, flyer or website as a one-off project, and they feel the need to 'spruce it up'. We might notice the extra detail, recognising how polished the project looks, but think nothing more of it – missing the opportunity to roll the designer details out elsewhere and strengthen our business' visual identity. As a Secret Service Marketer, be mindful of the marketing materials designed for your business and embrace the designer touches used to enhance them.

- **Photos** – Professional photos are the most important aspect of an SSB's visual identity but tend to be given the least consideration. A great photo gives an otherwise generic SSB personality and authenticity, invoking a powerful, emotional response from potential customers. But it's not any old stock photo or headshot that has this effect.

  The secret sauce of SSB branding and web design are photos of ourselves as the owner, and any key staff, that capture the essence of who we are and what we do; thus giving potential customers something *and someone* to connect to. This requires a distinct style of professional photography, revealed with specific instructions in *The Secret Service Website Formula*.

Note that amateur happy snaps won't cut it. Like copywriting, photography is a craft requiring thousands of hours to master. Professional photographers have an incredible way of bringing out the best in us, which brings out the best in our business by default. Attempting to handle the photography component of your visual identity yourself can have the exact opposite effect, so it's not worth contemplating.

Setting & Allocating a Branding Budget

To set a budget for branding, it's common to seek quotes for the design of a logo until we find one that seems reasonable, then the quoted price becomes our allotted budget. But this approach is problematic. It results in our entire branding budget being injected into the design of a logo – neglecting the elements of a brand that matter most.

The Secret Service approach to branding is more strategic. Comprising three stages, *The Brand Plan* (illustrated below) outlines who to involve, in what order, approximately how much time and money to allocate to each creative professional and what to ask of them to get the most from your branding budget. The process starts by engaging the services of a copywriter (for as little as a couple of hours work), followed by those of a graphic designer and, finally, a photographer. Each stage builds on the one before to create the strongest possible brand.

Figure 18: The Brand Plan - The creative functions required to build a strong SSB brand

Approximate proportion of total time and budget:

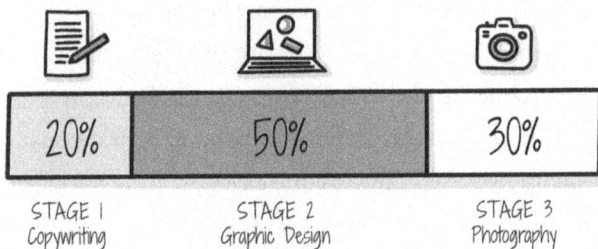

STAGE 1	STAGE 2	STAGE 3
20%	50%	30%
Copywriting	Graphic Design	Photography

Engage a **copywriter** to develop or refine your business name (if needed), a subline and slogan – having taken them through your business model in detail.

Engage a **graphic designer** to create a logo and business card and, budget permitting, a basic 'style guide' to identify and guide the use of colours, fonts and extra design elements. Ensure design files are provided in various formats and file types (including vector).

Engage a **photographer** to undertake a feel-the-love photoshoot (detailed in *The Secret Service Website Formula*), then edit and supply the final images (usually 10–20, with full licence to use and modify).

The Brand Plan tends to cost more than the 'logo only' approach but it's absolutely worth it. Factoring in copywriting and photography results in a stronger, more unified and engaging brand – a far cry from a brand built on graphic design alone.

Set It... But Don't Forget It

Once your brand basics and visual identity are in place, it's tempting to tick the branding box, breathe a sigh of relief and move on. But a brand isn't something to set and forget.

As a business evolves over time, its brand and marketing materials don't automatically keep up. Without reviewing them occasionally, we can become blind to the underlying meaning of words and images; oblivious to inconsistencies, outdated or irrelevant information, errors, omissions and operational over-sights. These can silently skew the perception of our business, causing confusion, misassumptions and lost leads.

To avoid this, check in on your brand at least once a year – reviewing it for relevance, possible misinterpretations and opportunities for improvement. It might need a small tweak (an incremental adjustment), a major brand overhaul to reflect a change in business model or be fine just as it is. The only way to know for sure is to gather up all the marketing materials you've got in use and consciously consider every detail.

The most vital thing to bear in mind about SSB branding is that an expensive, clever or quirky VI is not the be all and end all. Our corporate cousins spend millions of dollars on their visual identity because it's the face of their business. We don't need that. We have an actual face to represent our business... our own. A decent logo with an official suite of colours, fonts and designer details merely help put our best face forward.

CHAPTER 13.

THE WRONGS & RIGHTS OF WEBSITES

One of the main rules of modern marketing is 'a business needs a website' and it's unequivocally true. The internet has given us an incredible opportunity – to have the digital equivalent of an on-call, in-home sales representative available to potential customers, 24 hours a day, 7 days a week. But before we delve into what this means for the vast majority of SSBs, there are two scenarios in which a website is not necessary.

A business *does not* need a website if:

1. **Its owner feels 'enough is enough'** – Some of us are content with our business and how we acquire – or don't acquire – new customers. There's no desire to facilitate continual growth, longevity or the eventual sale of the business as an asset. Take Paul and Lesley, for example:

   Paul is a self-employed builder, nearing retirement, who employed people in the past but doesn't have the drive to do that anymore. He sees his work as more of a job than a business and stays busy enough with projects that come his way through pre-existing contacts. He plans to wind things down completely when he retires in three years.

Lesley is a family day care provider running a childcare service from home. She is authorised to care for seven children per working day but as she has two children of her own, she can only provide paid care for five per day. As a result of the leads she receives through a directory listing on a government-run childcare website, she is at capacity, with a long waiting list.

Neither Paul nor Lesley *need* a website. They are running at capacity with simple, yet effective, marketing systems in place.

2. **The business is a franchise outlet** – A franchisee is a person or company licensed by a franchisor to operate under a tried and tested formula, using its business model, systems and procedures, while capitalising on its brand, marketing and buying power. This usually includes a single, centrally managed website that presents a unified, corporate front. As such, franchisees do not need separate websites (although it's ideal to have their own personalised 'online hub' – as per the Breakout Box below).

FRANCHISE FRUSTRATION

Many **small skill-or-service franchisees** (SSFs) struggle just as much, if not more than other SSBs, due to the added burden of franchise fees and commissions. This occurs when a franchisor tries to follow the traditional franchise marketing model: the presentation of a unified, corporate front and as much mass marketing as the budget can allow, striving for brand saturation. For small franchises with a limited budget, this approach doesn't have the same impact as it once used to, because their efforts are drowned out – small franchises simply can't afford to compete at a level that keeps their brand top of mind, en masse. The key to overcoming this situation is for the franchisor to appreciate that their franchisees are SSBs in their own right, requiring a fusion of traditional and Secret Service Marketing for optimum results. This starts with the creation of individual, customisable pages branching off from the main site to act as the online hub for each SSF.

These exceptions aside, not having a website puts SSBs at a huge disadvantage, preventing them from enjoying the myriad marketing and operational benefits a website can offer. There are plenty of us in this boat, with a shockingly high percentage of small businesses (in the realms of 35–50%, depending on country of operation) still operating without a website.

No Website, Big Worries

Not having a website is a big deal for SSBs. Without a website, we're likely to:

- **Go sight unseen** – Not having a website slashes our chances of being found and considered by those outside our existing network.

- **Lose leads to competitors** – Without being online, we're not 'fishing where the fish are'. This gives web-savvy competitors the upper-hand and lion's share of leads.

- **Compete on price** – Without a website, we miss the opportunity to justify our value. If potential customers can't see or appreciate our value, they'll focus on price, putting us in a position to have to drop our prices to win them over.

- **Overspend on traditional advertising** – Without a website, we can find ourselves:
  - 'Stabbing in the dark', trying to find a means of advertising that works for us; or
  - Placing bigger, more frequent ads in local newspapers and other publications to generate the same exposure as smaller, less frequent ads once did.

- **Work harder to make a sale** – Not having a website puts us behind the eight-ball during the sales process. We have to work harder to be taken seriously and overcome scepticism associated with not being online.

- **Feel anxious and stressed** – Without a website, the Big 4 Frustrations and Busy/Slow Cycle are more pronounced, increasing the stress and strain of running a business.

- **Hit a plateau** – Not having a website can impede the profitability, growth and longevity of a business, as well as its value as a saleable asset.

Importantly, it's not just SSB owners *without* a website who are plagued by these afflictions. A huge proportion of those *with* a website suffer from them too. That's because, despite what we've been conditioned to believe, it's not a *website* that we need – it's the *sales leads* that a website has the capacity to deliver.

The Need for Leads

An SSB needs sales leads like a body needs water. Without tapping into a consistent supply of quality leads, it will dry up and die after a period of intense anguish and agony. To avoid this fate, we need a marketing system that allows leads to flow in organically, just as they did in the heyday of the Yellow Pages directory. It just so happens that nowadays, a website is the best, most cost effective tool for the job.

But it's not just any old website that has the capacity to generate leads for an SSB. With a run-of-the-mill, corporate-brochure-style website, our ability to drive leads is stunted; the marketing activities we pursue won't generate the leads they could, because our website isn't geared to convert interested service seekers into tangible leads. That's serious. It means that, instead of marketing activity being an investment that generates a measurable return, it's merely a pie-in-the-sky expense. Continuing to spend more money on marketing than it generates in return is not viable. On that trajectory, our business' growth and, ultimately, its existence, will be cut short.

It's in the subtle distinction between needing a website and needing an online marketing tool that drives leads to our business, that many of us run into trouble. Asking a web designer for 'a website' is simply too ambiguous. It leaves the purpose of our site open to the subjective interpretation of someone who has (most likely) been trained to prioritise design, not the generation of leads. To end up with a website that serves as the hub of our marketing efforts and produces tangible business results, we need to reframe what we ask for. SSB owners don't need a website, we need a *Lead Machine* – a website geared to drive leads to our business and (if applicable) customers to our door.

Leading the Way

To ask a web designer for a Lead Machine, we need to be clear about what we're asking for.

A lead itself (shortened from 'sales lead') is an enquiry, referral or other expression of interest, obtained through the internet, word of mouth, advertisements or other means, that *identifies* a potential customer (prospect). Every SSB has thousands of unidentified potential customers at any given moment. Until we obtain their contact details and determine them to be current, legitimate leads – rendering them 'pre-qualified' prospects – they're of no real value. If prospects aren't pre-qualified, we inevitably waste time and money trying to entice people who, for one reason or another, were never going to be our customers.

Pre-qualified prospects have the following characteristics:

1. They are **ready** to buy, within a reasonable timeframe;
2. They are **willing** to buy;

3. They have the **authority** to buy;

4. They have the **financial capacity** to buy; and

5. They have **not committed** to any other providers.

A lead with these attributes is a gift. However, it requires quick action and careful, considered attention via a sales process and service transaction, to unwrap its monetary potential. Without this, the gift evaporates into nothingness.

The Power of a Lead Machine

A Lead Machine differs from a standard website in that it generates pre-qualified leads by nature. It *leads* potential customers to us; engaging them, impressing them, then making it easy and inviting for them to get in touch.

When we get our website right, it relieves the burden of finding and pre-qualifying prospects. Pre-qualified leads flow in automatically, with minimal marketing activity, and we no longer have to try so hard (or drop our price) to convince them we're the best provider for the job. Where once we had to scrounge to find high-quality prospects, they now come to us with their contact details on a silver platter.

Start from Scratch or Work with What You've Got?

Sometimes it's possible to create a Lead Machine by overhauling a pre-existing website but it's rare. Websites are like houses; underlying structures and systems are in place to facilitate the final design and functionality. Just as a decision to move a bathroom from the front to the back of a house has major implications in terms of plumbing and framework, so too with the front-end components of a website – they can't be moved around without disrupting the systems supporting the site at the back-end. This makes overhauling an existing website to follow a specific design formula – namely, the Lead Machine Blueprint – near impossible.

Even if the front-end components of an existing website happen to be in the right place, the site won't work well as a Lead Machine if any of the following statements are true:

- **It's old (in dog years)** – If a website hasn't been overhauled since smartphones became mainstream, there's no way it will align with service seekers' expectations of a modern site. Most will draw the conclusion that our business is as old and out-of-touch as our website and click away to explore other options.

  Another indication of old age is that a website has sat dormant for years, requiring the cooperation, knowledge or skill of the original web designer to make changes to it. These days, it's standard practice for website owners to be able to make basic changes to page content (should we choose to) via a backend dashboard, accessed through an internet browser. If a website is so archaic that there's no online interface to work with, or no access instructions available from the designer, it's a sure sign that the site has passed its use-by date.

  In assessing the age of a website, it can help to apply the old rule of 'dog years' to get an indication of its perceived age. Using this method, one human year is equivalent to seven website years, so a website developed nine years ago is more like 63. Until the rapid pace of change in website technology and user expectations slows (if ever), there's little doubt that a 63-year-old website would be in need of an overhaul.[18]

- **It's broken** – As web development platforms and internet browsers are updated over time, they stop supporting outdated files and scripts of code. If that happens, websites requiring those files or scripts to function properly can stop working in one or more browsers. If unnoticed, a website can go weeks, months or even years without working properly, or at all.

  While some problems can be fixed or worked-around (such as a contact form not submitting), others can't, because the website is too dependent on the unsupported component. If your website is broken, and hasn't generated a lead in years anyway, there's no point bothering to repair it. Bite the bullet and build a Lead Machine.

- **It's not mobile-friendly** – Smartphones and tablets have become embedded in our social fabric at a staggeringly rapid pace. The use of smartphones to access the internet overtook that of desktop computers back in 2014 and continues to climb, so a mobile-friendly website is a must.

  If your website doesn't display on a mobile device (smartphone or tablet) without having to zoom in and move the screen manually to read the text, you need to take action – fast. In 2015, Google adjusted its algorithm to make life less frustrating for the growing number of mobile users. Since then, when a Google search is performed on a mobile device, only mobile-friendly websites are listed in search results. For an SSB owner whose website is not mobile-friendly, this is bad news. It means the chances of the site being found via a Google search are cut by *more than half*.

Depending how the existing website is built, a total rebuild is not the only means to achieve mobile-friendliness. A 'plugin' can often be used to create a mobile version of the site which displays automatically on mobile devices.

While a plugin can be a good temporary measure, be aware that sooner or later, you'll need to embrace **responsive web design** (RWD) – the current standard in mobile-friendly website development. Instead of having two versions of a website (to display on desktop and mobile screens), RWD rolls everything into one sophisticated site, which morphs fluidly to fit the size of the screen it's being viewed on. The shift to RWD has raised the bar of user expectation for SSB websites and, with the continued upsurge in the use of mobiles to search the internet, there's no going back.

- **It's too artistic** – One of the main factors distinguishing art from design is that art requires interpretation to be understood. There is little room for artistic licence when designing websites for SSBs because overtly artistic designs demand too much interpretation from website visitors. Before doing anything, visitors need to consciously interpret what they're seeing, which puts a giant roadblock in the way of taking action.

  The design of an SSB website needs to *comply* with human logic, not *challenge* it. If it's unusually quirky or clever, the site will hold the business back through unintentional obnoxiousness. Design features such as a flashy landing page with an 'enter here' button, the logo at the top right instead of the top left or the navigation menu in an unconventional position all make website visitors work harder than they need to. No matter how much you paid for it, if your website goes against the grain of user expectations, its ability to function as a Lead Machine is impeded and it's got to go.

While web design conventions and user expectations do evolve over time, it's not in an SSB owner's best interest to challenge them. Big businesses with unlimited budgets can do that. Those of us with limited resources are far better off following the design trails blazed by the big boys, than to go beating through the bush on our own.

- **It's a mess** – A website with no sense of structure, balance, style, order or flow has the same impact as art – requiring interpretation to be understood. A sensory overload of tiny text, lists and links, for example, will repel website visitors because it's too hard to visually and cognitively process.

  Messy websites are often the result of trying to force a square peg into a round hole; trying to make certain content fit a generic website template, for example. That means the problem exists at a design level and no amount of content tweaking will fix it. A clean, new site – built around the required content – is the only option.

- **It's slow** – When internet users want information, they want it *now*. If a website doesn't load quickly, they'll get frustrated and click away – never to return.

  A slow website that would otherwise serve as a Lead Machine, doesn't necessarily need to be scrapped. There are many things to try first, including reducing the size of images, migrating to a faster, closer web hosting service, and making ads and other marketing communications more enticing to motivate potential customers to wait a few extra seconds for the site to load. If all else fails, it's worth investing in a speedy new site – loading speed is simply too important to compromise on.

As covered in more detail in Chapter 20 of *The Secret Service Website Formula*, there are many free online tools available to test the speed of a website, including *PageSpeed Insights* at *https://pagespeed.web.dev.*

If your existing website is old, broken, not mobile-friendly, overly arty, messy or slow, it's doing your business a disservice. If there's nothing technically wrong with it but it's not serving as a Lead Machine, be open to scrapping it and starting from scratch anyway, in conjunction with the Secret Service Website Formula. Replacing an outdated, ineffective website with a site geared to serve your business, by actively driving leads, is one of the best business decisions you'll ever make.

From User Needs to Online Leads

Creating a Lead Machine is simple but not easy. On the back of considerable work and study in the fields of marketing and small business, it took me another seven years of coordinating website projects before landing on the Secret Service Website Formula. Seven years wondering why our innovative, attractive websites weren't generating leads. Seven years creating websites the traditional way. But during that time, pennies had subconsciously started to drop and – as soon as I niched to trade services – everything fell into place. Suddenly, I was liberated to stop approaching web design the traditional way, trust my marketing gut and follow a different formula; one with the best interest of our clients at its core.

Niching was the catalyst because – in order to overcome our niche's most painful problem (the Busy/Slow Cycle) – we were forced to shift the focus of our design. We had to stop designing for *us* and our project portfolio, stop seeking our client's direction on design and content, and start designing, wholly and solely, for our client's potential customers – the *users* who would experience the sites we designed.

This required a huge shift in priorities and perspective, from 'self-centric' design to 'service-centric' design. All artistic inclinations had to take a backseat to the intuitive consideration of **user experience (UX)**.

UX is the psychology of web design. It's the study of what, why, when, where and how internet users interact with websites. By better understanding the human motivations behind our potential customers' online behaviour, we can tailor our websites to drive more leads more often by giving them what *they need* rather than what *we think they want.* For SSBs, this change in approach can work wonders.

The key to UX web design is understanding and empathising with the needs of potential customers – not just the conscious need for a product or service but the intrinsic human needs that exist in all of us, deep below the surface. These needs are the hardwiring of humanity, subconsciously motivating everything we do. When SSB owners and web designers understand human motivation, we can gear our websites to connect with service seekers on a deeper level and gently guide them to take the desired action. It's a superpower; one we can harness to the benefit of our customers, communities and ourselves. So, let's get to it...

CHAPTER 14.

NEEDS TO KNOW

Abraham Maslow (1908–1970) was an American psychotherapist who had a profound impact on the field of psychology and, in turn, the field of marketing. As the founding father of the **positive psychology** movement, Maslow developed many groundbreaking theories on human motivation. Much of his work came about by observing 'successful individuals who aimed high but kept their feet on the ground'.[19]

One of Maslow's most important theories is depicted in a model known as the *Hierarchy of Needs*. Maslow's Hierarchy of Needs illustrates that as the lives of humans unfold, our needs evolve in various stages of motivation. These stages move from simple physiological needs such as air, food and sleep (**deficiency needs**) through to complex intellectual and spiritual needs (**growth needs**).[20] As one stage of needs reaches a point of being mostly satisfied, the motivation to satisfy the next stage emerges, however most stages are never entirely or permanently satisfied.

Figure 19: Maslow's Hierarchy of Needs – An illustrated representation

Maslow's Impact on Marketing

Although it wasn't Maslow's intention, the Hierarchy of Needs had a profound impact on the field of marketing. It helped shape a field of study known as ***consumer behaviour***; the study of what, why, when and how consumers make purchasing decisions. Corporate marketers have long known that by better understanding the human motivations behind consumer behaviour, they can tailor advertising campaigns to drive more purchases more often, by 'pushing the right buttons' in the minds of consumers – whether it's using fear to play on our safety needs, sexual appeal to play on our physiological needs (coining the phrase 'sex sells') or the depiction of an ideal social scenario to play on our love and belongingness needs. These, and others, are still highly effective advertising strategies used to this day by powerhouse consumer brands such as Coca-Cola and McDonalds.

However, in trying to apply these and other 'need-nudging' strategies to the design of websites for SSBs, I realised something was wrong. Not only were SSB owners hesitant to use them (feeling a sense of unease or awkwardness), visitors didn't seem engaged by them. For most SSBs, need-nudging didn't hit the mark... but what was the alternative? What would service seekers resonate with? What 'need' was I missing?

To answer these questions, I began researching the discoveries made about human needs *since* Maslow. I soon realised that in a few short decades, our understanding had come a long, long way.

The New Science of Social Needs

Aristotle once observed that 'man is by nature a social animal'. Fast forward some 2300 years and social scientists are only now exploring the depths of this statement, through a field of research called **social cognitive neuroscience** (SCN). SCN is the study of how brains engage in social activity. It has confirmed what Aristotle, Maslow and countless others have long known: that we are social beings, driven to attain a sense of love and belongingness through friendships, relationships, social groups and community integration.

But even the world's greatest minds may have underestimated the physiological importance of social connection. SCN research has revealed that humans need social connection like we need food and water. Our brains are hardwired to connect, to the extent that SCN pioneer, Professor Matthew Lieberman, suggests that social needs be moved to the bottom of the Hierarchy of Needs pyramid, forming the foundation on which every human life is built.

Lieberman's suggestion is reinforced by a tragic study. In 1945, psychoanalyst René Spitz tracked 91 babies in an orphanage, alongside a comparable group of babies at a prison. The physiological needs of all babies were met, however, there was a crucial difference. Once a day, the inmate mothers at the prison were allowed to visit, hold and play with their babies, while the orphaned babies were deprived of social interaction and visually segregated from their peers, with sheets hung between their cribs to mitigate the sharing of germs. By the age of two years, 34 babies out of the entire group had died and all 34 were from the orphanage.[21] Had the surviving orphans had no human interaction whatsoever (without being fed or changed), this 37% mortality rate would have been 100% within a matter of days, supporting Lieberman's point that connection comes before any other physiological human need, except air to breathe.

This need for social connection isn't something we grow out of either. Research shows that adult individuals with minimal social ties (in quantity or quality) are far more likely to experience certain health conditions – cardiovascular disease, high blood pressure, cancer and slow wound healing to name a few. What's even more alarming is that low social involvement increases the risk of premature death by at least 50%.[22] That means the socially isolated among us are twice as likely to die before we should. The risk of death from lack of social connection is 'comparable with well-established risk factors for mortality such as smoking and alcohol consumption, and exceed[s] the influence of other risk factors such as physical inactivity and obesity'.[23]

Bringing Maslow into the New Millennium

Now that the life-sustaining importance of social connection has come to light, updating Maslow's Hierarchy of Needs, as suggested by Lieberman, certainly seems necessary. Moving the need for love and belongingness to the bottom of the pyramid wouldn't quite cut it though, as that would have confusing implications higher up the pyramid. Instead, Maslow's model can be brought into the new millennium by adding a base stage of **connective needs**, along with a couple of tweaks elsewhere (explained in the Breakout Box below).

Connective needs encompass the need for physical contact, surface-level connections and interactions with other people *for the purpose of getting our higher level needs and wants met*. No man is an island. We all need the insight, knowledge and skills of others – facilitated through a mutually acceptable arrangement of supply, trade or exchange – to survive, create or maintain a suitable lifestyle and grow as individuals.

Figure 20: The Connective Hierarchy of Needs – A fresh take on Maslow's Hierarchy in light of more recent findings

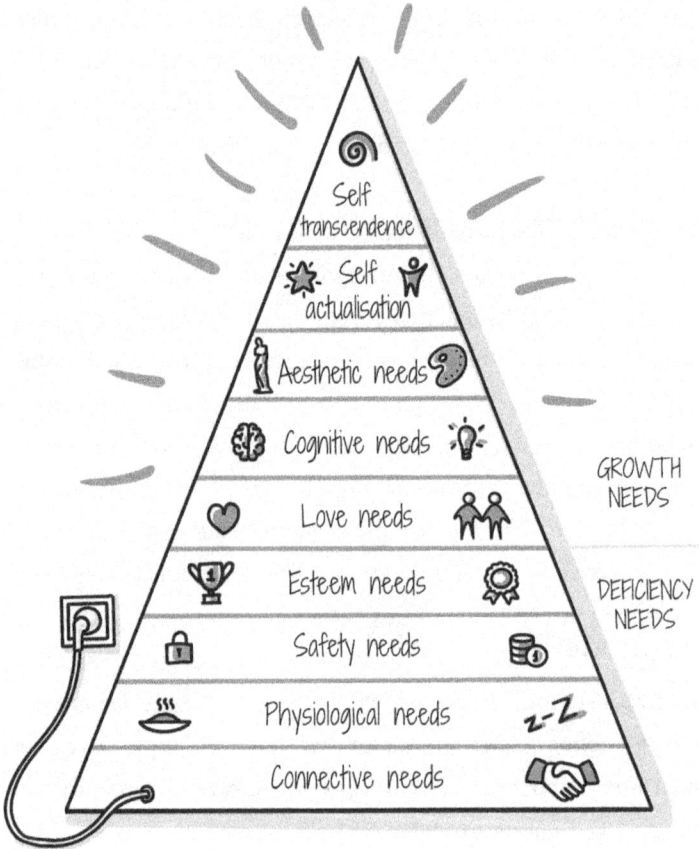

Self transcendence

Self actualisation

Aesthetic needs

Cognitive needs

Love needs

Esteem needs

Safety needs

Physiological needs

Connective needs

GROWTH NEEDS

DEFICIENCY NEEDS

OTHER CHANGES TO THE ORIGINAL HIERARCHY

Beyond the addition of connective needs, two extra changes bring Maslow's Hierarchy of Needs into closer alignment with modern schools of thought. These have been factored into the 'connective' version of the pyramid above.

1. **Removal of belongingness** – The desire to belong or fit in stems from ego, not love, so it makes sense to shift belongingness away from love and into esteem.

2. **Moving love up the ladder** – Having removed the needs for connectivity and belongingness from love and belongingness needs, love is no longer weighed down by self-serving, deficiency-motivated agendas and can step up to the realm of growth needs. This reflects the fact that the greatest personal growth comes as a result of showing, or being shown, love and kindness. It also allows love needs to take on a more altruistic interpretation, encompassing the desire for deep, genuine and meaningful relationships and the giving and receiving of compassion, empathy and acts of kindness.

Once these adjustments are made, three levels of social needs emerge: connective, esteem and love.

Every connection, interaction and relationship can be attributed to one of these categories: connective needs for the more shallow, temporary connections and interactions required to get our deficiency needs met and esteem and love needs for deeper, enduring relationships, roots and bonds. Whether a social need falls under esteem or love depends on the underlying intention of the connection or relationship. Esteem needs have predominantly self-serving (ego-based) intentions, while love needs have purer, more reciprocal intentions. For optimum social health, we need a balance of all three.

Adding connective needs to Maslow's Hierarchy is like plugging a lamp into mains power; all of a sudden, it works. A basic level of social connection is what makes the satisfaction of all other needs applicable and possible. It is the basis of human survival and the source of energy, in various forms, which enables us to grow.

The Business of Meeting Human Needs

In childhood, connective needs are satisfied by family (biological relatives and substitute carers). These individuals serve as human conduits between us and food, shelter, clothing, health, cleanliness, education and other basic goods and services that we need but are incapable of sourcing or satisfying independently. As we grow and our needs become more personalised and complex, they become our own responsibility. We reach a point where we must venture beyond our family for the human insight, intelligence, guidance, cooperation, supply, trade or exchange required to alleviate deficiencies and attain growth... and that's where SSBs come in.

SSBs exist to help humans get their needs met in exchange for monetary payment, when they don't have the capacity, connections, time or desire to get them met in other ways. We are paid to serve the needs of others; to fill the voids that a basic family network is not equipped, suitable and/or responsible to fill. That means SSBs have an incredibly important job. Collectively, we hold humanity's hand in helping her climb as high up the Hierarchy of Needs as possible, toward the summit of self transcendence.

As connective conduits, SSBs help customers satisfy all manner of needs in all manner of ways. Restaurants satisfy physiological and love needs (providing an environment to connect and bond with others); health professionals and property managers help satisfy safety needs; beauty stylists help satisfy esteem needs; fertility and adoption agencies help satisfy physiological and love needs; coaches and trainers help satisfy safety, esteem and cognitive needs; architects and builders help satisfy safety and aesthetic needs; therapists and counsellors help satisfy self actualisation needs... the list goes on.

But it is connectivity itself (the satisfaction of connective needs) that presents the greatest marketing opportunity for SSBs. Not only are connective needs the most primal and substantial of needs, they are needs that big businesses are not equipped to fill.

The importance of website users' connective needs to the marketing of SSBs was the link I was missing in the early days of Cyberstart. When I finally woke up to it and allowed connectivity to influence our website design and content decisions, the tables turned and leads began to flow.

Connective Needs & SSBs

The key to meeting the connective needs of those seeking our services is to invoke feelings of familiarity, trust and comfort – as if our business were an extension of a service seeker's own family. This requires consideration on two levels – an operational level (customer perception) and a marketing level (market perception).

Operational Connectivity

Operational connectivity is being of service to customers in the most attentive, effective, positive and personalised way possible. It's being physically available and emotionally present to determine and serve their higher-level needs. It's engaging our performance persona, and adapting our work performance, to provide a level and type of interaction that's pleasing to each individual customer. It's acknowledging them, appreciating them, genuinely wanting the best outcome, result or solution for them and taking the opportunity to serve them seriously.

Marketing Connectivity

Marketing connectivity is giving potential customers something human and familiar to connect with in our marketing communications, before they have the opportunity to connect with us in person. The aim of the game is to give them an insight into what engaging our services will look and feel like – enticing them with a feeling of human connection. The best way to present this is through a carefully crafted fusion of photographs, words and design on a website. As a portal available to anyone, at any time, anywhere, a website is the most effective means to achieve marketing connectivity, bar none.

Our potential customers are hardwired to want to connect with those who can help them fulfil their needs. That means they are hardwired to want to connect with *us*, the owners of SSBs. They want to feel an emotional connection with us but if our website doesn't meet them halfway – with humanity, personality, warmth and authenticity – they can't make this connection. There is nothing (or no one) to connect to, and therefore nothing to give them a sense of connective comfort.

Connective needs are mostly irrelevant to big business marketers, which is perhaps why consumer behaviour research never revealed a missing link in the Hierarchy of Needs. Connectivity requires a human presence and a concerted effort to understand and address an individual's needs, through the establishment of an emotional connection. This flies in the face of mass production and economies of scale. Continuing the sailing analogy from Chapter 11, connectivity is like a beach; the waters are warm and plentiful – perfect for our little SSB sailboats and, luckily for us, too shallow for corporate cruise liners to contemplate.

5 Other Needs Not to Ignore

Beyond connectivity, five human needs have important implications for SSBs at an operational and/or marketing level. These lurk silently behind every assumption potential customers make, and action they take, in the process of considering and engaging our services. Many of these needs have implications for our website (as the hub of our marketing efforts and the point where a first impression is formed, sealed and actioned). Others subtly influence the likelihood of customers returning second and subsequent times or spreading positive word of mouth – both of which impact the success and sustainability of an SSB.

1. Safety Needs

Safety needs drive us to attain a sense of security, stability and certainty in our ability to meet our most basic, physiological needs (food, water, warmth, etc). This results in a need for things like healthcare, shelter, money and employment. Many SSBs are built upon the sale of safety related services, from property management and trade service providers (for accommodation, water and energy, etc) to medical centres, employment agencies and insurance brokers.

One of the most satisfying things about running a business is the ability to help others satisfy their safety needs. Whether or not we sell safety for a living, we have a moral and legal requirement to provide any employees with a safe environment in which to work, and we all contribute to the safety needs of others through the distribution of money. This occurs naturally, through the procurement of goods and services and the employment of staff – we fund the monetary needs of others in exchange for the goods and services they provide.

But SSB owners have the power to contribute to safety needs in more subtle, psychological ways too. The most important of these is the provision of *value for money* to customers. As money is a safety need, it's important to deliver excellent value in exchange for the money we receive; going above and beyond to ensure the perceived value of the service we provide outweighs the price we charge for it. If we don't provide adequate value for money, customers can feel a sense of loss or anguish, having 'thrown away their hard-earned cash' – cash which could have contributed to the satisfaction of other needs. This can lead to resentment and negative word of mouth, with potentially dire consequences.

Taking safety needs into consideration is more important now than ever. The internet has brought with it a gamut of cybersecurity threats including identity theft, credit card fraud, phishing, hacking, grooming, malware and more. Savvy internet users have learned to be sceptical and defensive to keep themselves safe. This is crucial for SSB owners to know because it impacts the effectiveness of our online marketing efforts. Scepticism is not good for business. But by anticipating it, we can subvert it. Openly addressing common customer concerns and having adequate protection mechanisms in place (such as website security certificates) is often all it takes to reassure service seekers that they're in safe hands.

2. Esteem Needs

Every one of us needs to feel a sense of self worth. We satisfy this need both intrinsically – through a feeling of justification, competence or achievement and extrinsically – through receiving the attention, admiration, validation, recognition or respect of outside entities. As consumers, we seek out services such as personal trainers, beauty stylists, fancy restaurants, luxury resorts and cosmetic surgeons to maintain or improve our self esteem and, in one way or another, feel better about ourselves.

No matter what service it provides or what human need that service satisfies, every SSB stands to benefit by prioritising the esteem needs of its customers. Every time we go above and beyond to give our customers (past, present and prospective) our focused attention, validation and respect, we make them feel better about themselves. This, in turn, sets up a subconscious association between interacting or transacting with our business and 'feeling good', which brings them back again. Going the extra mile to fuel our customers self esteem can fuel our business by default.

This does not mean 'the customer is always right'. Far from it. Customers are human, with the capacity to behave irrationally or downright maliciously if their self esteem dips too low. Even the most self-assured of us can have bad days, causing us to be overly critical, condescending or judgemental. But the tipping point between a customer being right and being wrong is when our best efforts to resolve a situation are not enough – when the customer *repeatedly* or *relentlessly* complains, shames, blames or bullies, or when they feel the need to tear us or our staff down, for a temporary rush of superiority and self esteem. In these moments, we need to prioritise the esteem needs of us and our staff above those of the customer. Sometimes the best thing we can do is to sever the relationship – suggest they try elsewhere and genuinely wish them well.

When it comes to our website, the main implication of esteem needs comes from what psychologists call the ***halo effect***, which is 'the lasting effect of a first impression'.[24] The halo effect taints our ability to think and act neutrally beyond the moment in time in which a first impression is made. Our first impression of anyone or anything makes us look at them or it with either rose-coloured or jade-coloured glasses; it distorts our view in a positive or negative way to give us a greater chance of being proved 'right'. The halo effect occurs because the feeling of being right is nice – it fuels our ego. So, with every first impression we make, we form a cognitive bias, actively looking for things that support and substantiate our initial opinion and ignoring those that don't. Put in context, if a website visitor's first impression of our website is negative, their perception of it (and of our business) will likely stay negative and our chances of converting them into a customer will be slim.

3. Love Needs

Love needs drive us to build and maintain authentic connections with ourselves and others. This includes finding a sense of passion, purpose, intimacy, joy, depth and fulfilment in our personal endeavours and relationships – bonding with ourselves by exploring creative pursuits or interests (following our 'bliss') and bonding with others through shared experiences, vulnerability, mutual feelings of love and affection and acts of kindness and compassion.

SSBs that help service seekers satisfy love needs include restaurants, hotels and tourist operations, music teachers, matchmakers, psychologists and therapists, art studios and more, but an awareness of love needs is applicable to each and every one of us.

It's not that customers need to feel deeply loved by us. While it can happen, trying to create close bonds with every individual customer would be impractical and often awkward. It's also unnecessary – there are ways, means and apps to forge personal relationships. That's not the role of an SSB.

What SSBs contribute is a more superficial type of social connection; a *temporary escape* from the intensity and responsibilities of life, free of history, judgement, guilt and grudges. We offer a place for customers to feel visible and valued for who they want to be in that moment: a larrikin, an introvert, a VIP or something in between. By recognising and responding to a customer's social needs, we make them feel acknowledged and respected. From this, they derive a sense of validation and connectedness; a small but satisfying serving of the connectivity needed to live and grow.

The deepest love customers need to feel from us is the love we have for our work – both technically (the application of skill) and socially (being of service to others). The more passionate and positive we are about our work – in a grounded, authentic way – the more customers will be attracted to us; customers who care less about price and more about the value and experience of working with us specifically. While feeling the love for what we do day-to-day is essential to achieve this, it's not enough. To attract new customers, we need to capture and convey it in our marketing communications too (easiest to achieve by applying the Secret Service Website Formula).

4. Cognitive Needs

Humans are information addicts. We're naturally curious and crave knowledge, not only because knowledge is power, but because it gives us drug-like pleasure. Neuroscientists have found that the 'click' of grasping a new concept or discovering something new triggers a biochemical response that rewards our brains with a hit of natural opium-like substances.[25] In other words, the acquisition of knowledge makes us happy.

This discovery has a major implication for SSB owners. Keeping prospects and customers informed, updated and educated (about the status of their order or project, for example) does more than demonstrate our professionalism, it makes them happy. If we want happy customers, we need open lines of communication – taking the time to keep them in the loop and seeing issues, obstacles and delays as opportunities to inform and educate, not things to hide.

The human 'need to know' sparked and fuelled the Information Revolution, driving the rapid uptake of computers, the internet and, most recently, mobile devices. The more accessible information has become, the more we've craved and consumed it. Within less than two decades, we went from fumbling through reference books and microfiche records to having a world of information in our bag or pocket.

The human need to know and understand is the number one reason SSBs need a website. Our potential customers expect us to have an online hub of information that helps them understand who we are and what we do. Denying them that opportunity is the online equivalent to slamming a door in their face.

The need to know is also the reason our marketing activities need to direct potential customers to a website. Just knowing more information is available online – via a clear and concise website call-to-action in ads, on signage, etc – can be alluring, particularly if our ad or sign is the only one displaying a website address among others that don't. The mere presence of a website address can spark curiosity, compelling potential customers to take the first step towards engaging our services without even realising that's what's happening.

5. Aesthetic Needs

On our path to self actualisation, there comes a point where we start to appreciate beauty in our surroundings. From the natural beauty of a forest to the functional beauty of a tidy filing cabinet, we like things to look right and be visually pleasing.

Our aesthetic needs are responsible for the drive to straighten a crooked picture hanging on a wall, for example. Aesthetic needs are often gratified through structure, symmetry, alignment, order or a perceived sense of style, taste or appropriateness.

Aesthetic needs have a huge implication for SSBs. No matter what service we provide, customers visually and physically experience a long list of things in the process of considering and transacting with us, as itemised in Chapter 3 (page 36). Striving to systemise, organise and present these things in an aesthetically pleasing way is important. Making things 'look right' is not just a matter of professionalism, it satisfies an innate human need.

As the hub of our marketing efforts, it's crucial that our website makes an aesthetically pleasing first impression. The first glimpse of a site determines whether visitors hang around long enough to be engaged by its content or whether they hit the 'back' button to continue their search for services elsewhere. Research shows that this decision is made in as little as 50 milliseconds of the website coming into view – less than the blink of an eye.[26] So our website needs to fit the bill. If it's old, broken, not mobile-friendly, too artistic, messy or slow (as explained in Chapter 13), it won't meet the aesthetic needs of potential customers or perform as it should.

Savvy website users have become more and more puritan in their aesthetic preferences.[27] What 'looks right' to them has become increasingly clear-cut and they have little patience for unnecessary embellishments. They want a site that's well structured, streamlined and simple; one that guides them to the information they seek and makes it easy to interpret without forcing them to process more than they need to along the way.

An over-the-top design can stand in the way of that and end up doing more harm than good – especially for an SSB.

The halo effect, introduced earlier, compounds the implication and importance of aesthetic needs. If we can hook website visitors with a visually appealing design from the get-go, they'll be more likely to respond positively and take the desired action – ignoring the odd spelling error they noticed along the way. Conversely, if their first impression is negative, they'll feed on the faults, using them to validate their initial reaction. Then they'll leave, never to return, feeling justified in their decision – having proven themselves right.

SSBs & Customer Needs – The Bottom Line

For SSB owners, the Connective Hierarchy of Needs gives the term 'customer needs' a whole new meaning. Our customers' needs run so much deeper than the physical aspects of the goods or services they require. As we've seen, their subconscious safety, esteem, love, cognitive and aesthetic needs play a huge part in determining their behaviour, and their connective needs run so deep their survival depends on it. It's our job as SSB owners to appreciate these underlying needs and prioritise and practice connectivity; serving our customers with as much care and consideration as we'd have for members of our own family.

The New Benefactors of Consumer Behaviour

The wave of consumer behaviour research set in motion by Maslow was of enormous benefit to big business, but it's time for that tide to turn. With the emergence of research revealing the power of social connectivity, and the relevance of social connectivity to SSBs, the next few years might get interesting.

Once we, as a global collective of SSBs, realise our ability to thrive in the service of others, the tides of business will change forever. With a new-found appreciation for our customers' connective needs, along with a suite of straightforward Secret Service principles, we have the capacity to put Pareto in his place... shifting the balance of power from the corporate rich kids and rockstars to the humble SSB.

CHAPTER 15.

THE SOCIAL MEDIA TIMETRAP

This chapter may step on a few toes. It's not intended to compare different social media platforms, nor to provide strategies for getting more 'likes' or 'shares'. Rather, its aim is to present a more realistic perspective to that expressed by other business commentators; empowering SSB owners to pursue social media activity with clarity and purpose or move on to greener marketing pastures, guilt-free.

For many years, I towed the social media line. I recommended it to clients, promoted it in training workshops and even offered social media management as a service. But something didn't sit right. I was preaching that quality, consistency and persistence were the keys to social media success, encouraging a minimum of three carefully crafted posts per week. And yet, for the majority of SSB owners implementing this or an even more gruelling regime, social media success didn't come. Posts were met by general disinterest and audience size stagnated at 100–200 followers. Clinging to expert advice from myself and others, they felt compelled to continue, despite the lack of extra leads signalling that perhaps, for them, the 'ideal' use of social media was a poor investment of time and money.

And yet, for other SSB owners, social media was nothing short of a miracle. It provided a cost effective means to capture the attention of, connect and engage with their target market like never before. It enabled scores of talented individuals to convert skill-based side ventures – such as photography or cake making – into fully-fledged businesses, expanding their reach to thousands of fans and tapping into steady streams of leads and sales. For SSBs across the globe, social media activity was as revolutionary, if not more, than television advertising was for big brands in the 1950s.

So why the disparity? How can one small business soar on social media, while another fails to take off? The answer is *social suitability*.

Social Suitability for SSBs

Just like any other form of marketing, social media activity is a good fit for some SSBs but not for others. It can be unsuitable in one of two ways. Either the service an SSB provides is not a good fit for social media activity, or social media activity is not a good fit for the SSB owner.

Service Suitability

Social media users can be quite picky about the businesses they follow. Some won't follow an SSB because they don't want to publicly associate themselves with a service that could be deemed by peers as boring, embarrassing or agenda-driven. Others won't follow it because they don't want their newsfeed encroached upon by local service providers with sales-driven ulterior motives. Ultimately, it boils down to social media users having more fulfilling uses of their time online, than receiving constant updates from service providers with nothing genuinely 'social' to share. Some services are simply more social than others.

Five key characteristics determine a service's suitability for social media activity. The quiz below is geared to assess these characteristics, helping you determine if social media is a good fit for your service... or not so much.

NOTE: This tool relates specifically to personal social networking sites, such as Facebook and Instagram, as opposed to the professional networking site LinkedIn, which all SSB owners should explore.

**Figure 21: The Social Suitability Quiz – For determining how
well social media activity suits your business**

Characteristic	Question Respond with a score of 1 (low) to 5 (high)	Example 1 Financial Adviser	Example 2 Baby Photographer
Visual Interest	How visually interesting / photogenic is the outcome or end product of your service?	SCORE: 1 A financial adviser does not produce a visually interesting outcome or photogenic end product (at least not one that clients would feel comfortable sharing publicly), making it difficult to generate social traction.	SCORE: 5 The outcome of a baby photographer's service is highly visual. Photos themselves are the end product, so there's always something engaging to share.
Visual Dynamism	How much does the outcome or end product change from one customer or project, to another?	SCORE: 1 Other than the appearance of the clients themselves, the outcome of the service doesn't change, at least not in a way that can be captured visually.	SCORE: 4 Despite a level of sameness due to the 'baby' niche, every photograph, therefore every social media post, is different. As such, a baby photographer's work is very dynamic.
Social Relatability	How big is the online population that can socially relate to your product or service and how strong is that relatability?	SCORE: 2 Although financial advice is relevant to a substantial proportion of the population, most people won't relate to it until they have a specific need.	SCORE: 5 The target market for baby photography (impending/ new parents) is highly active on social media and the service is extremely relatable and shareworthy.

Characteristic	Question Respond with a score of 1 (low) to 5 (high)	Example 1 Financial Adviser	Example 2 Baby Photographer
Social Substance	To what extent are you able to create and contribute unique, engaging content (posts) with no expectation of return (as opposed to blatant promotion of your services)?	SCORE: 1 Financial services are highly regulated, making it difficult to give free, unsolicited advice. This limits a financial adviser's ability to share engaging content and makes them more likely to post promotional posts.	SCORE: 5 Photographers contribute engaging content by simply sharing their work. They have little need to actively spruik their services, as the photos tend to speak for themselves.
Social Acceptance	How comfortable would your target market feel being seen associating with your business (following it, liking posts, sharing posts, etc) by their friends or family?	SCORE: 2 Many people like to keep their financial affairs private and may feel uncomfortable endorsing or sharing their financial adviser's posts on social media.	SCORE: 5 Images of people are one of the main things that make social media 'social'. Photos of newborn babies are highly social, likeable and shareworthy.
		TOTAL – 7 POINTS	TOTAL – 24 POINTS
RESULTS	5–11 Low social media suitability 12–17 Medium social media suitability 18–25 High social media suitability		

Self Suitability

A business can be suitable for social media marketing in theory, but not in practice. That's because, for SSBs, social media success tends to hinge on the hands-on involvement, on-the-ground access and quasi-celebrity appeal of the owner.

People connect on social media to get a window into each other's lives. We're curious to see:

1. What they do;
2. Where they go;
3. Who they associate with;
4. What they have to say;
5. What others think of what they do, where they go, who they see and what they have to say, via likes and comments.

Connecting with a business on social media is no different. When someone follows our business (or contemplates it), they scan our social media page, looking for posts that satisfy their social curiosity – to see what we do (the process and outcome of our service), where we go (in our workplace, at events, etc), who we associate with (us with staff and clients), what we have to say (our insights and experiences) and what others seem to think of us. This is a subconscious, human assessment; one that is not satisfied by faceless, corporate style imagery, promotional posts or 'activity for the sake of being active'.

SSB owners who benefit the most from social media are those who:

- **Make it personal** – Their identity and personality flows through every post on their social media page – text, image or video. Their authenticity, transparency, accessibility and confidence makes their business profile endearing and engaging; it's what makes it human and therefore, 'social'. If an SSB's posts aren't social, they are merely ads... and poorly placed ones at that.

- **Keep it real** – They don't hide behind staff, a social media manager or a generic, corporate façade. They handle or closely oversee the function of content creation, rather than delegating or outsourcing it to others, knowing that delegating it would sever the genuine relationship and direct line of communication between them and their audience, largely defeating the purpose and opportunity of social media activity.

- **Keep their feet on the ground** – SSB owners with high social media appeal are acutely aware that – although their social media activity may imply it – it's *not* 'all about them'. In fact, it's not about them at all – it's about the needs and perceptions of their target audience. Every post is filtered for the greater good and best interest of the audience, in terms of frequency, value and relevance.

- **Do it for love, not money** – They're active on social media first and foremost to serve the collective human needs of their online audience; providing knowledge (through insight, education and inspiration) and social connection, while rewarding their audience for taking an interest in them and their business. Although money flows from this, it's not the main reward – that stems from the thrill of entertaining, educating and inspiring their audience.

No matter how well suited an SSB is to social media activity, if the pressure to post new content feels like a constant burden, it won't have the desired effect. If we're not feeling it, we'll struggle to create fresh content, find the time to post and get audience engagement, all because our energy isn't right; we'll be coming from a sense of 'force', not a sense of 'flow'.

When we force social media activity – creating posts and persisting out of obligation or desperation – it has a negative effect on market perception. Social media users sense it and won't engage. That's why relentless, agenda-driven activity doesn't gain traction and why its reach tends to remain limited to a small, supportive group of family and friends (many of whom subconsciously cringe when yet another post appears from our business in their news feed).

Finding Your Social Flow

Social media activity should challenge our social fears but it should *never* feel forced or fake. If it does, it means you probably don't have the energy required for social media activity to flow at such a high rate – at least not right now. It'll likely come with time, as your business model falls into place and you find a stronger sense of business purpose.

In the meantime, a lack of suitability is no excuse to ignore social media. Ignoring it can taint market perception as much, if not more, than forcing it can.

So, what's a savvy SSB owner to do, if we can't force social media activity but we can't ignore it either?

We just need to find our *social flow* – the rate of social media activity that's right for us. This ideal is found somewhere between the two extremes of 'ignoring it' and 'forcing it', where our investment of time and energy is: 1) realistic, and 2) justifiable (in terms of market perception and return on investment). Depending on our social suitability, this can equate to a non-active presence, a highly active presence or something in between.

Figure 22: The spectrum of SSB social media activity

Social Strategies for SSBs

Along the spectrum of social media activity, there are three main strategies to choose from:

Social Strategy 1. The Listing Presence

Creating a basic social media presence involves setting up or claiming a business profile on a relevant platform, typically Facebook, Instagram and/or LinkedIn. Once set up, that's it. There's no flow of social media activity. It simply sits there, serving the functional purpose of an online business directory listing, hence the name *listing presence*. This subtly contributes to a business' findability – helping it get slightly more exposure in search engines, providing a link to its website (beneficial for SEO purposes) and giving potential customers the option to make contact via social media, if they prefer.

While a listing presence can make a business slightly more accessible online, it has a major drawback in that it can hinder market perception. With no social media activity, a business' profile page has no 'social history' for potential customers to explore. This can give rise to feelings of doubt or scepticism, weakening market perception and sabotaging sales opportunities before they come to light. However, it doesn't take much to transform a listing presence into a ***supporting presence***, which contributes to market perception without demanding too much time or energy.

Social Strategy 2. The Supporting Presence

A supporting presence is created by posting high-quality content at low-frequency intervals, e.g. every 1–2 months. This can be done on one or more social media platforms – whatever platforms our target market is most active on. The aim of this strategy is not to maximise followers or likes, nor to generate leads or sales, but simply to build a history through occasional use. A supporting presence gives potential customers an alternate view of an SSB and the opportunity to validate its history and existence; much like giving them the chance to peer through a window. It doesn't take long for a history to build up and be quite impressive to those who are investigating the business with a view to engaging its services.

When planning any social media activity, it's crucial to understand that social media is highly visual. On Facebook, for example, posts with pictures get a whopping 2.3 times (230%) more engagement.[28] That's why every post *must* contain an image, whether it's a photo of the service being delivered, the outcome of the service, participation in special events, etc.

Note that photos with people in them get substantially more engagement than those without (it is *social* media after all), so it's important to include yourself, staff and customers in photos whenever possible.

Other than the inclusion of images, key things to note when opting for a supporting presence are:

- **All give, no take** – A supporting presence on social media is *not* for spruiking your services through a timeline of agenda-driven promotional posts. That will undermine market perception and turn potential customers off. What it *is* for, is strengthening your business' online presence by injecting a sense of personality, reliability and longevity into your business' social profiles. That's only possible by posting high-quality content with no expectation of return or reciprocation.

- **Be original** – If you're only posting every 1–2 months, there's no room for unoriginal content. Third party posts, photos, memes or videos will only dilute your online presence, so ensure you are the creator of all shared content.

- **Schedule it** – If social media isn't your number one marketing priority, it's easy for months to pass by without a single post. To prevent this, set a monthly reminder on your calendar or phone.

No matter your social suitability, a supporting presence is worth the small investment of time and energy to create and maintain it. Not only does a supporting presence contribute to a business' findability, it boosts its credibility, making a worthwhile contribution to market perception.

Social Strategy 3. The Driving Presence

If your social suitability is high (the main indicator being that social media marketing feels somewhat easy and enjoyable), opt for a *driving presence* – using social media activity as one of the main spokes of your Marketing Wheel. To get off to a solid start with this:

- **Pick your platforms** – Choose one or two social media platforms that align with the online habits of your target market. Note that it's better to 'go deep' on one or two platforms with distinct communication styles and goals for each, than to share the same posts across multiple platforms.

- **Learn the ropes** – Learn everything you can about your platforms of choice from SSB owners and entrepreneurs who've had success with them. Read articles and books (such as *Jab, Jab, Jab, Right Hook: How to Tell Your Story in a Noisy Social World* by Gary Vaynerchuk) and take advantage of free online courses and webinars to learn strategies of relevance to your audience. Don't feel pressured to buy every follow-up course or program though – embrace the chunks of information that resonate with you and shelve the rest.

- **Post at your own pace** – Social influencers don't post to a robotic routine – they post when they've got interesting, relevant, original content to share. The same goes for SSBs. Don't worry if there's a lull between updates. Just be sure to set a maximum lull time (be it days or weeks) to prevent your audience from assuming you've vanished completely.

- **Drive home to a hub** – While the majority of your social media posts should be 'jabs' that provide in-situ content, less frequent 'right hooks' need to drive potential customers back to your website, where they stand a greater chance of being converted into leads.[29] This is done by gearing the post as a 'teaser', with the 'main event' (the bulk of content – be it an article, photo gallery or video – and a clear sales-oriented call-to-action) located in a blog post on your website, accessed via a link. Without doing this, scores of opportunities to convert followers into customers will be missed.

- **Evolve and adapt** – Follow the cues of your audience and adapt your communication style accordingly. Give more of what they 'like' (literally) and less of what they don't.

- **Avoid social spamming** – Posting too much or too often can have the same effect as junk mail. Just as we skim through junk mail and disregard it (recognising that we're either being sold to, or scammed), social media users scroll past 'spammy' posts in their news feeds. If your business posts are too frequent or look too similar, they run the risk of losing their appeal and being dismissed as social spam. Aspiring entrepreneurs posting regular 'on-the-run' style videos – such as those shared through the Facebook Live video feature – often experience this. Although video posts can be incredibly powerful, used too often, or with the same background from one video to the next, they can be a waste of time and energy – no matter how insightful, generous or educational the content may be. So bear in mind that if you persist with the same frequency or style of post despite a lack of traction, you're likely to be perceived as intrusive and narcissistic... two characteristics you definitely don't want associated with your business.

The Sweet Spot of Social Media Activity

The optimal social media strategy is not black or white – the sweet spot for most SSB owners is a shade of grey. It's found by using a process of trial and error; setting up a profile, posting occasionally but consistently, speeding it up, slowing it down, posting different types of content in different formats, all while monitoring the effect these changes have on audience engagement, leads and sales.

If posting multiple times per day or week, the result of slowing down can be surprising. The old saying 'quality over quantity' is relevant to every facet of social media, be it the number and type of platforms we select, the updates we post, the followers we acquire or the time and effort we invest. One highly engaging post per week is better than seven boring ones, just as hundreds of authentic relationships are better than tens of thousands bought through a 'follower farm'. When trying to find your sweet spot of social media activity, opt for quality over quantity and you can't go too far wrong.

Socially Acceptable Behaviour

In any society, online or offline, acceptance and inclusion is a privilege. Certain standards of behaviour must be upheld to retain our social privilege for the greater good. Defying these standards gets our privileges revoked.

Social media is a society like any other with connection and contribution as its standards of behaviour. If we approach social media activity as an opportunity for promotion rather than an opportunity for connection and contribution, we will be rejected (ignored) for defying social convention and left disappointed with our return on investment.

The societal nature of social media presents a unique marketing challenge for SSBs. Leads and sales don't come rolling in as soon as we create a social media profile (like they can when commencing other marketing activities), nor is it socially acceptable to push for sales (like we do with paid ads). With social media activity, monetary gratification is delayed. It takes time to generate interest, build trust and get traction – just like it does to build a business in the real world.

Our business is more than its promotional messages. It is us (the owner and heart of the business), our staff and customers, interactions and transactions, service outcomes and results, premises, processes, assets, values, events and more. The aim of social media activity is to build an online presence that reflects the humanity and vibrancy of this offline presence; a perpetual, visual record of our business' existence. This is only possible when we see our social media followers as people, not walking wallets.

Escape the Timetrap

Slipping into the social media timetrap stems from believing our only options – in terms of the time and energy we invest in social media – are 'all' or 'nothing'. Many of us choose 'all' (a driving presence) out of perceived obligation, then force ourselves to comply with idealistic strategies and schedules rather than trusting our gut. Only *we* can determine if social media activity is right for our business and if so, how much.

A supporting presence is an excellent middle ground between all and nothing. If you've been forcing a driving presence, hating every second of it or not gaining traction – shift down a gear. The effectiveness of a social media strategy comes down to the leads and sales it generates, weighed up against the time and energy invested in it. If maintaining a driving presence is costing more than it's generating, scale it back to a supporting presence. Not only will this release any feelings of force or frustration you've come to associate with social media, it will give you the time to work out what's going wrong; to reassess your business model, review your website and explore other spokes of the Marketing Wheel.

To be clear, we don't go to hell in a handbasket if we choose not to use social media religiously. It just means we're choosing a different marketing path – one which makes the most of our time and energy and isn't reliant on likes or shares to define our business' success.

RECOVERY MISSION 4

Chapter 12 – The Truth About Branding

- **Basic recall** – On a single page, type out the basic text elements of your brand: your business name, subline, slogan and contact details as they currently stand.
- **Compile your comms** – Gather together the marketing communications you currently use: business cards, flyers, website, quote template, photos of signage, etc, along with your page of brand basics. Lay them out alongside each other.
- **Spot the saboteurs** – Review the above in conjunction with Chapter 12, noting any inconsistencies, errors, oversights or potential causes of confusion.
- **Craft a brand plan** – Determine what changes would strengthen your brand and consider engaging the services of a copywriter, graphic designer and/or photographer to fill the gaps (but be sure to read *The Secret Service Website Formula* first).

Chapter 13 – The Wrongs & Rights of Websites

- **Do a site assessment** – With the criteria on pages 233–237 for reference, review your website (if you have one) and decide whether it needs an upgrade or overhaul to serve as a Lead Machine.
- **Secure the site plan** – If any changes to your website are required (especially the development of a new site), source *The Secret Service Website Formula*, ready to read next.

Chapter 14 – Needs to Know

- **Access Unlocked** – Download and print the Connective Hierarchy of Needs file from *www.secretservice.biz/downloads*.
- **Climb time** – Working your way up the Connective Hierarchy of Needs pyramid, determine which needs your business satisfies for customers. For each one (particularly connective, safety, esteem, love, cognitive and aesthetic needs), consider what you could do to meet the need in spades.

Chapter 15 – The Social Media Timetrap

- **Crack the social code** – Take the Social Suitability Quiz on page 262. Then, if your service is well suited to social media activity, consider your 'self suitability' (page 264). Do you have what it takes to make social media activity work?
- **Get a head-start** – In light of the above, start considering your social media strategy: a listing presence, supporting presence or driving presence, and on which social media platforms. There's no need to commit to a social strategy now though – your plans may change after you've read and implemented *The Secret Service Website Formula*.

PART FIVE

WANTED: NEW CUSTOMERS

'Build it and they will come', or so they say. Although this can hold true for some, the reality is that it requires strong, pre-existing demand for a good or service for customers to engage with a business of their own volition. For most business owners, the reality is more like this:

- **Determine** who 'they' (ideal customers) are and what they need – beyond what they *think* they need.
- **Design** a business model that draws them in, gives them cause to part with their money and keeps them coming back.
- **Build it** and they will come.
- **Continually improve and maintain it** and they will stay, and/or spread the word to others who'll come too.

When contrasted with the original cliché, it becomes clear why so many SSB owners struggle. When we build anything without a clear plan, we're more likely to make mistakes, waste time and give up. Add to that, the fact that most of us assume the marketing function is solely about attracting *new* customers when that aspect of it – the 'draw them in' part – is just the tip of the iceberg. It's little wonder so many SSBs fail the test of time.

With these common business-building inclinations in mind, the topic of acquiring new customers has been left until last. If it had been covered upfront, it might have been tempting to put the book down too soon – inspired with ideas to increase market awareness and sales conversions but still lacking the insights to improve the trajectory of your SSB. Now, however, we've established what it takes to create and grow a successful SSB, above and beyond the acquisition of new customers, so we can zoom in on it without losing sight of the big picture.

Acquiring new customers is crucial for every SSB in every industry. Without new customers, SSBs stagnate, both energetically and financially. A business with a base of regular, high-paying customers, such as an accounting practice, will last longer without new customers than one that relies on small sales from scores of walk-in customers, such as a café. But sooner or later, both will reach an insurmountable performance plateau.

With the Secret Service approach, three things are needed to acquire new customers:

1. **Marketing activities** – Tactics that make our business visible to its target market; generating awareness, attracting interest and encouraging an initial action, such as clicking a link or phoning us. Marketing activities enable our business to become visible to the right people in the right places at the right time.

2. **Marketing tools** – Resources that help us convert interested service seekers into paying customers.

3. **A lead-to-sale strategy** – A system to convert potential customers into paying customers. A successful lead-to sale cycle initiates a service transaction: the exchange of goods or services for money.

With a constant stream of new customers, every day presents an opportunity to build a better business. It's a chance to implement new strategies and systems, improve customer perception and increase customer retention. New customers play an important role in shifting the energy of an SSB from 'going through the motions' to serving with personality, passion and purpose.

So, let's get to it...

CHAPTER 16.

THE MODERN MARKETING ARSENAL

*** NOTE ***

This chapter is an abridged version of the third book in the Secret Service Business Series, 'The Modern Marketing Arsenal: Ways & Means to Promote a Small Skill-or-Service Business (& Which to Choose to Get the Most Bang for Your Marketing Buck)'. If you like what you read... you'll like the full book more.

In the modern world of small business, the ways and means to attract new customers can seem overwhelming and endless. Every day, new business-boosting ideas and opportunities present themselves and with each one we ignore, many of us feel a pang of guilt that we're not doing as much for our business, or bank account, as we should be.

But the good news is that most of these ideas and opportunities are irrelevant. They're geared for goods-based, internet marketing or small businesses generally – not the highly specific needs of SSBs.

When the mud and murk of irrelevant ideas and opportunities are cleared away, there are a finite number of marketing activities worthy of our consideration, which can be boiled down to just 10 types. These comprise the spokes of the Secret Service Marketing Wheel, introduced in Chapter 3 and recapped for quick reference below.

Recap: The Secret Service Marketing Wheel

The Secret Service Marketing Wheel presents the marketing activities available for SSBs to attract the attention of service seekers, along with the fundamental tools and steps required to convert them into paying customers. The Wheel is designed to help SSB owners make smarter marketing decisions; decisions that have the capacity to boost business momentum with little to no increase in marketing expenditure.

Figure 23: The Secret Service Marketing Wheel (a repeat of Figure 10 for quick reference)

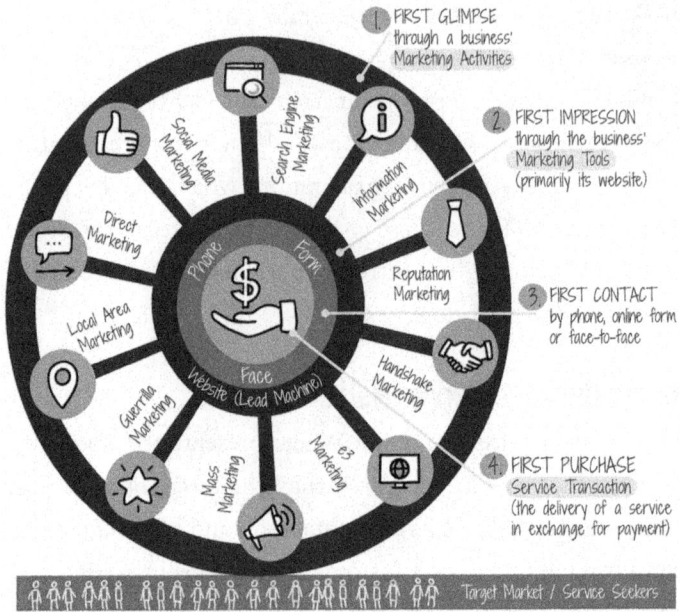

1. FIRST GLIMPSE
through a business'
Marketing Activities

2. FIRST IMPRESSION
through the business'
Marketing Tools
(primarily its website)

3. FIRST CONTACT
by phone, online form
or face-to-face

4. FIRST PURCHASE
Service Transaction
(the delivery of a service
in exchange for payment)

Target Market / Service Seekers

How the Wheel Works

With the Secret Service approach to marketing, service seekers are funnelled through a series of 'firsts', from unidentified members of a target market through to paying customers. The spokes of *marketing activity* generate awareness of, and interest in, the business' offering – giving service seekers a *first glimpse* of a possible solution. These activities drive traffic to a *website*, which has the pivotal role of connecting with, convincing and converting potential customers into leads through the creation of a favourable *first impression*. From there, leads flow in via website enquiry *form submissions, phone calls* and *face-to-face 'walk-in' enquiries*. This is the all-important **first contact**, which – if handled well and followed up appropriately – can culminate in a *service transaction* or **first purchase**.

The Activity Arsenal

Most SSB owners have a preconceived idea about what marketing activity should look like and how much it should cost as a percentage of revenue. But such rigid business beliefs no longer serve us. The game of marketing has changed – *in our favour*. We have more power than we ever dreamed possible, but putting it into play takes awareness and practice. Only by recognising the opportunities available to us and making tactical moves can we access our share of the spoils.

Modern marketing requires a carefully considered gameplan. Observing and imitating the manoeuvres made by big businesses is no longer the smartest play. SSBs are not big businesses – nor are the majority ever intended to be. Seeking to play the game like the big boys on the business field is a surefire way to lose. To win, we need an entirely different approach and attitude; embracing our small size and limited resources as opportunities, not blaming them for our lack of business traction to date.

Building a thriving SSB with next to no ongoing marketing costs is no longer a pipedream. With a Secret Service mindset, a strong business model, a Lead Machine website and a carefully selected suite of marketing activities, we can kick more goals than we ever thought possible.

In order to select the right marketing activities for our business, we first need to know what opportunities are available to us and how to choose between them. This is the purpose of the third book in the *Secret Service Business Series* – *The Modern Marketing Arsenal*.

But in the meantime, let's shine a light on the arsenal of options at our disposal – the 10 broad types of marketing activity available to SSBs (aka the 10 spokes of the Marketing Wheel).

1. Handshake Marketing

It's only fitting to kick things off with the oldest marketing activity in human history and, arguably, the most crucial to SSB survival. *Handshake marketing* is any marketing activity that involves the development and nourishment of business relationships through one-on-one interaction and connection. It has existed for thousands of years and is as relevant now as it ever was – in the form of *networking*, *manual sales prospecting*, *alliance building* and exhibiting at *expos or trade shows*.

2. e3 Marketing

From the oldest form of marketing to one of the newest... *e3 marketing* is a means of generating traffic, leads or sales, through an electronic (e), third party (3) website service. These third party sites exist to serve as intermediaries between buyers and sellers in specific industries or markets. They range from broad marketplaces, like Gumtree, to niche comparator websites such as 'Compare the Market' for insurance. Each e3 site serves as a conduit between buyers and sellers, bringing them together via an online hub. Ideally, the

site's brand awareness, buyer database and resources generate a flow of traffic, leads or sales for sellers. The e3 marketing platforms of most relevance to SSBs are *online business directories*, *comparator websites* and *group buying ('daily deal') websites*.

3. Reputation Marketing

Reputation marketing is an ongoing activity aimed to build and preserve a business' public image. At the core of reputation marketing is the familiar concept of *word of mouth*. Word of mouth occurs when customers are so satisfied (or dissatisfied) with our service that they recommend (or disparage) us to their friends, family, associates, or even strangers. Positive word of mouth can be encouraged but it can't be commanded or controlled. To a large extent, it is what it is. However, what we *can* do is capitalise on it (and any other positive events and occurrences) through two free activities: *online review management* and *public relations (PR) management*.

4. Information Marketing

Information marketing is the sharing of rich, valuable information with an online or offline audience – informing, educating and/or empowering them to become more capable or successful in some way. Empowering your audience to undertake a project or achieve a certain outcome for themselves might sound counterintuitive – on par with revealing the ingredients in a secret sauce. But, in actuality, spilling a few beans can prove incredibly lucrative and generate

far more momentum than spilling none at all. The information marketing activities of most relevance to SSBs include *content marketing*, *group training* and the development and dissemination of *information products*.

5. Search Engine Marketing

Search engine marketing makes the most of search engines (Google, Bing, DuckDuckGo and others) to help businesses get found by internet users who are actively searching for goods, services or solutions online. There are two modes of search engine marketing: *search engine optimisation (SEO)*, which seeks to help a business' website rank higher in the natural or 'organic' list of search results displayed for relevant search terms, and *search engine advertising (SEA)*, which generates exposure through paid advertising.

6. Social Media Marketing

The term social media refers to online platforms (sites and applications) that allow users to create and share content with a pool of friends or followers, for the purposes of social connection and amusement. Popular social networks include Facebook, Instagram, YouTube, LinkedIn, TikTok, X (formerly Twitter) and Pinterest. *Social media marketing* uses one or more of these platforms to reach and engage with a targeted audience. As with search engine marketing, there are two ways to make a business visible to users on social media: the free way, *social media activity* and the paid way, *social media advertising*.

7. Direct Marketing

Direct marketing involves communicating with potential or past customers and contacts via a one-to-one medium of communication – email, phone or mail. The boundaries of direct marketing have been blurred over the years, however the most practical way to define it is a marketing activity that: 1) requires a database or list of individual contact details to initiate, or 2) is triggered by an individual taking a certain technological action (such as subscribing to a mailing list or phoning a business to make an enquiry). As such, direct marketing encompasses the activities of *telemarketing*, *email marketing*, *mobile marketing* and *snail mail marketing*.

8. Local Area Marketing

Local area marketing refers to activities geared to capture the attention and interest of offline buyers within a localised geographic area. This includes *point of sale (POS) promotion*, *asset advertising*, *community facility advertising*, *resident distribution advertising* and *local markets*. The majority of these activities are best suited to businesses that are operationally confined to a particular region due to the delivery of in-person or on-site services (e.g. beauty salons, cafés and trade services).

9. Guerrilla Marketing

Guerrilla marketing is a means of generating public attention and interest by thinking outside the marketing box. It's about creating

opportunities to stand out from the crowd; initiating – or capitalising on – events and occurrences that are impressive, memorable and unique. For SSBs, these opportunities tend to fall into three categories: *celebrity appeal marketing*, *viral marketing* and *street marketing*.

10. Mass Marketing

Mass marketing encompasses activities geared to push an advertising message out to the general public via traditional advertising mediums – mainstream television, radio, print and/or outdoor advertising (billboards, ambient media etc) – referred to collectively as *mainstream media advertising*. The aim of mass marketing is to generate awareness, interest and desire for a product or service, en masse. While it's one of the most expensive forms of marketing activity, the shift away from it (to online modes of marketing) has rendered some mainstream advertising opportunities more accessible to SSBs than ever before. As such, it's still worth considering.

A Secret Service Marketer's arsenal is made up of the marketing activities that fall into these 10 categories (explained in detail in book three), plus six marketing tools to be summarised shortly.

To be clear, no business needs all marketing activities. You'd be silly (and broke) if you tried. Instead, the aim of the game is to find the best mix to sustain or grow your business without breaking the bank. This optimum arsenal of activities is different for every business. For some SSBs with a strong business model, it can comprise little more than a few free activities. For others, more trial and error, time, money and business model refinement is required to strike the right balance. There is no 'one size fits all' mix of marketing activities, only one tailored to fit the needs, objectives and resources of a particular business and, importantly, the capabilities and personality of its owner.

Where to Begin

All marketing activities are not created equal. Some are essential while others are entirely optional. Some are free, requiring little time or money to implement, while others can quickly blow your budget. As Secret Service Marketers, we need to take this into account – prioritising essential, low-cost activities first, and optional, expensive activities last. Book three makes this much easier by breaking activities down into four types: *survival*, *no-brainer*, *cheap but challenging* and *upper end*, starting with those freely available to any business owner with the initiative to embrace and action them.

The Secret Service Six

While some marketing activities can be effective in isolation (typically 'survival' activities), most require the active support of one or more marketing *tools* to unleash their performance power.

Marketing tools are physical or digital apparatus geared to capitalise on the attention induced by marketing activity. There are six tools in the Secret Service arsenal:

1. A Lead Machine (website geared to drive leads)
2. A sales kit
3. Automated phone messages
4. Email signatures and canned responses
5. Business cards
6. Promotional products

Of these six tools, the aim of the first four is to engage, educate and inspire *immediate* action from prospective customers. The last two (business cards and promotional products) serve better as reminder mechanisms – helping a business stay in prospects' minds to prompt action at some point *in the future*.

Marketing activities and marketing tools (aka the *Secret Service Six*) need each other. They are interdependent and intrinsically linked. Focusing on one over the other (like many of us do when building a website – expecting leads to start rolling in without determining where the traffic necessary for that to happen will come from) is the equivalent of SSB self-sabotage. Without marketing tools, we undermine the effectiveness of our marketing activity and without marketing activity, we undermine the effectiveness of our marketing tools. So, we need both.

When it comes to organising and implementing our marketing arsenal however, tools take priority. Marketing tools are the key to capitalising on marketing activity, so it's ideal that they be in place before an activity commences, or as soon as possible after recognising they are missing.

In order of importance, a rundown of the Secret Service Six (including where to find further information) is provided below.

A Lead Machine (website geared to drive leads)

While all six marketing tools are important, one – a Lead Machine – stands head and shoulders above the rest, surpassing all others in its ability to change the game for a struggling SSB.

As explained in Chapter 13 – and down to the finest detail in *The Secret Service Website Formula* – a Lead Machine is a website designed to convert traffic into leads. It's also the single greatest marketing investment an SSB owner can make. Having a well-functioning Lead Machine is the only way we can rely on no-brainer marketing activities to organically acquire new customers. Without it, we have to spend much more time or money to get anywhere near the same result.

A Sales Kit

The tools and techniques used to present an offer to a prospective customer in a sales meeting go a long way to determining whether they'll convert into paying clients. For some SSBs, the sales meeting takes the form of a phone call – answering a few simple questions, providing reassurance and booking an appointment. For others, it's a lengthy face-to-face consultation – guiding a prospect through a structured sales presentation, or introducing a menu and a set of daily specials. Whatever the sales process that's most appropriate for our business (covered in Chapter 17), we mustn't skimp on it; taking the time to consider the structure of our sales meetings and to develop a suite of supporting resources called a *sales kit*. A comprehensive, well-considered sales kit equips us to present our goods or services in the best possible light.

It helps ensure everything that needs to be covered in a sales meeting gets covered; freeing us to be the most authentic, consistent and high-performing salesperson we can be.

A sales kit is one of the most powerful, yet overlooked marketing tools for SSBs and, as such, is the sole focus of Chapter 18.

Automated Phone Messages

As explained in Chapter 6, the phone is a pivotal point of contact between service seekers and an SSB, but one that many of us take for granted. To that end, the following scenarios are incredibly common in small business:

- Calls going unanswered without giving potential customers the opportunity to leave a message;
- Calls not being returned quickly, or worse, not being returned at all;
- Callers being spoken to coldly or bluntly – as if they are an inconvenience;
- Callers being put on hold – left listening to mind-numbing music or empty silence, often wondering if the call has been disconnected.

To avoid undesirable phone experiences, we need to check our phone systems and procedures carefully. For the three main factors to consider, refer to Chapter 6 of book three. A little bit of consideration about the phone experience of our potential customers – and the infrastructure to enhance it – can go a long way to increasing leads, sales and customer satisfaction.

Email Signatures & Canned Responses

An *email signature* is a block of text and images that gets added automatically to the end of our emails. It identifies us and our business – branding our email messages while serving as a digital business card. Among other things, an email signature provides an opportunity to:

- Make your contact details easily accessible;
- Educate recipients about your services, accomplishments and affiliations; and
- Drive traffic to your website and social media pages.

For context, imagine your business has 10 employees, each sending 10 emails a day, 250 days per year. That's 25,000 extra impressions of your logo, contact and service details that wouldn't have otherwise existed, all for no extra work or financial outlay.

For a list of details that can be included in an email signature, refer to Chapter 6 of book three.

Essentially, an email signature is a free ad. It's an opportunity to enhance the effectiveness of our email communications, requiring a miniscule amount of effort and no extra cost. As such, it's an opportunity that SSB owners are wise not to waste.

Canned email responses are essentially email templates, created in response to common enquiries or questions. Rather than responding to common enquiries from scratch each and every time they are received, the appropriate canned response is selected, personalised and sent. This can save hours of time per week and countless hours per year, while significantly reducing a business' risk of human error and oversight.

Setting up email signatures and canned responses is relatively easy if using a mainstream email platform, but all systems have their quirks. To navigate these, simply search Google or YouTube for instructions specific to your platform of choice (e.g. 'How to set up canned responses in Outlook?'). Failing that, hiring an IT professional – to set up an initial signature and canned response and teach you how to use them – would be well worth it; a small investment for a huge boost in professionalism and efficiency.

Business Cards

Once upon a time, a full suite of professionally printed stationery – business cards, letterheads, 'with compliments' slips and envelopes – was essential for SSBs to present a professional image. With advancements in DIY desktop publishing, printing and, more recently, digital communication and file storage, this has all changed. Now, most physical, bulk printed stationery does little more than gather dust... with one exception.

Business cards are as important to SSBs as they ever were. They are fundamental to handshake marketing as well as many other marketing activities – group training, free community facility advertising and point of sale promotion to name a few. They can also serve the dual purpose of a customer service tool – designed with lines on the back to write the date and time of a customer's next appointment.

The quality and professionalism of a business card says a lot about the business it represents, so it's worth investing in a set of decent ones. That said, when starting out in business on a tight budget, a short run of cheap, generic cards can be the wisest option. Investing too much on physical marketing tools too soon, can hold SSB owners back – deterring us from adapting our business model to better position our business for success. Once our business model has stabilised and it's less likely that the design and detail of our business card will change, we can invest more on unique, high-quality design and printing to produce a card that does our business justice.

Before finalising the design of a business card, refer back to Chapter 12 to ensure the basics of your brand are clear and strong, and all essential elements are included.

Promotional Products

Whether it's a pen, mug, stubby holder, keyring, notepad, fridge magnet, power bank or other item of practical use, a branded ***promotional product*** can be a clever addition to an SSB's marketing arsenal. Although entirely optional, promotional products can be a perfect complement to handshake marketing, point of sale and other face-to-face marketing activities, serving as a semi-permanent bridge between a prospective customer and a business.

Like business cards, promotional products are a physical marketing tool with the capacity to prompt leads and sales into the future. A simple item – such as a branded fridge magnet or mug – can be an excellent way of generating repeat business from first-time or occasional clients, keeping the business top of mind for months or even years. The right promotional product serves as a powerful reminder mechanism, providing constant brand exposure in homes and workplaces. In a welcome way, it infiltrates a prospect's personal environment – boosting brand recognition and recall for far longer than most advertising opportunities.

For guidance on the selection and design of promotional products, refer to Chapter 6 of book three.

Strong Tools Rule

The strength of our marketing tools goes a long way to determining the success of the marketing activities we pursue. With a website that applies the Secret Service Website Formula, a well-planned sales kit, a professional email signature, an appropriate suite of automated phone messages and canned email responses, decent business cards and, optionally, a promotional product or two, our marketing arsenal is exponentially stronger. That means the marketing activities we engage in have the capacity to work better than they otherwise would. We can generate more leads and sales from them with less input, effort and risk... the ultimate no-brainer, really.

Marketing Decisions Made Easier

As you familiarise yourself with the marketing tools and activities at your disposal, another can of worms opens up. 'How many activities does my business need? Which activities should I try first? Should I focus on free opportunities or skip straight to paid advertising? Is it better to prioritise online or offline marketing?' and more. The final chapter of book three addresses all these questions and more, including how to assess the viability of a paid marketing activity before committing to it, and how to know if that activity is benefiting your business or holding it back.

When the foundations are laid for a successful SSB using the first two books of the *Secret Service Business Series*, the third book, *The Modern Marketing Arsenal*, is the place to turn. No one can tell you the exact combination of marketing activities that will fuel the growth and success of your business but

The Modern Marketing Arsenal will serve as a handy reference point, so you know what you've got in your arsenal and where to start to make the biggest bang.

CHAPTER 17.

MAKE THE MOST OF FRESH LEADS

*** WARNING! DETAIL AHEAD ***

This chapter contains detailed instructions that may be overwhelming at first. If you get bogged down in it, switch to skim reading and return to each section as it becomes applicable.

For most SSB owners, leads are the lifeblood of business. But the only leads that really count are those converted into sales. Without culminating in a sale, a lead is not only worthless, it can drain us; sapping us of time and energy that could be spent generating another form of income.

For low-risk services (restaurants, beauty services and dry cleaners, for example), leads usually take the form of enquiries, which are relatively quick and easy to convert into bookings and sales. For these businesses, the mere fact that a potential customer has made contact indicates they are ready and willing to engage its services. All that's needed to get the booking over the line is a little validation – positivity, professionalism and common courtesy.

For higher risk services (such as design and construction services), leads tend to be more prospective in nature. Each one requires a significant investment of time and expertise to qualify it, scope the project and quote on a solution before the prospective customer can seriously consider engaging the business' services. Selling a high-risk service is usually more complex and time-consuming than selling a low-risk service, but the sale amount is typically much higher, making it worth the extra effort.

Sales Snags

Selling low-risk services may sound easier than selling high-risk services but both present challenges that can hold us back from realising our sales potential.

Low-Risk Services

The lead-to-sale cycle for low-risk services (restaurants, etc) usually starts with an enquiry, which, if handled effectively, results in either an on-the-spot service transaction, or a booking for the service at a mutually convenient time and place. As simple as this sounds, handling enquiries effectively isn't easy. More often than not, office or floor staff are tasked with the responsibility of answering phone or email enquiries, with no sales training beyond how to process a booking. They're not conscious of the fact that they're salespeople, with one of the most important tasks in the business... turning today's enquiries into tomorrow's wages.

Many SSB owners assume office and floor staff know how to handle phone enquiries because 'everyone knows how to answer a phone'. However, with no sales training, employees can come to believe that the phone ringing is an annoying and unwanted inconvenience. This negative attitude can infiltrate their phone manner, causing them to come across as annoyed or arrogant. The only thing worse is when the phone is left to ring out.

Whether or not the business has staff, the main mistake low-risk service providers make is not having a documented sales process, or *lead-to-sale strategy*. With no lead-to-sale strategy, leads are handled inconsistently. Sales communications – particularly emails – are more likely to be slow and sloppy, with precious time wasted crafting individual communications from scratch. What's more, leads are more likely to be overlooked or lost during busy periods – having been put aside for later follow-up – and potential customers will often forget they made an appointment or booking, resulting in costly 'no-shows'.

For low-risk services, a steadfast lead-to-sale strategy, well-trained staff and a couple of canned email and SMS communications can be all that's needed to make a stronger first impression, increase sales conversions and dramatically boost the business' bottom line.

High-Risk Services

When selling high-risk services, the most common mistake SSB owners make is not adequately preparing for price discussions. Benjamin Franklin famously said, 'By failing to prepare, you are preparing to fail' and this certainly holds true for the sale of services. The higher the perceived risk, the more 'proof' a prospect needs to feel comfortable proceeding with a service transaction. The more proof *they* need, the more consideration and preparation *we* need, to present an appealing offer and, ultimately, close the sale.

All too often, we approach the crucial price conversation by 'winging it'. There's little, if any, structure to the conversation, let alone the use of any sales tools, besides a written quote. For high-risk services, winging it doesn't cut it – neither does sending through a quote by email and crossing our fingers the prospect replies with a 'yes'. Both these approaches rely on hope – and hope is not a strategy.

The second common mistake that sellers of high-risk services make is giving up on leads too soon. It's believed to take between 6 and 12 communications with a potential customer to build the trust required to make a sale. This number can be significantly reduced using the Secret Service Website Formula to induce a sense of trust and connection prior to the first contact but nevertheless, it's essential to persist until a definite answer is received.

With the sale of high-risk services, preparation and persistence go a long way. It wasn't until I incorporated them into my own business' lead-to-sale strategy, that I realised I'd been expecting my sales prospects to take my business seriously, when I hadn't been. In not preparing for price discussions or persisting in following up afterwards, I had been shooting myself in the foot – wasting time and money, opportunity after opportunity, year after year.

Becoming Lead-to-Sale Savvy

Whether our services are low- or high-risk, the series of actions we take upon receiving a fresh lead determines our likelihood of converting that lead into a sale. An off-the-cuff approach minimises our chances. A carefully considered, strategic approach maximises them. Taking a considered approach to sales opportunities makes the sales function more logical and less emotional. Sales become measurable, predictable numbers and ratios over which we have insight and control, rather than random events that seem to hinge on dumb luck.

In order to increase sales conversions, we need to set ourselves a challenge: to make purchasing our offering seem like an obvious decision – as close to a no-brainer as possible. This is done by using a combination of sales tools and procedures to communicate and reinforce the value of the offering so clearly that prospects feel it would be silly to go elsewhere.

Creating a no-brainer sales environment has nothing to do with luck and everything to do with an effective *lead-to-sale strategy*. A lead-to-sale strategy is the flow of tasks and interactions that take place upon receipt of a lead. It is best presented in a flowchart format, so it's clear to see what to do, in what order, to boost our chances of sales success.

The Benefits of a Strong Lead-to-Sale Strategy

There are plenty of reasons to get a lead-to-sale strategy in place ASAP. For one, the mere process of mapping out the interactions that take place upon receipt of a lead makes us more conscious of them. Amidst the day-to-day running of a business, it's easy to get complacent about the odd sales call or email, but each and every one is important. The composition and quality of every little interaction counts; impacting our conversion rates for better or worse.

Mapping out the interactions in our sales process also paves the way to greater efficiency. With conscious consideration, many steps in our lead-to-sale strategy can be systemised and streamlined through the use of tools and resources, such as canned email responses or booking software. This frees us up to focus on building an emotional connection with our prospects and tailoring our offerings and sales pitches to optimise our sales performance.

Beyond its initial implementation, benefits of a strong lead-to-sale strategy include:

1. **Connective professionalism** – Carefully considered interactions during the sales process make us appear highly professional, yet personal and attentive, reinforcing the sense of familial connection and trust (connectivity) generated by our website.

2. **Fewer errors and oversights** – A clear lead-to-sale strategy reduces the potential for human error and lost leads.

3. **Higher revenue potential** – Knowing what's necessary at each step of the sales process helps keep the time and energy invested in leads to a minimum. When every action is predetermined, there's no need to consider what to do next – you just follow the steps. This speeds up the sales cycle, thereby boosting a business' revenue potential.

Implemented well, the right lead-to-sale strategy can dramatically improve customer perception and sales performance while streamlining back-end operations – making a striking difference to a business' profitability and capacity for growth.

Selecting the Right Lead-to-Sale Strategy

There's no one-size-fits-all lead-to-sale strategy for SSBs but the options *can* be narrowed down to four. Determining an appropriate strategy requires two variables: the perceived risk of the service (low or high, as per Chapter 8) and the approach taken to pricing (post-op or preset, explained in Chapter 10). With these, you can use the matrix below to pinpoint a suitable strategy.

Figure 24: The Lead-to-Sale Strategy Selection Matrix

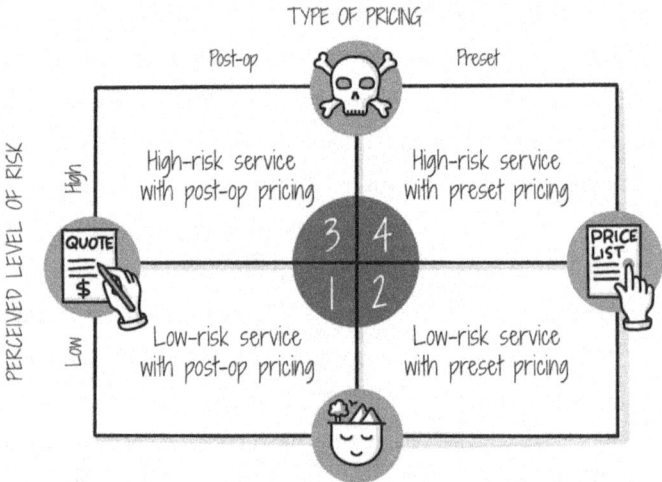

Once you've identified the applicable strategy (number 1–4) for your business, refer to the corresponding flowchart. Note that this chart should be considered as a starting point; a means to incorporate structure and attention to detail into your sales process. It is a theoretical ideal and will likely need to be adapted to suit the intricacies of your business.

STRATEGY 1

Figure 25: Lead-to-Sale Strategy 1 – For SSBs selling low-risk services with post-op pricing

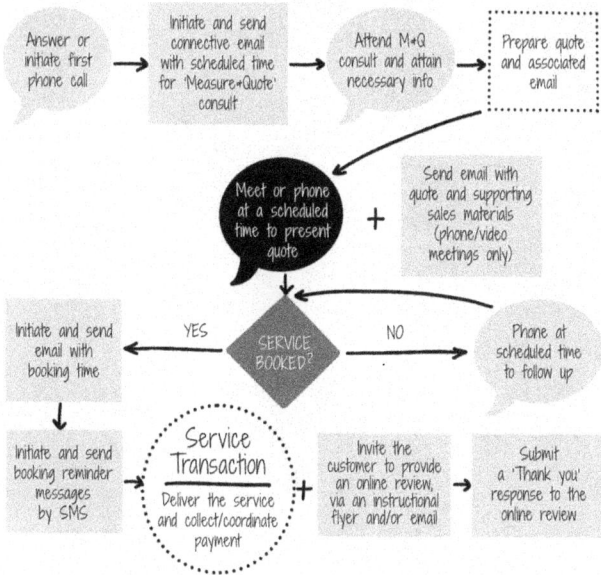

To interpret the symbols in this chart, refer to the key on page 313.

STRATEGY 2

Figure 26: Lead-to-Sale Strategy 2 – For SSBs selling low-risk services with preset pricing

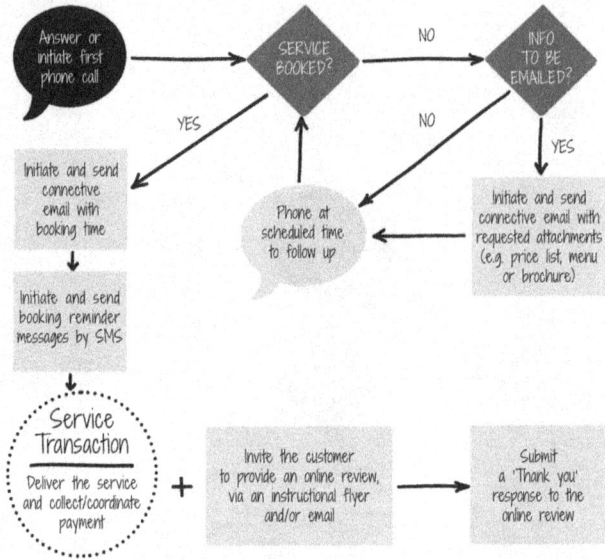

To interpret the symbols in this chart, refer to the key on page 313.

STRATEGY 3

Figure 27: Lead-to-Sale Strategy 3 - For SSBs selling high-risk services with post-op pricing

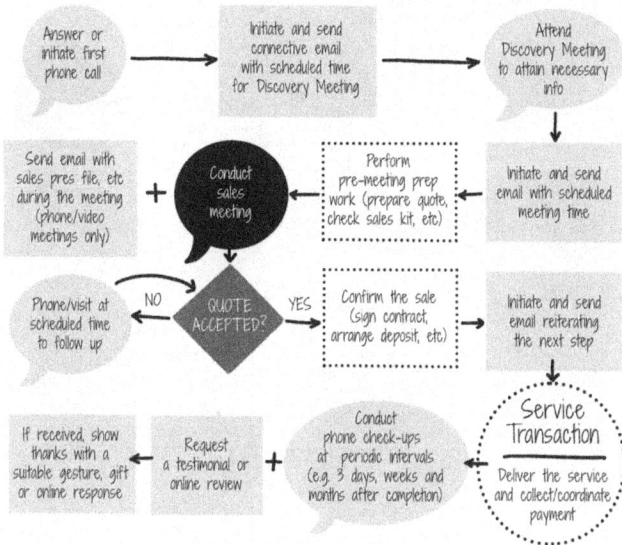

To interpret the symbols in this chart, refer to the key on page 313.

STRATEGY 4

Figure 28: Lead-to-Sale Strategy 4 – For SSBs selling high-risk services with preset pricing

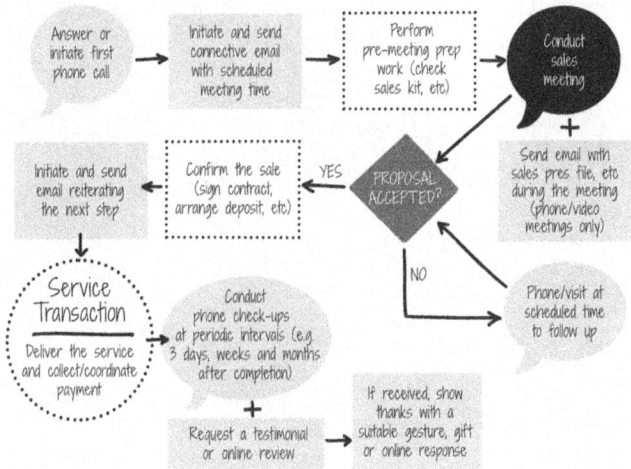

To interpret the symbols in this chart, refer to the key on the next page.

KEY

Figure 29: The symbols used in the Lead-to-Sale Strategy charts

Symbol	Meaning
Answer or initiate first phone call	In each chart, the most prominent speech bubble signifies the all-important *sales meeting*. This conversation is paramount. It's when the value proposition (from Chapter 8) is presented, the proposed solution and price are outlined and a 'close' attempted, with the aim of getting the prospect's agreement to proceed with a purchase.
Answer or initiate first phone call	A pale grey speech bubble signifies a *two-way, real-time conversation* conducted face-to-face or by phone or video conference. Each conversation is an opportunity to make a human connection and, as such, plays a vital role in the lead-to-sale process. It should not be substituted for email or text messaging unless absolutely unavoidable.
Initiate and send email with booking time	A pale grey box signifies a *one-way communication*, usually via email or SMS, often using a canned response (pre-prepared template). Each communication plays an important supporting role in the lead-to-sale process.
Prepare quote and associated email	A box with a dotted border signifies *pre-sale preparation or paperwork* – investigating, measuring, preparing reports and quotes, signing contracts, etc.
Service Transaction — Deliver the service and collect/coordinate payment	The circle with a dotted border in each chart signifies the *service transaction*. This is the pinnacle of the lead-to-sale process where an exchange of goods or services for money takes place.

While certain steps in our lead-to-sale strategy may seem straightforward and self-explanatory, the importance we place on them, and how we execute them, can make a world of difference to our sales results... starting from the very first phone call.

The First Phone Call

No matter what you're selling, or with which lead-to-sale strategy, it's always preferable to respond to remote sales enquiries by phone. The phone facilitates a two-way conversation in real time, which fuels human connection. An email or text message does not. Email or SMS communication is one-way, faceless and often delayed – making it easy for potential customers to disassociate from it. An actual human voice on the end of a phone line is much harder to ignore. This makes the phone the ideal tool for kicking off the lead-to-sale cycle.

There are two main exceptions to the 'respond by phone' rule: 1) if the prospect has specifically requested email communication, or 2) if they've provided a false phone number. These are signs that the prospect is either price-shopping or not ready to buy, so avoid spending too much time crafting an email response. Note that the number of requests for email-only communication tend to diminish as a natural by-product of launching a Lead Machine.

When to Call

It's common to think that phoning a lead too soon after receiving an enquiry makes us appear desperate. However, research shows that attempts to contact online leads within five minutes of receiving them are 900% (nine times) more successful than those contacted after 20 hours.[30] The early bird really does catch the worm, so call as soon as possible after receiving a lead. If the prospect doesn't answer, continue phoning at increasing intervals of several hours over the following days, resisting the urge to leave voicemail messages every time (as that *will* make us appear desperate... and slightly unhinged).

Only Sell the Next Step

To be clear, the purpose of the first phone call is *not* to make a sale – it's to introduce ourselves and demonstrate that we're responsive to, and focused on, our potential customer's needs. Above all else though, the aim is to **sell the next step.** This means securing the customer's commitment in one of two ways: 1) scheduling a booking to provide/deliver the service, or 2) scheduling a time for the next two-way, real time communication (face-to-face or phone).

For low-risk services with preset pricing (Lead-to-Sale Strategy 2), the first phone call is often the only chance to discuss a service before delivering it, so it is the equivalent of a sales meeting. However, as mentioned earlier, by the time a prospect enquires about a low-risk service, they are usually ready to commit. By this stage, little is needed to get the booking over the line. Being friendly, attentive and professional – guiding the prospect towards making a booking – is enough.

So, no matter your lead-to-sale strategy... relax. The first phone call is *not* a sales call. It's a time to be your best self, to connect and listen – giving just enough away to make the prospect excited to meet with you.

Script for the First Phone Call

The first phone call can be broken down into a series of eight steps

1. **Introduce** – Formally introduce yourself to the prospect, then, if you initiated the call, remind them of the action they took to prompt it. For example 'Hi, I'm Julian from G Flat Construction. You submitted an enquiry form through our website about half an hour ago?' Wait for confirmation before proceeding.

2. **Appreciate and validate** – Thank them for getting in touch, then start the conversation by referencing their enquiry in the form of a question: 'So, you're looking at building a granny flat?' Respond to their answer with a suitable level of enthusiasm and reassurance. 'Oh, fantastic. That's exciting. Well, you've come to the right place.'

3. **Question** – In order to ascertain the prospect's knowledge, needs and expectations, and subtly demonstrate your expertise, have a series of questions ready. Ask each question (adding or avoiding certain ones, where necessary, to tailor the conversation around the prospect's specific circumstance) and really listen to the answers. In particular, listen out for any fears, concerns, likes and dislikes. Utilising a pre-prepared *customer enquiry form* (paper-based or digital) is a great way to ensure all relevant questions are asked and the answers recorded for later reference.

   Taking notes is important, not only to assist with scoping the work, but to provide attentive, personal communication moving forward. Nothing surprises and delights customers more than when you recall highly specific details they'd forgotten they shared with you (such as the name of their partner or child, where they work, etc).

It's also beneficial to stop and summarise what the prospect is telling you by saying 'So if I understand correctly...' or 'So what you're saying is...' This shows you've heard and understood them.

For high-risk service providers, it's important to note that if what *you think* the prospect needs differs from what *they say* they need, the first phone call is not the time to convince them otherwise. The point of the call is to sell the next step, not to close a sale. Be an active listener, not a convincer.

4. **Answer** – Embrace the opportunity to answer questions, as they are a strong sign of a prospect's keenness to proceed. Dignify every question with a clear, confident response, taking the opportunity to sell the next step where possible.

   More often than not, the burning question is 'How much will it cost?' For SSB owners following Lead-to-Sale Strategy 2, be upfront about the price but don't linger on it. State it matter-of-factly and move on. Those following other lead-to-sale strategies can provide an indicative price range if necessary (to help qualify the prospect), however, it's better to channel the question into selling the next step. For example, 'There are quite a few variables involved in determining that, but once we've gone into a little more detail in our discovery session, I'll be able to give you a fixed price.'

5. **Suggest and steer** – Outline the next step in the sales process and get consent to proceed with it. For example:

- 'What I'd like to do is schedule a discovery session with you – at no charge – to determine exactly what's needed to achieve the result you're after. Does that sound helpful?'
- 'How about we meet on site later this week? I'll take some measurements and show you some materials, then we can narrow down your preferences and I can put a proposal together. Would that suit you?'
- 'From here, I'll put a quote together for you and phone you tomorrow afternoon to take you through it... would 2:30pm work for you?'

6. **Confirm** – Confirm the date and time of the next two-way communication.

7. **Collect** – Collect or confirm the prospect's contact details, including their name, phone number, physical address if required and an email address for sending a message of confirmation.

   Avoid asking the prospect to send their details to you via a text message. While this may save time and effort for you, it burdens the potential customer with an extra job. This is unprofessional, inappropriate and can undermine your conversational efforts.

8. **Conclude** – To end the call, thank the prospect again, reiterate the scheduled date/time for the next interaction and advise that an email will be sent shortly containing the details for their calendar.

The First Email

Immediately after the first phone call, an easy extra step can be taken to reinforce the prospect's decision to meet or book in with us and reduce the likelihood of them changing their mind. This involves the transmission of a connective, introductory email, geared to bolster the human connection established to that point.

Connective Emails

A connective email contains a more engaging, human energy than a standard business email, through the strategic use of images and words. The key ingredients in a connective first email are:

1. **A feel-the-love photo** – A pivotal element of a connective email is a feel-the-love photo[31] of the person who the prospect is scheduled to meet with next (either you, or the technician scheduled to deliver the service). This serves a strategic purpose; humanising and validating the business, while fueling a sense of connection and trust.

2. **A personal note of welcome and introduction** – The email should 1) convey a sense of gratitude for the opportunity to be of service, 2) touch briefly on the prospect's specific situation, values or needs, and 3) state the scheduled day and time of the next meeting or booking, using a friendly, conversational tone.

To save time and reduce the likelihood of human error, this email can be canned: prepared in advance and saved as a template – ready to customise and send as soon as possible after the first phone call.

A connective, introductory email will come as a welcome surprise to your sales prospects. Not only will it make them feel like a genuine priority – which is rare in this fast-paced world – it will serve a strategic business purpose; reducing the likelihood of costly no-shows and cancellations.

Sending Prices via Email

For some SSBs, sending prices, quotes or other proposals via email works well. For others, it's a barrier to sales. Email is a detached form of communication – not the best for revealing prices. It's easy for a prospect (the email recipient) to dismiss an email on the basis of price, give us no response or right of reply and cut off all communications; avoiding the discomfort of rejecting our proposal directly.

If sending prices by email is causing leads to go AWOL, a shake up in your lead-to-sale strategy might be in order. The first thing to try is a connective *pricing* email instead of a connective *introductory* email. Including a feel-the-love photo and personal note with your proposal or quote has the power to shift a prospect's focus from the price to your social and technical proficiency, making the proposal harder to flippantly dismiss. Note that with a connective *pricing* email, the introductory email can be scaled back to basic details, or scrapped if it becomes superfluous to the process.

If a connective pricing email doesn't help, another change may be in order. Instead of emailing the quote as soon as it's ready, try waiting until the prospect is physically on the phone, at the agreed time. This will give you the chance to:

- **Verbally expand on the quote** – emphasising the quality of the inclusions or any time or money saving benefits, as you walk them through the proposal over the phone;
- **Ease into the numbers** – softening the impact of the price by emphasising the value of the service or, if sensing price is an issue, explaining that certain features can be cut out to bring the price down;
- **Transmit and present a sales presentation file first** – to inform, educate and influence the prospect *before* presenting the price;
- **Seal the deal** – getting the go-ahead to provide the service if possible (thereby closing the sale).

Whether it's via a connective pricing email or a combined phone/email presentation, these alternatives to a standard pricing email work by putting the price into context and respectfully commanding that your proposal be given the consideration it deserves.

The Preliminary Meeting

For SSBs using post-op pricing, the sales process often involves a preliminary face-to-face consultation to discuss and assess the potential customer's needs. In trade services, for example, this consultation is the 'measuring' part of a free measure and quote. In my line of work (B2B services), I call it a ***discovery meeting***.

For many SSBs, a preliminary consultation is a vital part of the lead-to-sale cycle. For others, it can be overkill. Few of us give due consideration to the relevance, content or structure of our preliminary meetings but, with some focused attention, they can either be tweaked to be more effective or eradicated completely.

The Fast Track to a Shorter, Smoother Lead-to-Sale Cycle

A quick way to negate the need for preliminary meetings and other quoting rigmarole is to convert from post-op to preset pricing. With preset pricing, it's possible to merge the preliminary meeting and sales meeting into one single consultation. Not only does this reduce the number of face-to-face and phone interactions required to get a sale over the line, it dramatically reduces the amount of time spent travelling to meetings, costing projects and preparing quotes behind-the-scenes.

In my experience, the fastest route to a shorter, smoother lead-to-sale cycle was the adoption of *business level niching* with *preset packages*. Preset pricing without niching didn't work for me, but every industry and every business is different. For some SSBs, preset pricing will work without niching and for others, it won't be feasible or desirable at all, in which case preliminary meetings could still be an integral part of the process.

Preliminary Meetings for Low-Risk Services

For low-risk services such as carpet cleaning or lawn mowing, it can be tempting to offer a free measure and quote to encourage leads, but doing so has a downside. Scheduling, travelling to and attending preliminary consultations chews into profits. If these extra sales costs are built into the price of our services, that's okay – but only if we're happy to accept the added pressure and responsibility of positioning ourselves as a premium provider. If not, providing preliminary consultations to every prospect is dangerous territory and best avoided.

Instead of face-to-face preliminary meetings, it's worthwhile considering alternative ways to determine and present prices. In the case of a carpet cleaner or lawn mower, an incentive such as a discount or bonus service could be offered for prospects to provide accurate measurements, allowing quotes to be prepared site unseen. Alternatively, quotes could be calculated and presented differently – as a variable estimate or a price dependent on certain criteria, instead of a fixed price. With a bit of out-of-the-box thinking, the traditional, costly measure and quote can be replaced by a couple of phone conversations and a same-day 'quick quote', sent as a connective pricing email. When we strike the right combination of lead-to-sale interactions it can change the game; saving time, money and a whole lot of messing about.

Preliminary Meetings for High-Risk Services

For high-risk services with post-op pricing, one or more preliminary, face-to-face consultations are usually required to scope the requirements of a project before formulating a detailed proposal – particularly for custom design and construction projects. Without a thorough assessment of the foundations and constraints we'll be working with, and a clear understanding of the needs and preferences of the client, it's near impossible to provide an accurate indication of price.

The preliminary meeting is crucial to the sale of customised, high-risk services for another, equally important reason – it plays a vital role in converting prospects into paying customers. A preliminary meeting gives a prospect a clear idea of whether or not they're prepared to trust us with their project. If they're not, it won't matter what our service offering is, they'll deem it unacceptable and won't proceed to the next step.

Winning the prospect's trust is not hard but it does take some conscious consideration. The preliminary meeting can be thought of as an expanded, face-to-face version of the first phone call. It requires an awareness of, and genuine interest in, the prospect's needs, including their underlying need for connectivity. To maximise our chances of meeting these needs, we need to plan our approach.

Planning the Preliminary Meeting

A preliminary meeting has exactly the same structure as the first phone call (introduce, appreciate and validate, etc). The difference is, it needs to facilitate a deeper level of enquiry through more in-depth questioning and/or a physical assessment (taking measurements, making observations, etc). As with the first phone call, it pays to have a pre-prepared list of questions, a clipboard and pen at the ready. A generic form, completed by us during the consultation, is an invaluable addition to a preliminary meeting to guide the conversation and keep both parties on track, while ensuring all necessary data is collected.

The Sales Meeting

The most pivotal of all steps in the lead-to-sale cycle is the *sales meeting* (or *sales call*). For the purposes of SSB sales, a sales meeting is the phone or face-to-face discussion in which price is verbally communicated. Whether it's a two-minute phone call in which a hairdresser relays the price of a cut-and-colour, or a two-hour consultation in which a builder presents an intricate proposal for a whole-home renovation, the sales meeting is the main chance to secure a sale. It's the heart of the sales process and, as such, needs to be taken seriously.

For lower risk services, the term 'sales meeting' or 'sales call' may sound too cheesy or official but it's beneficial to use the proper term, and only necessary behind closed doors.[32] Calling it a sales meeting or sales call ensures that this important discussion is given the consideration it deserves and that we make the most of every opportunity to make a sale.

For the providers of higher risk services, the sales meeting step of the process becomes much easier and more effective with the help of a sales kit – the focus of the next chapter.

In the meantime, the most important thing for high-risk service providers to note about sales meetings is that nothing beats meeting in person. While the capabilities of online conferencing platforms are excellent, being face-to-face in a shared environment is always preferable. Face-to-face is more conducive to creating a strong emotional connection as we behave more naturally and are more attentive to the other person's needs and cues. It allows us to read their body language (uninhibited by technology), offer or accept refreshments and enjoy some casual banter before and after the meeting; seemingly small social nuances that can play a big role in building a relationship.

If distance renders face-to-face meetings impossible, online video conferencing is the logical alternative. Video conferencing technologies such as Zoom, Google Meet and Microsoft Teams Meetings have come a long way. Businesses rely on them everyday to facilitate global communications – particularly since the COVID-19 pandemic. However, using them to facilitate sales communications comes with a word of warning – be sure that your sales prospect is comfortable with your software of choice and that they won't be suffering the inconvenience or anxiety of trialling a foreign system just to accommodate one sales meeting.

I learned this lesson the hard way. With a growing number of interstate clients back in 2013, I started to insist on video-based sales meetings in an effort to move with the times. The result? We lost leads in droves. Prospects would avoid committing to a time for the meeting, become difficult to contact and eventually drop off the radar. As soon as I realised what was happening, I changed tactics – opting for phone/email meetings (transmitting a sales presentation in PDF format via email at the start of the phone call, then guiding the prospect through each page in real time). For my time-strapped, often tech-averse target market, this simpler approach was infinitely more effective.

This experience taught me that for SSBs, it's necessary to take a 'gently gently' approach to new communication technologies. Human connection and relationships are far too important to us to force the adoption of an innovative communication method – particularly at the pivotal sales meeting step of the lead-to-sale cycle.

Following Up

The goal or 'plan A' of a sales meeting – and all communications thereafter – is to get the go-ahead to proceed with a service transaction. But that's not always practical. Sometimes the prospect just isn't ready to commit and continuing to push for the sale beyond a certain point can do more harm than good. Before reaching that point, it's time to switch to 'plan B' – setting the date and time for the next face-to-face or phone communication. For example, 'How about I call you at 2pm on Thursday?'

This small commitment serves as a bridge between one communication and the next, helping to prevent the lead from falling in the water.

If you make contact at the agreed time and the prospect still isn't ready to commit, it doesn't necessarily mean you've lost the sale. It means fears, concerns or other objections are standing in the way of a 'yes'. Ask questions and read between the lines until you identify and overcome the sticking points. Never assume the price is too high or that the prospect can't afford what you're selling. Unless they tell you otherwise (and even if they do), they may simply need extra reassurance in order to proceed. Supplying the phone numbers of a few happy clients (with their permission) can be all it takes – equipping the prospect to verify you independently.

Until a firm answer is received, don't give up. That means not leaving the ball in the prospect's court. At the end of every phone or face-to-face meeting, schedule the date and time for the next communication. Continue contacting them as scheduled – using each communication as an opportunity to identify and overcome objections and reiterate/add value (as explained in the next chapter) – until a definitive 'yes' or 'no' is received. Tenacity is a powerful tool. As stated earlier, it traditionally takes between 6 and 12 communications to build the trust required to make a sale, so those with the tenacity to follow up make more sales than those who don't. That said, with the right business model, you don't have to force sales. Follow up? Absolutely. Flog a dead horse? Never.

If the final answer is 'no' – because they've decided to proceed with another service provider, for example – don't burn any bridges. Be polite, thank the prospect for the opportunity to be considered and genuinely wish them luck with their project. Leave the door open for them to come back if need be, for example 'If you have any concerns or need a second opinion, I'm always here'. Secondly, be sure to keep their contact details on file. A couple of informative emails over the coming months may be all that's needed to turn that 'no' into a resounding 'yes', should their current plans fall through. Customer relationship management (CRM) software can make this – and the whole lead-to-sale cycle – a lot easier to manage; prompting us when it's time to perform follow-up tasks and even performing certain tasks (such as the transmission of emails) on autopilot.

Following Through

When a prospect agrees to buy from us, the time comes to follow through on our marketing and sales promises. This means engaging in a *service transaction* – delivering the required service in exchange for money.

Figure 30: The service transaction – A basic exchange

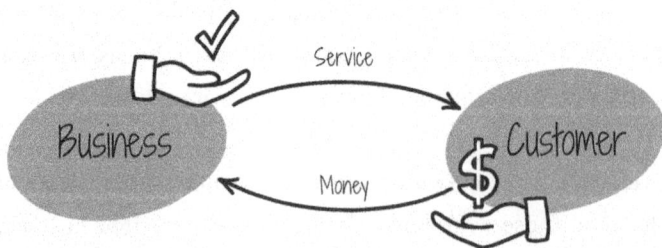

For many of us, the service transaction is the easy part – or so we think. The delivery of our service is the core of our expertise after all, and who doesn't like receiving money? Unfortunately however, good intentions are not enough to ensure service transactions run smoothly. The service transaction is where any managerial inadequacies or incongruences between our pre-sale promises and physical capabilities come to light. It's when our business' true colours are revealed. This entire book is geared to help those colours shine as brightly as possible but there are a few extra things we can do to help the course of business run smooth:

1. **Act with integrity** – Making a sale is a two-way commitment that's not to be taken lightly. Never enter into a service transaction if the business is not equipped or available to deliver on it (e.g. don't accept payment for a gift voucher if the business is soon to close down).

2. **Get covered** – Ensure the business has suitable insurance as well as a good quality, legally-binding contract of sale. For low-risk providers, this can be as simple as a 'terms and conditions' document, which stipulates the obligations of both parties.

3. **Run a tight ship** – Make the service delivery process as simple and streamlined as possible. Document the process (in the form of a flowchart or step-by-step checklist) and seek to eliminate or automate excess steps.

4. **Make paying painless** – Provide convenient payment options so there are no barriers to getting paid. Avoid forcing customers to pay 'cash only' (no matter how small the transaction may be), as it can deter them from proceeding or returning.

Post-Service Communication

Once the service transaction step of the lead-to-sale cycle is over, it doesn't mean our relationship with, or responsibilities to, the customer are over. For high-risk services, contact should be initiated by phone at one or more predetermined intervals after the service has been completed (three days then three weeks and three months after the completion of a kitchen renovation project, for example) to check how things are going and uncover and resolve outstanding issues.

Post-service communication is not as practical for low-risk services with high customer turnover but that doesn't mean it should be disregarded. There is much to be gained from checking in with selected customers (be it first-time customers, corporate customers, potential 'big spenders' or other VIPs) via a quick phone call, a day or so after delivery of the service.

For any SSB, post-service communication can be extremely powerful – demonstrating that we value our customers and aren't just 'in it for the money'. It also:

- Ends the customer experience on a high note, leaving the customer with residual feelings of connectivity and satisfaction;
- Boosts the chances they'll use our services again;
- Boosts the chances they'll recommend our business to others via word of mouth and online reviews;
- Enables us to identify opportunities for improvement;
- Provides the chance to leverage the transaction for future marketing endeavours by obtaining feedback for a testimonial or case study (with customer consent).

The sum of these effects can have a profound impact on the viability, growth and success of a business – all from making a couple of extra phone calls.

If the thought of contacting customers post-service invokes a sense of dread, there's a problem. It's an indication that deep down, you're not satisfied with the service you are delivering and that improvement is needed – likely at a business model level – to ensure your personal integrity aligns with the calibre of service the business provides.

Measuring Sales Success

When a lead-to-sale strategy is implemented, the difference can be profound. For some, seeing and feeling the improvement is enough. But for those who appreciate facts, figures and black and white proof, it's easy to calculate the effectiveness of the change. All you need to do is calculate your *sales conversion rate* for the month or quarter before the new approach and compare it to that of the month or quarter after, as shown below:

SALES CONVERSION RATE BEFORE LEAD-TO-SALE STRATEGY

$$\frac{\text{Total \# of sales in the period before the change}}{\text{Total \# of leads in the period before the change}} \times 100$$

e.g. 8/20 x 100 = 40% conversion rate

SALES CONVERSION RATE AFTER LEAD-TO-SALE STRATEGY

$$\frac{\text{Total \# of sales in the period after the change}}{\text{Total \# of leads in the period after the change}} \times 100$$

e.g. 13/20 x 100 = 65% conversion rate (a 62.5% increase)

It's useful not only to compare your before and after sales conversion rates, but to compare them with the average conversion rate for your industry, if available. To attain this and other figures for comparison, start by searching online for 'small business benchmarks'. Failing that, an accountant or applicable industry association may be able to help.

Making the most of fresh leads does not happen by accident. It takes an open mind and a degree of humility to admit we've been letting ourselves, our business and our potential customers down by failing to respond to leads in a systematic way. It then takes drive and determination to go from winging the steps in our sales process to bringing a sense of structure to it – particularly for the providers of high-risk services, as explained in the next chapter. But it's unequivocally worth the effort. Not only does overhauling our lead-to-sale strategy increase sales conversions and facilitate business growth, it demonstrates (in a universal sense) that we value and appreciate leads, which tends to attract more by default. The compounded impact of this energetic shift makes a lead-to-sale overhaul one of the most rewarding marketing projects we can undertake.

CHAPTER 18

SUPERCHARGE YOUR SALES MEETINGS

*** WARNING! DETAIL AHEAD ***

This chapter contains detailed instructions that
may be overwhelming at first. If you get bogged
down in it, switch to skim reading and return
to each section as it becomes applicable.

As the heart of the sales process, the sales meeting is critical. When we avoid sales meetings or get them wrong, we're dismissed on the basis of price; having failed to create a strong enough human connection or perception of value. When we embrace them and get them right, not only can sales skyrocket, but the dreaded sales meeting can become infinitely more enjoyable... even exciting.

Getting sales meetings right takes some initiative. For low-risk services, this can be as simple as pinning a 'customer enquiry procedure' up near the phone to navigate first phone calls – ensuring important questions are asked and prospects are steered towards making bookings.

For other SSBs, sales meetings need more preparation. When selling high-risk services, prospects tend to require more convincing to overcome the perceived risk of proceeding. While it's possible to do this through verbal persuasion alone, it's a tough gig. In the modern era of consumer scepticism, fancy words and slick sales tactics no longer cut it. Prospects need physical proof of our professionalism and capacity to deliver. Meeting this need requires preparation in two parts: 1) preparing a *sales kit*, and 2) preparing for *individual sales meetings*.

Preparing a Sales Kit

A sales kit is a suite of sales tools that helps us make the most of sales opportunities. Searching for 'sales tools' online generates a landslide of information about sales apps and programs, but these are *not* the sales tools to be concerned about at this point. What SSBs benefit from the most are simpler, more tangible tools; ones that provide a visual point of reference in sales meetings. Good sales tools draw the eye, guide the conversation, demonstrate professionalism and boost the power of the spoken word to maximise engagement with prospects. They can include brochures, menus, function packages, price lists, material samples, colour charts, forms and contracts, business cards, promotional items and – most importantly for many SSBs – a sales presentation folder or file. A well-prepared sales kit, with a carefully considered sales presentation folder, is one of the most powerful marketing tools in the Secret Service arsenal – second only to a Lead Machine.

The Sales Presentation

A sales presentation is the part of a sales meeting geared to induce a sale. It's 'a *planned process*, made up of a series of steps that *build one upon another*' – explained best as 'the *commencement of a relationship*, sealed by a sale'.[33] A sales presentation folder or file is so powerful because it guides and supports this process, paving the way for sales meetings that are quicker, clearer and substantially more persuasive than those without.

A sales presentation folder (or 'file' if designed to display on screen) is essential to the sale of high-risk services and beneficial to the sale of many low-risk services. Often, creating and implementing one is all it takes to catapult sales conversions to record levels. It does this by taking a proactive, 'front foot' approach to sales opportunities: answering questions before they're asked, overcoming objections before they arise and providing visual and social proof that our business can be trusted to deliver a service – all the while making us look highly organised and professional in comparison to other providers vying for the job.

Folder or file?

A printed presentation in a smart, leather folder (available off-the-shelf from an office supply store) is ideal for small, face-to-face sales meetings, while an on-screen presentation (a digital file presented via PowerPoint, Google Slides, Keynote or a simple PDF) is more practical for group or remote meetings. A sales folder is preferable for small meetings, not only because it's less susceptible to user error or technical glitches, but because it's more tactile and versatile. It provides a visual aid to touch, point at and peruse, which grounds a service offering (and its provider) in reality. It also makes it easy to mould sales presentations around the needs of individual prospects or embrace the flow of a conversation by flicking back and forth between pages and ignoring sections that aren't applicable.

No matter its format, a sales folder or file doesn't just make the sales presentation more strategic and engaging, it makes the entire sales meeting easier and, dare I say it... fun. A well-planned sales folder or file directs the content and structure of sales meetings; freeing us up mentally and emotionally to focus on building a human connection with the prospect. It also allows us to take charge of the discussion without appearing too pushy or self-concerned.

Like a Lead Machine, a good sales folder or file takes a bit of work to create but once it's done it only requires occasional updates.

The content of a sales folder

An engaging sales presentation folder or file may include the following:

- **Title page** – Featuring the business' logo, subline and slogan.
- **Mission statement** – A brief statement about who you serve and how (as in Chapter 11). This is best presented as a pull-quote, alongside a feel-the-love photo.
- **Media articles/clippings/mentions about you or your business** – to leverage any direct media attention.
- **Media or research articles about the problems or challenges faced by your target market, or the shortcomings of your industry** – to use as a segue into the solutions you provide.

- **Educational tidbits** – In most fields of service, there are things prospective customers need to know to 'compare apples with apples' or, in other words, to compare the service offerings of various providers on more than price alone. These are usually simple things that seem like mute points when you've been in a field of service for years, but come as revelations to those new to the market.

  In web design, for example, an educational tidbit is that a great SSB website is not determined by how unique or artistic it is, but by how many leads it generates. Snippets of general content like this are incredibly powerful as they can change the way a prospect weighs up their options.

  Educational tidbits may require one page of your folder or several, depending on the number of points you need to make – bearing in mind that one concise point per page has far more impact than a long-winded paragraph.

- **Value proposition** – As explained in Chapter 8, a value proposition (VP) spells out how you provide value to your customers. While a shortened teaser or 'canapé' VP is ideal for marketing communications and initial conversations, the sales presentation is the time to roll out your extended or 'banquet' VP, backed by facts, figures, models and examples to substantiate your canapé claim.

  Presenting a mix of monetary and emotive incentives (where possible) creates the most persuasive VP. It builds both financial and emotional value in the prospect's mind, leaving no stone unturned. If the prospect is highly logical, they'll respond to financial intelligence and if they're highly emotional (motivated by a desire for pleasure or a means to escape pain), they'll respond to emotional intelligence. Most prospects fall somewhere between these two extremes, which is why a hybrid or double whammy VP works so well; covering both bases and amplifying the perception of value.

- **Price** – The best time to reveal the price of your services is immediately after the VP, when perceived value is at its highest. Ideally, the presented value should be high enough that the price looks reasonable, or even generous, in comparison.

  In a sit-down sales meeting, the price usually takes one of two forms:

  a. A selection of preset packages (outlined clearly in the sales folder), or

  b. A custom quote (prepared as a one-off, separate document).

  Either way, it's best to present the proposed offering as a list of individual components with a sum total underneath, rather than a single, all-inclusive amount. Listing each component separately conveys higher value for money. It also creates room in the presentation to emphasise the importance of each component, the quality of the materials involved, etc – helping to substantiate the price.

- **Portfolio** – If the end product or outcome of your service is visual in nature, the inclusion of photographs or pictorial evidence is a must. This visual portfolio can span several pages of the sales folder or, depending how many examples you have to display, may require a separate, dedicated folder.

Not every image needs to be shown to every sales prospect. Fanning through an extensive portfolio to locate particular images can be more powerful than lingering on every page. Select the images most relevant to the prospect's situation or requirements and focus on those.

Photographs should be captured, edited and laid out as professionally as possible, in high resolution and full colour. With a reasonable camera and a little practice, portfolio shots can be snapped yourself. DIY 'before and after' shots can be an excellent tool for SSBs specialising in any form of rejuvenation or enhancement, such as building renovations or pre-sale property styling. That said, hiring a professional to photograph the occasional significant project is an excellent investment. This is explored further in *The Secret Service Website Formula*, along with DIY photography tips.

If your service is not particularly visual (e.g. accounting or finance brokerage), it pays to consider other ways to create a portfolio, such as photos of satisfied customers or the logos of business clients (with their permission). Any pictorial evidence of past projects adds visual interest, demonstrates aptitude and experience and provides a valuable talking point. Above all else, it delivers tangible social proof – evidence that others trust you with their needs and money, so your sales prospects can too.

- **Testimonials** – Written testimonials from happy customers make all the difference to a sales presentation, particularly when incorporated into the visual portfolio

– each one featured as a pull-quote alongside a photo of the applicable job or project.

There are many things you can do to maximise the power of testimonials as social proof in your presentation.

1. Opt for quality over quantity – four or five authentic, glowing testimonials is ideal;

2. Feature one testimonial per page, in an easy-to-read font, size 16–18;

3. Use quotation marks (' ' or " ") around each testimonial so it's obviously a direct quote;

4. Humanise and legitimise the testimonial by including the customer's name, position title/business name (if applicable), suburb/state, the month/year the service was delivered and if applicable, a brief summary of the project (all with the customer's permission). For even greater impact, include a photo of the person being quoted.

5. Highlight poignant words and phrases with bold text or colour (much to the horror of your graphic designer). This draws attention to key points while creating visual interest, making the words easier to absorb.

6. Don't read all testimonials to the prospect out loud. Instead, focus on one or two that are most closely related to their needs or situation – honing in on words and phrases that have the greatest impact.

For more information about testimonials – including the questions to ask of customers to cultivate excellent ones – refer to Chapter 10 of *The Secret Service Website Formula*.

- **'What to expect' process chart** – An effective way to conclude a sales presentation is a chart or diagram outlining the service process from 'kick-off' to 'completion'. For Cyberstart, this took the form of a colourful table, simplified down to four steps (Plan, Prepare, Produce and Go Live). Each step had a small list of dot-points, outlining what would happen and in what order, should the prospect choose to proceed.

A process chart benefits both the prospect and salesperson. For the prospect, it prompts the visualisation of steps involved, while instilling a sense of confidence and certainty in the service provider's approach. This reduces the perceived risk of the service and makes the whole proposition seem less daunting. Meanwhile, for the salesperson, it provides a handy segue to the all-important but often neglected *close*.

In a sales meeting, closing a sale means getting the prospect to agree to proceed with a purchase. A successful close doesn't happen by accident. Sometimes, the prospect will take the lead by saying, 'Great, so where to from here?' or 'Where do I sign?' but, more often than not, the salesperson has to initiate a close by tactfully (and sometimes repeatedly) asking for the sale. This can range from a gentle, 'So, how would you feel about moving forward?' (known as a 'trial close' – used to ascertain and address any remaining objections) to a more assuming, 'So, let's get the ball rolling, shall we?'

With a process chart at the end of the presentation, these closing questions roll off the tongue quite naturally, when they could otherwise sound awkward or pushy. Upon presenting the chart, a void opens up between the present moment and the first step of the process;

a void that can only be bridged by the prospect's decision to proceed. This void prompts a dialogue about the elephant in the room – the prospect's willingness to buy. Many of us avoid this pivotal conversation out of fear or embarrassment but, with a 'what to expect' process chart at the end of your sales folder, it happens organically – allowing you to embrace the close with unwavering confidence.

The single most important thing to remember when preparing a sales folder is to go light on text and heavy on imagery. As with slides in a PowerPoint presentation, the words in a sales folder should serve as a prompting mechanism only, not a script to read out loud. Humans are visual creatures – processing and reacting to visual data much quicker and easier than written words. Images, charts, diagrams and sensory experiences such as fabric samples or taste tests (if applicable) are infinitely more engaging and effective than long sentences and blocks of text. They take sales meetings to a whole other level.

Preparing for a Sales Meeting

Once the sales kit is ready, it's not enough to roll a generic sales presentation out at every sales meeting. That may inform and educate the prospect but it won't meet their connective needs. To do this, we need to show we care about them as an individual – customising the presentation to demonstrate our understanding of their specific situation. This customisation means preparation; allowing a window of time before each sales meeting to personalise it.

Pre-meeting prep-work boils down to five tasks:

1. **Reviewing for relevance** – Looking through the sales presentation folder with the customer in mind to determine what pages will be relevant to them: which photos and testimonials to emphasise, which ones to skip, what package to recommend, etc.

2. **Restocking** – Checking there are ample supplies of supporting tools in the sales kit, such as brochures, business cards and service agreements.

3. **Quoting (if applicable)** – Costing the project (if using post-op pricing), then preparing and printing a quote or proposal.

4. **Report running (if applicable)** – Preparing a personalised report that highlights facts or figures specific to the prospect's current situation.

5. **Pointy end prepping** – We'll look at this shortly.

A little pre-meeting prep-work makes a big difference to the energy and outcome of a sales meeting. This work can take anywhere from two minutes to several hours or days, depending on the pricing method at play, the value of the project and the availability of customer or market intelligence to produce a personalised report.

The Power of a Personalised Report

Real estate agents arrive at each sales meeting (aka 'property valuation') armed with a report, specific to the property in question, for a reason: it dramatically boosts the odds of winning the listing.

For providers of high-risk necessities, presenting specific, factual information about a prospect's current situation in the form of a report vastly increases the likelihood of a sale. When shared at the start of a sales presentation, a personalised report tends to change the dynamic of a sales meeting from a one-way pitch to a two-way consultation. It provides an unsolicited jolt of value by implying that:

- You know your stuff;
- You're an expert in your field;
- You've done your homework;
- You're generous with your time and knowledge;
- You have your prospect's best interests at heart;
- You are an ally – it's safe for them to let their guard down and be honest about their circumstances, fears and concerns; and
- They need to act quickly to improve their (now undeniable) situation.

For these reasons and more, presenting a personalised report is the most powerful way to customise a sales meeting. But there's a catch... prospect-specific facts and figures are the foundation for a personalised report, and they can be hard to come by. If there's no market data pertaining to a prospect's current situation, there's no basis for a report. Sometimes, though, there's more data available than you think.

Sources for finding prospect-specific information include:

- **Industry databases and records** (often requiring special access or a paid subscription)
- **Online assessment tools and calculators**
- **The prospect's own website or web presence**
- **Search engine results**
- **Business benchmark data** (often available through accountants or industry associations)

Property and web marketing services are two high-risk necessities that are well suited to using customised reports as a sales tool due to the accessibility of third party data. However, any business with access to useful intelligence or insights can craft it into a short, personalised report and reap the resounding benefits.

The Pointy End of a Sales Meeting

After the sales presentation comes a stage in the meeting that can be quite intimidating as it can take careful mediation. This is the point at which we endeavour to reach an agreement with the prospect. It can feel intimidating because, having just presented our offering, we are at our most vulnerable – all our cards are on the table and the outcome is entirely dependent on the prospect's willingness to make their feelings known... unless we have a couple of aces up our sleeve, through the 'pointy end prepping' mentioned earlier.

Preparing to Seal the Deal

To be prepared for the pointy end of a sales meeting, the first aspect to consider is the action we want the prospect to take to symbolically seal the deal. While a verbal agreement is fine for many services, a written agreement is preferable for others – particularly those with a high perceived risk.

Signing an agreement has a powerful psychological effect on a prospect, as it literally *signifies* their decision to proceed. However, to avoid putting them off, the document needs to be carefully structured – short enough to be read on the spot (so it doesn't provide an excuse to leave without committing) and long enough to cover all applicable legal bases. The best way to get around this dilemma (subject to the independent advice of a lawyer) is to use two separate but interrelated documents: 1) a short sales agreement on which the signature is collected, and 2) an appendix terms and conditions document that the prospect can take and read during a prescribed 'cooling off' period of approximately three business days.

Preparing to Overcome Objections

While some prospects will be eager to sign on the dotted line, most will have questions and concerns (objections) preventing them from moving forward. How well we respond to these can make or break our sales goals.

Addressing objections is where the 'risk listing' task from Recovery Mission 3 comes into play. An analysis of the risks that may be associated with your goods or services prepares you to answer questions and address concerns, so you're ready to respond when they arise in sales meetings. Performed thoroughly, and reviewed periodically, it equips you to meet prospects' objections with a potent blend of empathy and logic – backed by a deep understanding of the fears and insecurities that drive them.

When price is the sticking point, and no amount of empathy or logic can overcome the objection, a change of tact can be necessary. It's crucial to note that concerns around price rarely stem from the prospect being short of funds. Rather, they stem from us failing to provide or communicate sufficient value to justify the price we're asking. Until the prospect's perception of the value of an offering exceeds the presented price, there will be no sale.

To navigate this situation, one of four courses of action can be taken:

1. **Add value without adding to your workload** – Boosting perceived value can sometimes be as simple as reiterating your VP more clearly, providing a strong guarantee or simply taking the time to build trust over coming weeks and months through 'random acts of value', patience and persistence.

2. **Negotiate on price** – The decision to reduce the price of your services to land a sale is not one to take lightly, nor one to make in the heat of the moment. A 10% discount may not sound like much but if your profit margin is 20%, that's the equivalent of a 50/50 profit share arrangement with the customer; the generosity of which they will never appreciate.

   Negotiating on price is a dangerous habit for SSB owners to get into. Regular price reductions temporarily advantage the customer (providing a financial saving and a perceived 'win') but they permanently disadvantage the business. Not only do discounts eat into the all-important profit margin, they can undermine the value of our services, cheapen our brand, skew the balance of power in the customer/provider relationship, cause resentment towards the customer (leading to impeded performance and results) and muddy the waters for future transactions by setting a precedent for discounting.

   That said, the occasional, carefully considered price negotiation can be a good move, *if* the proposed transaction stands to provide a juicy benefit to the business, over and above cash flow. If the transaction is going to provide valuable experience, exposure, or a foot in the door of a desirable niche, for example, a price reduction can be a wise business move.

If prepared to negotiate on price, undesirable side effects can be reduced by:

- **Setting a baseline** – Be sure to crunch the numbers ahead of time to determine the lowest price point at which a project will be financially feasible.

- **Explaining your decision** – Always give a reason for offering a discount, such as 'I've been looking to work with a company in your industry, of your size and ethos, for quite some time, so I'm prepared to offer you a heavily reduced price, as a one time only opportunity...' Expressing a strong reason for reducing your price can prevent you coming across as a pushover and giving too much power to the prospect.

- **Asking something in return** – Put a caveat or condition on the price reduction, such as the prospect agreeing to participate in a case study, be photographed or provide a testimonial. This makes the negotiation a trade of benefits in itself and boosts the chances of the discounted transaction working out well for both parties.

- **Reporting discounts as expenses** – Every discount should be recorded as an expense for accounting purposes. This enables the financial impact of your discounting decisions to be monitored, ensuring it doesn't get out of hand.

3. **Negotiate on inclusions** – The preferable alternative to negotiating on price is negotiating on inclusions; adding,

removing, upgrading or downgrading components of the offering to reach an agreement that both parties feel is fair.

If a prospect is lingering on the brink of proceeding – with no major objections but lacking the desire to commit – sweetening the deal with an extra inclusion can work wonders. This means offering a pre-determined bonus or incentive such as an extra service or complimentary upgrade to a better quality material – something you know is quick, easy and cost effective to deliver but provides a distinct benefit with high perceived value. This unexpected, last-minute injection of value can be all it takes to get a sale over the line; reaping the same (or greater) psychological benefit as price negotiation, without the undesirable side effects.

If the prospect still insists the price is beyond their means, scale the offering back; removing or downgrading certain inclusions (services, components or materials) and reducing the price accordingly. Scaling back the offer is a way to negotiate without taking a hit to your profit margins or power base. You may end up with a smaller project than anticipated but – depending on your business model – a smaller, profitable sale is better than a large, heavily discounted one, or no sale at all.

If negotiating on inclusions is not enough to seal the deal on the spot, the meeting can be drawn to an end by putting a time limit on the offer (such as seven days) and scheduling the date and time for a phone or face-to-face follow-up. Giving the offer an expiry date reinforces its legitimacy, sparks a fear of missing out and forces a decision within a reasonable timeframe, while the value proposition is still fresh in their mind.

4. **Walk away** – The final course of action is to stick to your guns on the stipulated price – to the extent that you're prepared to walk away. This can be more powerful than negotiating, especially when dealing with experienced hagglers who are used to pushing salespeople to their limits. Being prepared to walk away without a sale demonstrates confidence in the value of your services. It's a powerful stance, devoid of desperation, which can motivate a bargain-hungry prospect to bite the bullet and pay full price.

To engage in any form of negotiation at the pointy end of a sales meeting, preparation is a must. We need to know what we're prepared to compromise on, and to what extent, to avoid shooting ourselves in the foot. This means crunching the 'negotiation numbers' ahead of time; determining exactly what we can use or propose to sweeten or scale back a deal and how these adjustments will impact our bottom line, so there are no nasty surprises in our financial reports.

The Social Etiquette of a Sales Meeting

While a sales kit and pre-meeting preparation can supercharge sales performance, a lack of social etiquette can flatline it. The neglect of common courtesies and seemingly trivial niceties are social red flags that can stifle connectivity and undermine any amount of sales preparation. The more red flags we spark, the more trust we need to build and value we need to demonstrate during the meeting to stand a chance of making up for it.

Simple things you can do to be socially savvy in sales meetings, are:

- **Start on time** – Arriving late to a sales meeting is like starting a race on the wrong foot. It can negatively impact the rhythm, feel and flow of the meeting, not to mention the prospect's perception (due to the halo effect of a first impression, presented earlier). This can determine the outcome of the race before it's even run.

- **Keep them posted** – If plans change or you're running late (even 5 minutes), phone the prospect as soon as possible before the scheduled start time. Explain, apologise and confirm that it's okay to start the meeting slightly later than arranged. Not only is this courteous, it satisfies the human need to know, which can turn a red flag into a green one.

- **Look the part** – Be well-groomed and dressed appropriately for your line of work.

- **Play the part** – Activating your performance persona is crucial for any interaction with a prospective customer but particularly for a sales meeting. Strive to be in top form... warm and natural, with the prospect's needs and situation top of mind. With sufficient pre-meeting prep work and a pre-performance routine – such as putting on a particular jacket and playing a favourite song on repeat – this will happen organically.

- **Make them comfortable** – Be observant and considerate of any physical needs the prospect may have: offering to hang up a wet coat or umbrella, pointing out where the toilets are, removing dirty boots before entering their home or putting your dirty coffee cup in the sink before you leave, for example.

- **Offer/accept refreshments** – If meeting at your premises or on mutual ground (such as a café), always offer to make or buy the prospect a drink. If in *their* home or workplace and they offer refreshments, graciously accept. Be aware that they may be offering refreshments not only out of social courtesy, but to create a comfortable transition into the meeting. They could be feeling slightly nervous, not knowing what to expect, and having an activity to focus on (preparing their guest a drink) can help set the stage for a relaxed, friendly interaction. Many trade service workers (builders, for example) decline refreshments to their own detriment. Turning down a drink sets a tone of rejection ('no'), instead of acceptance ('yes'). It also passes up a valuable opportunity to create a personal connection before getting into the nitty gritty of the meeting.

- **Put the prospect first** – Never get so caught up in a sales pitch that you forget it's about *them*, not *you*. Listen attentively and watch their body language to pick up on any objections or commitment cues. Ask questions to get their input and feedback, like 'Is this what you had in mind?' or 'What do you think of that one?' to ensure the meeting is a two-way dialogue, not a one-way pitch.

- **Don't be a victim** – No matter how bad your day, week or year has been, or how much your competitor irritates you, suppress any urge to whinge, complain, blame or gossip. As the salesperson, it's your responsibility to set the tone for the meeting. Negativity depletes connectivity, making the prospect less likely to place their trust in you.

If you ever doubt your sales skills or compare yourself to those renowned for their ability to 'sell ice to eskimos'... don't. Few SSB owners are born with sales prowess pumping through their veins. Selling is a learned skill that, like any other, requires good technique, resources and practice to master. Where many of us go wrong is practising without good technique (a clear lead-to-sale strategy) or resources (sales kit). We beat ourselves up, assuming a lack of charisma or intelligence is to blame, when we're actually missing two pieces of a three-piece puzzle.

So rest assured, you don't need the God-given ability to sell ice to eskimos. Just preparation, positivity and practice.

RECOVERY MISSION 5

Chapter 16 - The Modern Marketing Arsenal

- **Open to the options** – Start considering the marketing activities that could be a good fit for your business. There's no need to make decisions yet – just get your head in the game.
- **Acquire a full copy** – Add *The Modern Marketing Arsenal* (the third book in the *Secret Service Business Series*) to your reading list.
- **Reserve your resources** – Put a savings plan in place so, when the time comes, you're ready to invest in some decent marketing tools.

Chapter 17 - Make the Most of Fresh Leads

- **Recall your approach** – Draw a rough flowchart of your current sales process.
- **Enter the matrix** – Use the Lead-to-Sale Strategy Selection Matrix on page 308 to determine the strategy/ flowchart of most relevance to your business.
- **Stack up the systems** – Compare your hand-drawn process chart with the suggested lead-to-sale strategy chart, identifying any shortfalls or opportunities for improvement.
- **Action stations** – Write a list of actions required to transform your sales process into an effective lead-to-sale strategy, e.g. '1) Write a list of questions to ask a prospective customer in the first phone call, 2) Prepare a discovery questionnaire for preliminary meetings, 3) Write canned email responses for situations A, B and C'.

- **Know your hit rate** – Using the formula on page 331, calculate your current sales conversion rate.

Chapter 18 – Supercharge Your Sales Meetings

- **Prepare your props** – Determine the suite of tools required to support the sales meeting phase of your lead-to-sale strategy. This could be as little as a procedural poster or customer enquiry form, through to a comprehensive sales kit with a contract of sale and appendix terms and conditions document.
- **Find the folder** – If you have in-person sales meetings, purchase a smart, leather-look A4 folder from an office supply store.
- **Build a compelling case** – Start collecting/designing the content for your sales presentation folder or file:
  - Title page
  - Mission statement
  - Media/research articles or mentions
  - Educational tidbits
  - Value proposition
  - Price (a summary of preset packages or a placeholder page for the inclusion of a custom quote)
  - Portfolio (images)
  - Testimonials
  - 'What to expect' process chart
- **Plan to get personal** – Determine the elements of the sales presentation that need to be customised for each prospect and what information is available to produce a personalised report.

- **Roll out the red carpet** – Start preparing for individual sales meetings and using your sales tools. After each sales meeting, stop and reflect on its effectiveness and make improvements to the process or sales kit if required.
- **Re-run your hit rate** – After a period of time, calculate your new sales conversion rate as well as the percentage increase in sales conversions since putting the new tools and processes in place.

MISSION INCOMPLETE

If the responsibilities, rigours and rewards of SSB ownership had to be summed up in a single word, I'd have to call it a ***mission***. Defined as:

- 'an important goal or purpose accompanied by strong conviction'
- 'a challenging, long-term assignment'
- 'a strongly felt aim, ambition or calling'

I believe there are few words that encapsulate modern-day SSB ownership quite so succinctly.

Answering the Call

Only those who have experienced the burning desire to start an SSB or inspire a social movement can understand how it equates to a calling. Like an unquenchable thirst, it's a feeling that can only be satisfied by moving towards a vision for a future that's in some way better or brighter than the reality that exists today.

Not only is the desire to operate an SSB a calling, it's a *call to a life of service*. That might seem sacrilegious to those who associate this phrase with the religious devotion of priests, nuns and monks. But joining a holy order is not the only way to live a life of service. There are other ways, which (thankfully, in my opinion) do not require a vow of chastity, poverty or obedience.

A life of service is simply an attitude; one that prioritises integrity, humility, connectivity and joyful contribution to others. We can commit to a life of service at any time – no matter who we are, what skills we have and what we do for a living.

An SSB is merely a conduit for living a life of service in the mainstream, modern world, without relying on a middleman for remuneration. It's a self-orchestrated means to transform our skills and talents into the life-sustaining energy of money. How successfully we do this is determined by our attitude and our ability to recognise and respond to the needs of those we seek to serve. It requires us to adapt and evolve over time, constantly seeking to serve better and contribute more – trusting that we will be remunerated in accordance with the depth and breadth of our contribution.

Walking the Wire of Give & Take

Running an SSB requires sacrifice but it shouldn't feel like slavery or a relentless burden. Contrary to popular belief, living a life of service does *not* require us to give limitlessly of ourselves without expectation of return. Whether in business or any other area of life, constantly giving without receiving (undervaluing our time, skill and effort) is not sustainable. Neither is constantly receiving without giving back, nor gaining at the expense of others (underdelivering on promises or short-changing those we serve). Unless we strike a balance between giving and receiving, sooner or later, we'll face energetic and material consequences: discomfort, distress, disappointment, disassociation, disease and/or the inability to strike a viable balance between the demand and supply of our services – ultimately leading to business demise.

There are many philosophies developed by business, scientific and spiritual leaders that could be used to explain this phenomenon. Some might refer to a law of cause and effect, correspondence or reciprocity and some to a law of attraction, vibration or duality; others might refer more specifically to a law or science of service. The common thread running through these philosophies is that we are all energetically connected or, in other words, we are all 'one'. If we are one, we can deduce that in providing benefit to others we must benefit ourselves – and vice versa. If we don't actively seek to strike this balance, the consequences will kick in, our sense of connection to the universal 'oneness' will weaken and our capacity to realise our personal and business potential will be lost.

Defying Monetary Limits

For the provision of our skill or service to be viable as a business, the energy of each transaction must be positive and reciprocal. A vital component of this is money – society's designated medium of exchange; merely a quantifiable, measurable type of energy.

But there's more to the energy of a service transaction than money. What matters most is the *emotion* associated with the transaction – the perceptions and resultant feelings experienced before, during and after the exchange, by both the skill or service provider and customer. Ideally, the energy of the transaction should not only feel 'fair', it should spark feelings of gratitude and satisfaction on both sides, with a mutual sense of joy being the best possible outcome. The more we strive for and achieve this ideal, the more viable our business will become.

Consistently achieving positive energetic outcomes is only possible as a result of acting in the best interest of our customers. This means:

- Considering each prospect as a person with physical and emotional needs;
- Connecting with them from the get-go, through smart marketing, clearly defined sale and service processes and the activation of our performance persona;
- Continually improving ourselves and our business, working towards a business model that facilitates the greatest societal contribution.

When we're truly acting in the best interest of our customers, the price they pay for our service will pale in comparison to the sense of value they experience. Reaching this point does not happen automatically, or overnight. It only becomes possible when we start thinking beyond the customer's physical needs to their deeper, emotional needs – their aesthetic, knowledge and self-esteem needs and, above all else, their need for *connectivity*. Once we grasp the significance of our customers' emotional needs, and shift our attitude and approach accordingly, the energy of service transactions will surge by default.

Lifeforce Mission Critical

It's no secret that the era of information and technology we exist in has enhanced our ability to communicate, yet simultaneously stifled opportunities to connect in person. Once upon a time, satisfying our need for connectivity occurred organically while going about our day. We'd pay our bills at the local post office, withdraw funds at the bank and seek the assistance of a real life person to bridge a product, knowledge or skill gap. Interacting with our community was part and parcel of living. Now, with bills paid online, ATMs, self-serve checkouts and the ease with which we can access products, information and instructions online, many basic opportunities to interact and connect with others have become obsolete.

Although this may not sound like a big deal, loneliness has reached epidemic proportions. A recent study found that one in two adults (50.5%) feel lonely at least one day a week, while one in four (27.6%) feel lonely for three or more days per week.[34] This is reflective of a growing worldwide trend – an incredibly concerning one, due to its impact on human health and well-being. The influence of social isolation on health and wellbeing is 'comparable with well-established risk factors for mortality such as smoking and alcohol consumption and exceeds the influence of other risk factors such as physical inactivity and obesity'.[35] In other words, loneliness is deadly.

This stands to worsen in coming decades, as society is infil-trated by artificial intelligence (AI). Handy technologies such as Siri, Alexa and text generation phenomenon ChatGPT are merely the tip of the AI iceberg; an iceberg that – if left unchecked – could sink humanity, according to modern-day masterminds Professor Stephen Hawkings and Elon Musk. Hawkings predicted that, 'The development of full artificial intelligence could spell the end of the human race. [...] Humans, who are limited by slow biological evolution, couldn't compete and would be superseded'.[36] More recently, Elon Musk described AI as humanity's 'biggest existential threat' and likened its continual development (uninhibited by government regulation and close supervision) to 'summoning the demon'.[37]

If these globally respected thought leaders are correct, heeding the call to a life of service is more important now than ever before – not only to help preserve human connection, but to preserve humanity.

Together, we must rise up to meet the cold, corporate threats of AI, economies of scale and mass marketing; banding together to create an upsurge of human energy through conscious reconnection. Contributing to this movement is as easy as being of service to others more consciously and more often. Founding or refining an SSB is a means to take this 'recon' mission up a notch, creating a vehicle through which we can serve, inspire and impact the world in a way that's uniquely our own, while making a living commensurate with our contribution. And to be clear, getting paid for what we do does not undermine or offset this contribution – it funds it, making it plausible and sustainable.

For established SSBs, just activating our performance persona – consciously and consistently presenting our best, most service-centric self – is a powerful act of service with a considerable energetic impact. The more of us who do this, the more our impact will amplify. Given that SSBs comprise almost three quarters of the business population and counting, we have the capacity to incite a monumental energetic shift, to the benefit of all humanity.

As tempting as it was to call this final chapter 'Mission Complete', it would have been misleading. Living a life of service is a mission that's never complete. There's always an opportunity to serve others better or in a more impactful way. As long as we do the right thing for the right reason, are willing to listen, learn, adapt and evolve, serve as authentically and wholeheartedly as we can and trust that it will all pay off – then it will.

While an SSB owner's mission may not be as riveting as that of Indiana Jones or James Bond, it's a means to enormous real-life reward. Building a successful business on a foundation of authenticity and integrity can be a long, hard road but it's one of the fastest roads to self discovery, fulfilment and abundance. As Mahatma Gandhi said, 'The best way to find yourself is to lose yourself in the service of others.' Service is key to self-actualisation, so when the road of business gets dark and rocky, return to it. Acts of selfless service will light your way.

Big business can keep its robots, economies of scale and multi-million dollar marketing budgets. The life force of SSBs is infinitely more powerful. To wield our share of this collective power, all we need is mastery of our vocation, strong values, a few smart systems and strategies and an unwavering commitment to connectivity. With these, even if we don't change the world, we're sure to leave a legacy – shaking up the status quo, living a bountiful life of service and giving Indiana Jones a run for his money, as the hero of our own awe-inspiring action-adventure.

YOUR MICRO MISSION

Congratulations! You finished *Secret Service Marketing* – book one of three in the *Secret Service Business Series.*

To help the Secret Service approach gain momentum, there are a few things you can do:

1. **Share the love** – Post a short review of this book (complete with a photo or two) on your social media platform of choice, or wherever you bought it online. This is one of the best ways to help others discover the series for themselves.
2. **Lend, gift or recommend** the book to a struggling SSB owner, designer or content creator.
3. **Look local** – Ask your community bookshop or library to stock the Secret Service Business Series, if they don't already.
4. **Loop yourself in** – Join the Secret Service revolution by subscribing to occasional updates via *www.secretservice.biz* (scan the code and sign up now).

See you in book two (*The Secret Service Website Formula*) where you'll learn how to land a website that drives leads to your inbox and happier, high-paying customers to your door.

Laura de Lacy
Author & Secret Service Marketer

ACKNOWLEDGEMENTS

Producing the Secret Service Business Series was a mission made possible by many. A huge thank you to Isabelle Russell, Gianna Grbich and Tatsiana Teush for your dedication and expertise; David, Jessica and Keely at Green Hill Publishing for your patience and professionalism; Nett Hulse, Natasha Pintaric, Gianna, Michelle Ridland, Jason Lehman and Thomas Le Coz for your support and valued contributions over the years; the small business owners I've had the privilege to work with – each one instrumental in nutting out the Secret Service approach; Graham McGuiggan; Peter Daniels and Brett McFall for your trust and tutelage; Gordon Kay for proving that integrity and generosity **do** belong in business (when I was starting to doubt it); Brad, Corinne and Caro for your strength and inspiration, in life and from above; Billy for believing in me before I was ready to; Ellie and Evie for being our village; Lovell and Jacqui (my earth angels) for paying it forward; the de Lacy and Braithwaite clans – my family and best mates; And last but not least, William Devlin… 'I may have given you life, but you gave me mine'.

INDEX

ENDNOTES

1   Australian Small Business & Family Enterprise Ombudsman (2016), *Small Business Counts: Small Business in the Australian Economy*, p8

2   DIISRTE (2012), Australian Small Business Key Statistics & Analysis Report, p30

Percentage of total small businesses 'Services' category (83.9%) less Retail Trade (6.5%) and Wholesale Trade (3.6%) = 73.8%

3   Based on Australia's population of approximately 25 million people.

4   House of Representatives Standing Committee EFPA (2007), Services Export Report – *Servicing Our Future*, Chapter 2 – Overview of Australia's Services Sector, Sections 2.56 & 2.63 https://www.aph.gov.au/parliamentary_business/committees/house_of_representatives_committees?url=efpa/services/report.htm

5   Melbourne Institute of Applied Economic & Social Research (2018), *The Phases of Business Cycles in Australia 1960 – 2018*

6   Baden-Fuller C, MacMillan I, Demil B, Lecocq X, 'See *Long Range Planning* call for papers for the Special Issue on 'Business Models" as referenced in: Casadesus-Masanell R, Enric Ricart J (2009), *From Strategy to Business Models and to Tactics* (working paper), p7 www.hbs.edu/ris/Publication%20Files/10-036.pdf

7   Cision PR Newswire (10 Mar 2010), *Nearly All Consumers Now Use Online Media to Shop Locally*, www.prnewswire.com/news-releases/nearly-all-consumers-97-now-use-online-media-to-shop-locally-according-to-biakelsey-and-constat-87221242.html

8   Crosley H (26 Feb 2010), *Beyoncé Says She 'Killed' Sasha Fierce*, MTV News http://www.mtv.com/news/1632774/ beyonce-says-she-killed-sasha-fierce/

9   Lieberman MD (2015), *Social: Why our brains are wired to connect*, Oxford University Press, p258-259

10   Lieberman MD (2015), as previously referenced, p268

11   Lieberman MD (2015), as previously referenced, p265

12   For Australia, the rules and regulations for email, SMS and MMS marketing can be found online via www.acma.gov.au/avoid-sending-spam. Determining the regulatory body and regulations in other countries will require independent research.

13   Metzger M (2015), *Human Error No.1 Cause of Data Loss, Say IT Professionals*, SC Media via www.scmagazineuk.com

14   The marketing mix was first expressed in 1960 by E. Jerome McCarthy in his book *Basic Marketing – A Managerial Approach* and popularised through many marketing textbooks.

15   Satir V, et al (1991) *The Satir Model: Family Therapy and Beyond*, Science and Behavior Books

16   United Nations Development Program (1992), *Human Development Report 1992: Global Dimensions of Human Development* www.hdr.undp.org/en/reports/global/hdr1992

17 Bunkley N (3 Mar 2008), *Joseph Juran, 103, Pioneer in Quality Control, Dies*, The New York Times www.nytimes.com/2008/03/03/business/03juran.html

18 Note that the seven year 'rule of paw' for calculating a dog's age has been disproved and refined to a more accurate system, which takes into account that dogs mature much earlier than humans – Cell Press (2 Jul 2020), *How old is your dog in human years? New method better than 'multiply by 7'* via ScienceDaily www.sciencedaily.com/releases/2020/07/200702113649.htm

19 Collin C, Benson N, Ginsburg J, Grand V, Lazyan M, Weeks M (2012), *The Psychology Book*, Dorling Kindersley Limited, London, p138-139

20 NOTE: The Hierarchy of Needs model has been adapted by others over time, from five levels to eight (reflecting Maslow's theories about the composition of growth needs, which he rolled into one all-encompassing category of 'self actualisation' in the original model). Key references:

Maslow AH (1943), *A Theory of Human Motivation*, originally published in the Psychological Review, 50(4), 370-96
Maslow AH (1962), *Toward a Psychology of Being*, originally published by D. Van Nostrand Company, New York

21 Krznaric R (2015), *Empathy: Why it matters, and how to get it*, The Random House Group Limited, p14

22 Umberson D, Karas Montez J (2010), *Social Relationships & Health: A Flashpoint for Health Policy*, Journal of Health and Social Behaviour 51(S) S54-S66, American Sociological Association https://journals.sagepub.com/doi/pdf/10.1177/0022146510383501

23 Holt-Lunstad J, Smith TB, Layton JB (2010), *Social Relationships and Mortality Risk: A Meta-analytic Review*, PLoS Med 7(7): e1000316 https://doi.org/10.1371/journal.pmed.1000316

24 Hopkin M (13 Jan 2006), *Web users judge sites in the blink of an eye*, Nature www.nature.com/news/2006/060109/full/news060109-13.html

25 Biederman I, Vessel E (2006), *Perceptual Pleasure and the Brain*, American Scientist Journal, Volume 94/3, p247 www.americanscientist.org/article/perceptual-pleasure-and-the-brain

26 Hopkin M (2006), as previously referenced

27 Hopkin M (2006), as previously referenced

28 Pinantoan A (2015), *How to Massively Boost Your Blog Traffic With These 5 Awesome Image Stats*, BuzzSumo http://buzzsumo.com/blog/how-to-massively-boost-your-blog-traffic-with-these-5-awesome-image-stats/

29 Vaynerchuk G (2013), *Jab, Jab, Jab, Right Hook: How to Tell Your Story in a Noisy Social World*, Harper Business

30 Insidesales.com (2009), *The Lead Response Management Study*, www.leadresponsemanagement.org/lrm_study

31 Captured by applying the Feel-the-Love Photoshoot Formula, published in book two of the *Secret Service Business Series – The Secret Service Website Formula*.

32 NOTE: Although we all sell to survive, the terms 'sales meeting', 'sales call' or 'sales presentation' have a negative connotation of self-interest. That's why it's important to only use these terms behind closed doors... not with potential customers themselves.

33 Daniels P (2020), The Sales Leadership Program, Lead Australia

34 Australian Psychological Society (2018), *Australian Loneliness Report*, https://psychweek. org.au/wp/wp-content/uploads/2018/11/Psychology-Week-2018-Australian-Loneliness-Report-1.pdf

35 Olien J (23 Aug 2013), *Loneliness is Deadly*, Medical Examiner, The Slate Group www. slate.com/articles/health_and_science/medical_examiner/2013/08/dangers_of_ loneliness_social_isolation_is_deadlier_than_obesity.html

Holt-Lunstad J, Smith TB, Layton JB (2010), as previously referenced

36 Cellan-Jones R (2 Dec 2014), *Stephen Hawking warns artificial intelligence could end mankind*, BBC News www.bbc.com/news/technology-30290540

37 Piper K (2 Nov 2018), *Why Elon Musk fears artificial intelligence*, Vox Media www.vox. com/future-perfect/2018/11/2/18053418/elon-musk-artificial-intelligence-google-deepmind-openai

www.ingramcontent.com/pod-product-compliance
Lightning Source LLC
Chambersburg PA
CBHW030538210326
41597CB00014B/1197